Studies in Social Policy and Welfare XXIV

COMPARING WELFARE STATES AND THEIR FUTURES

Studies in Social Policy and Welfare

COMPARING WELFARE STATES AND THEIR FUTURES

Edited by Else Øyen

Gower

Published by
Gower Publishing Company Limited,
Gower House, Croft Road,
Aldershot, Hants GU11 3HR,
England

and

Gower Publishing Company,
Old Post Road, Brookfield,
Vermont 05036,
U.S.A.

British Library Cataloguing in Publication Data

Comparing welfare states and their futures. —
   (Studies in social policy and welfare; 24)
   1. Social policy
   I. Øyen, Else   II. Series
   361.6'1   HN18

   ISBN 0-566-00910-2

Printed and bound in Great Britain at
The University Press, Cambridge

Contents

Preface

The future of the welfare state is being decided on here and now, but much of the decision-making goes unseen. The grand visions of the welfare state as a lodestar have faded and have been replaced by many small and unrelated decisions, the sum of which is staking out a path we might not have followed had we known where it was leading us. Many are now worried about the future of the welfare state. The authors of this book share these worries, both as concerned human beings and as puzzled social scientists groping for an understanding of the processes guiding this development.

This book evolved from these worries — which multiplied as our work progressed. The terrain we have moved into is not only difficult to force intellectually. It is also difficult to penetrate politically because of the many economic, moral, private and public interests tied into the welfare state, which constitute efficient barriers to investigation and lead the analysis into detours and blind alleys.

But the challenge is there to be met. Our analysis is a step towards a better understanding of the many different forms of welfare distribution and their future. On our way we have sought comfort in the words of Theon, philosopher and director of the University in Alexandria in Egypt c. 380 BC, who advised his daughter Hypatia: 'Reserve your right to think, for even to think wrongly is better than not to think at all.' It is less comforting to know she took up the challenge — and was stoned to death by an outraged mob, manipulated by the moral and financial powers of that time.

The initiative for the book was taken by The Research Committee on Poverty, Social Welfare and Social Policy of The International Sociological Association. Its members met at the Xth World Congress of Sociology held in Mexico in 1982, and made comparisons of future welfare state development, one of the main topics of discussion. The work continued throughout the following year when Universität Bielefeld, the Federal Republic of Germany, generously provided hospitality and a grant which made it possible for the authors to meet at Zentrum für Interdisziplinäre Forschung, Bielefeld, to discuss the problems raised and make comparisons across national boundaries.

The book is an invitation to use comparative research as a basis for a theoretical approach which is not tied to national welfare states. It is also an invitation to understand better how national welfare states can be brought out of their cocoons and comprehend the need for an *international* welfare state, bridging the gap between the haves and the have-nots.

ELSE ØYEN
University of Bergen, Norway

To the Children of the Welfare State because

'It takes all the running you can do to keep in the same place . . . . If you want to get somewhere else you must run at least twice as fast as that'.

(The Red Queen to Alice, in *Through the Looking-Glass* by Lewis Carroll)

Part I Trends and Problems in Common for the Welfare States

1 Identifying the Future of the Welfare State
Else Øyen

Introduction

The future of the welfare state concerns so many people and their well-being that it has to be considered seriously. Research on the welfare state has been a neglected area of study and it is only during the last decade that sociologists, political scientists, historians, philosophers and economists have turned their attention in that direction. The attention is clearly related to the 'crisis' of the welfare state — whether the phenomenon is seen as a crisis *of*, a crisis *in*, or a crisis *by* the welfare state; or a crisis located in capitalism — i.e. construction of the state or the national/international economy spilling over into the welfare state. The crisis phenomenon has so dominated our way of thinking that much of the basic thinking as to *why* the welfare state was constructed in the first place, is getting lost. The call for immediate solutions by politicians and influential groups over-shadow the long-term functions of the welfare state and this ahistorical and limited perspective is now a much greater threat to the welfare state than pending financial problems and unsupportable unemployment rates.

This diversion from the ideological rationale for the welfare state makes it all the more important to concentrate on its future. But for this kind of research there is neither a coherent analytical framework nor an adequate methodology. Instruments for short-term planning and predictions have been developed, but the more the time horizon is expanded the more unreliable such instruments become. But it is still possible to go beyond educated guesses.

One way of doing so is to extrapolate historical and recent trends and evaluate under which conditions these trends will continue. Another way is to identify the processes underlying the welfare state and ask whether they are so inherent in our culture that they will persist in the future. Still another way of approaching the problem is to ask how universal these processes are, given different models of the welfare state.

In this book we are using all three approaches. We accept that there is no one unifying model which allows us to compare welfare states across national boundaries (Heidenheimer *et al.*, 1975). We also acknowledge that different welfare systems are designed and implemented on a national scale, thereby almost defying comparison and the concept of the welfare state. But in our search for unifying frames of analysis we have been struck again and again by the fact that it seems to be *the same underlying processes which guide the future of the welfare states*, regardless of their cultural context or their stage of development. Therefore, it is to these processes we address ourselves, trying to identify them in the historical development of different welfare states and in the mounting pressures which are now surrounding many welfare states. For this purpose we have selected countries with very dissimilar developments and nestled in very different cultures, using various theoretical approaches and empirical documentation.

We are aware of the fact that the concept of the welfare state is a poor analytical concept. But since it is crucial to the ongoing debate we still chose to use it. The core idea of the welfare state is that of a state providing for citizens who are not able to cover basic needs. Basic needs are defined within a cultural context and vary from a daily ration of rice to universal economic security measured in relation to a national income. The set of welfare institutions constructed to meet basic needs is one of several operational definitions of a welfare state. The role of the state can be either that of organising, guaranteeing or acknowledging these institutions. As the concept of basic needs expands, the welfare institutions grow more comprehensive and diversified, and the role of the welfare state merges with the role of the state.

The selection of countries presented represents the embryonic welfare state, the pending welfare state and the well developed welfare state, each with their specific sets of welfare institutions.

How real is the crisis?

Much of the research so far has taken for granted that the crisis of the welfare state is real, but this raises several questions. First, it is important to distinguish between crisis symptoms and systemic crisis. Second, it is necessary to analyse the relationship between social change and crisis. And third, it is important to ask why we, at this stage in time, are confronted with a crisis definition and what the underlying forces of such a definition are. Only when approaching these questions can we gain insight into whether the future of the welfare state is at stake, whether it needs to be dismantled to meet the crisis or whether it needs strengthening, protection or change in order to meet challenges ahead.

Society is composed of a number of systems and sub-systems which are interwoven and dependent upon each other. Changes in one of the systems are likely to bring about changes in other systems, and society is constantly adapting to these changes. Some of the systems are stable, while others undergo fundamental changes which make them lose their original content and functions. A crisis can be seen in this perspective. If one of the systems is threatened by changes that makes it lose its original content and functions, then this system is in crisis. Other systems in society can be threatened by this crisis to such an extent that they also become crisis prone. And if enough of the systems enter into a crisis, society itself will be thrown into a crisis.

Historically we can see that social change, and even rapid social change, has been a feature of all industrialised countries, and is increasingly becoming so in the developing countries. Some of this change is being absorbed in established systems, while other systems have been transformed into systems with entirely new characteristics; or have been irretrievably lost. Looking back, we can say that the latter systems were in crisis. Looking forward, we can say that social change has become inherent in all modern societies, but it is difficult to know when penetrating social change becomes a crisis and how this crisis spreads to other systems. One approach, which has been utterly misused because it has not been rooted in coherent theories about social change, is to look for crisis indicators.

In discussing social change we are not only facing methodological and theoretical considerations. We are also facing normative issues. An evaluation of the value of social change will always raise the question as to whether the change is 'better' or 'worse' than maintaining the status quo, or provoking a crisis. We shall try to leave the moral question aside here, but let the problem be mentioned.

The present crisis has been defined largely as an economic crisis, or by some, as a crisis of the management of the economy. Much of the responsibility for the crisis is being placed within the welfare state which is demanding still larger shares of the national economy. While there is little doubt that social expenditure constitutes a growing part of the national budgets (cf. Chapters 7, 9, 11 and 12), one may question whether this is an indication of a crisis in the welfare state or of the poverty of the economic models used. Demographers have forecast changes in the composition of the population which would put heavy demands on social expenditures (Chapter 7), but the economists have not incorporated in their models the micro- and macro-economics of the welfare state. For example, while unemployment is a central variable, expenditure for unemployment benefits is a peripheral variable, as is the economic behaviour of the unemployed. It seems that social change has come so rapidly that the economists have not been able to cope with it intellectually. An easy, but much too simplistic explanation is to define the welfare state as being in crisis.

Nevertheless the economists are not alone. Mishra (Chapter 2) shows how sociologists have ignored the analysis of the welfare state and instead focus on social problems, social policies and institutional analysis. Although sociologists are trained to analyse the structure and functioning of society as a whole, they have not developed theories of the welfare state which can help us in the present situation. There is no precise definition of a welfare state, although there is widespread agreement on its functions. Also, it should be borne in mind, that the welfare state may not even be a useful analytical concept, however popular it is, because many of the functions of the welfare state cannot be separated from other political and economic responsibilities of the national state. The East-European countries, for example, do not use the concept of the welfare state — admittedly for ideological reasons — but their range of social provisions for their citizens reaches far beyond that of countries which regard themselves as true welfare states (Chapter 10). The Japanese welfare provisions, though well developed, are not organised in the context of the national state (see Chapter 8).

Himmelstrand (Chapter 3) argues that it is not the welfare state as such which is in crisis but the mature capitalistic society and the way we have arranged vital functions around the capitalistic way of life, which are in jeopardy. He points to the growing number of 'external effects' of capitalist production which the welfare state slowly and reluctantly is being forced to take over. One of the basic functions of the welfare state was to shield marginal individuals from the impact of the market forces. But the welfare state now encompasses the majority of the population and through its emphasis on quality of life and social rights acts both as a buffer between capitalistic interests and a vehicle of these interests, thereby creating internal contradictions which society has no model for coping with.

Rupesinghe (Chapter 15) shows in his analysis of Sri Lanka how the introduction of an international capitalistic culture not only breaks down an established and modest welfare state based on benefits in kind, but actually demands that the majority of benefits be abolished in order for the new society to take over. This introduction of crisis in the welfare system seems to have severe repercussions for other parts of society, especially the political system, thereby creating a political instability which might undermine the 'modernising' of the economy and throw the whole society into crisis.

Piven and Cloward (Chapter 4) give a historical account of how the ideological and structural separation of the economic from the political system both strengthened capitalist society and delayed the advancement of a welfare state in the USA. People participated in 'politics', but it was not a politics of property and redistribution, and social problems were excluded as irrelevant to the public economy. However, as the US economy expanded in the twentieth century, so did the 'externalities' and the business community's need for state intervention. The crisis in the economic system between the two world wars brought about profound changes in the political system and popular demands for state intervention in favour of unemployment benefits, pensions for the aged, low-cost housing, legislation regulating the work sphere, etc., challenged the *laissez-faire* ideology.

Here, as in many other countries, the crisis in the economic system actually acted as 'midwife' to the welfare state. The Reagan administration has been trying to restore the ideology of less state intervention in order to save the economy from what is defined as a crisis. But US social programmes now constitute a large and intricate apparatus of governmental and quasi-governmental organisations that are interwoven in the political system. Therefore, they are more difficult to dismantle and less crisis prone than before.

Heinze, Hinrichs and Olk (Chapter 5) locate the crisis in the administrative organisation of the welfare state which was created for other purposes and now is incapable of handling the complex problems which face it. The example they use is the fragmented organisational system for controlling unemployment in West Germany which used to be an administration of unemployment benefits. The many actors involved respond rationally within their own sub-system, but the sum of their decision-making creates an irrational response which defeats efficient action. They argue that the continuation of the welfare state in its present form depends on a sufficient demand for labour since individual income is distributed through participation in the labour market. While Piven and Cloward (Chapter 4) stress the fact that it is in the interest of capitalism to keep unemployment rates high, Heinze, Hinrichs and Olk stress the fact that structural barriers undermine the consensus and innovation which the political administrative system needs in order to solve the transnational problem of threatening unemployment rates.

What we are witnessing are societies in rapid change, which are subject to forces we know much too little about, whether it be the impact of new technology, complex decision-making processes, demands for extended democratic rights, demographic changes, unfamiliar political and economic constellations or new channels for information, etc. The welfare state is affected by these forces, as is the rest of society. But why is it that the welfare state becomes the main object of a crisis definition and a prime target for criticism?

One answer could be that the modern welfare state now involves such a large number of citizens that the concern is more widespread. However, these people also have a stake in defending their rights under the welfare state. Opinion polls made in several western countries show that the majority of the population is against changes that will impede these rights. Still the welfare state is under attack. It is accused of *creating* a crisis, through high social expenditures which undermine and twist the national economy (whether in Sri Lanka or the USA), through the level of unemployment benefits which is seen to contribute to unemployment and distortion of the labour market, and through its ideology which is considered contradictory to important social goals. The welfare state is also accused of *being* in crisis because of lack of financing, rigid organisation, poor delivery of services, unsolved problems, and never ending needs for expansion.

All these arguments are no doubt valid, but the sum of the argument does not necessarily reveal a welfare state in crisis.

Historically, none of the arguments are new — only the vocabulary and the sophistication of the statements have changed. This, of course, is closely related to the very nature of the welfare state, the initial struggle for its development and the challenges which emerging and more developed welfare states still face — and will still face in the future.

Much of the recent literature on social policy and the welfare state has defined the functions (both intended and unintended) of specific social programmes and the welfare state as a macro-social phenomenon. Most of the authors see the welfare state as a way of bridging conflicts of interest, between classes, different distributional systems, market forces and human needs, majority and marginal groups, and between interests of specific kinds. More generally, the welfare state is seen as setting the limits to the degree of social distance which a society can accept without conflict emerging. At the same time the welfare state serves as a frame for bridging all these conflicts *and* a legitimation of the political and economic arrangements and institutions which represent these interests (Dahrendorf 1958; Titmuss 1958; Rex 1961; Piven and Cloward 1971; Øyen 1974; Korpi 1978; Flora and Heidenheimer 1981; Mishra 1981).

However, the welfare state is far from being a perfect vehicle for bridging the kinds of conflict which seem to be part of all societies. Welfare states vary in the degree to which they have confined the conflicts in institutional forms, and to the degree the redistributional measures have been accepted by the parties involved. But within them all are ongoing battles as to how far redistribution should go, how far social rights should be extended, what kind of new beneficiaries should be included, how much state intervention should be allowed, and who should give up privileges in order to extend the welfare state. Some of the battles have been violent; some have been forced to the surface by the underprivileged themselves, while others have been taken up by intellectuals and the middle class and turned into universalistic programmes.

The interests of capital, represented by the business community, the industrialists and the conservative forces, have always seen the welfare state as a threat to their interests, and with good reason since the welfare state sprung out of an effort to curb these same interests. Through compromises and indirect means of control they have influenced the shape of the welfare state and incorporated their interests in such a way that the welfare state provides part of the infrastructure of capitalism, and capitalistic ideology has become part of the welfare state (Chapter 3).

During the 1960s and early 1970s radicals in most of the Western welfare states attacked their governments for not having gone far enough in solving social problems, abandoning class differences, incorporating minorities and creating a more just basis for income distribution and social wages. In the forefront were social scientists who exposed poverty, inequalities, lack of opportunities and the vicious circle of maldevelopment. The welfare states certainly expanded during this period, as the increases in social expenditure, coverage of people, quantity of social programmes and the number of employees working for the welfare state reveal. But it is probably fair to add that this expansion was more a result of a general expansion in the economy rather than of the efforts of radicals and social scientists.

When the economy receded the scales tipped and the more conservative forces took over with the crisis definition of the welfare state. The radicals withdrew their criticism for fear of an unholy alliance which would harm the welfare state. However, they had helped lay the foundation for the conservative critics and their argument that there was a crisis *in* the welfare state in that it was not meeting social needs, which was transformed into a claim that there was a crisis *of* the welfare state and an economic crisis created *by* the welfare state. The crisis definition is now being used as an ideological basis for reducing social expenditure, changing redistributive patterns in disfavour of the marginal groups and reducing government responsibility in social policy. This attitude may be seen in relation to a more general social change from labour intensive to capital intensive industries which in principle render the pacifying power of the welfare state more insignificant. For some it becomes profitable to define the crisis as so 'real' that drastic measures have to be taken in order to halt the expansion of the welfare state — or better, reverse its development.

Besides these traditional actors on the arena of the welfare state, there are also other actors who have a vested interest in the future of the welfare state and who will throw their strength into keeping the status quo or changing the discourse according to which most serves their interests. The labour unions, for example, have taken very different roles: in Scandinavia they have aided the development of the welfare state; in the USA they have taken over welfare rights; and in Australia they have remained on the side line of the welfare state. Now labour unions in these countries, as well as in many other countries, realise that social wages are a very important supplement to ordinary wages and are worth fighting for. The professionals, as well as the bureaucrats who make a living and a meaningful existence through the welfare state, have a heavy interest in keeping the status quo. Even the medical associations which in all countries have fought against in-corporation in the welfare state services, are now realising that competition among medical doctors in the industrialised countries is growing fierce and a closer integration into the welfare state is offering their group a certain economic protection. Voluntary agencies, ideo-logical societies, self-help groups and other private organisations try to sell their services through the welfare state. Hospitals as well as research units depend on the welfare state for funding and try to bend the welfare state to suit their purposes. For many groups wage settlements are no longer a two party agreement between employers and em-ployees, but a three party negotiation with welfare benefits as a mediating element.

For analysts of the welfare state the outcomes of all these activities are difficult to evaluate. We know much too little about the changes of composition of the groups involved, the nature of their ideologies, the immanent contradictions of their behaviour, the intensity and impact of their activities and the channels through which their influence is directed.

The strength of the activity of all these interest groups is hardly surprising. The welfare state is turning into one of the most important institutions of redistribution, second only to the labour market and the family and is gaining on both these institutions. In some countries social expenditure constitutes up to a third of all public expenditure, one fifth of the population get their entire economic support in benefits in cash, while many more receive benefits in kind through institutional care, health services, etc. The rewards of managing to define a group as 'needy' under a well developed welfare state can be profitable for its members, especially if individual taxes are high and progressive. Much can also be gained if competing groups can be squeezed out of the welfare market or their rights be questioned. When this happens in a poorly developed welfare state, the loss of a group being excluded in this way can be a matter of life or death (see Chapter 15).

The welfare state has become an instrument of power, through the number of citizens it affects, the size of its economy and the interests vested in it, and as such, it has also become part of a power game. A crisis definition, for example, can be seen as part of this power game — as can calls to support the present welfare state. The rules by which to play the game are partly institutionalised, but much of the scene is left for innovative and unorthodox behaviour from pressure group activities outside accepted channels, the labelling of 'enemies' as misusers, and depicting imagined and undocumented consequences of social security spending.

The scene is complex, and it is this unruly kaleidoscope of actors, activities and external forces which we are facing when we try to probe into the future of the welfare state.

The search for new solutions
The welfare state is not built upon an inner logic from which policy decisions can be deduced. Although some of the more developed welfare states have a dominant ideology, the implementation does not reflect a coherent system of social programmes. Since the welfare state has grown out of the many conflicting interests, it has also coopted and integrated them into its system. In the process the welfare state has become an extremely complex organisation of programmes, legislation and ideologies, the internal logic of which is at best difficult to discern, and at worst directly counteractive to the idea of a welfare state. This complexity has become a distinct feature of the welfare states. It only adds to the complexity discussed earlier in relation to the many interest groups involved in the welfare scene and the rapid social changes confronting most countries.

Faced with this complexity and a range of problems for which there are no precedents, it seems that governments are turning to the past for solutions when pushed to make decisions on the welfare state. The disturbing uncertainty of future challenges are met with the security of former time, although the old solutions hardly seem to solve the problems. The very market forces that the welfare state was developed to curb, are called upon again in order to meet the 'crisis'. State intervention which developed as a guarantee for equal access to welfare provisions, is to be reduced, private organisations and the family are again seen as the most adequate units for extending welfare, while self-help groups are being encouraged. Centralised responsibility for social programmes is being returned to the local communities, now under the label of democratic reforms, and hard-won universalistic measures are being questioned. Redistributional systems in favour of the less privileged are slackened. High unemployment rates are now defined as tolerable and even necessary for a healthy national economy, while unemployment compensations are decreasing.

Altogether, it looks like these 'solutions' have swept over the world, regardless of the size and content of the problems they are intended to solve.

The intricate question is not only whether these responses are adequate solutions to perceived and real problems. It is also important to ask if the processes underlying these solutions are related to the welfare state as such, and what are the implications for the future of the welfare state in the implementation of such solutions.

In all the countries surveyed in this book the call for these kinds of solutions has increased strongly during the last few years, the only exception being Japan. The demands for the solutions have been set forward independent of the degree of development of the welfare states or the colour of the political party in power. They have also been forwarded independent of whether economic difficulties have penetrated the national economies or only touched upon the fringes, whether state intervention and bureaucratic responsibility are extensive or limited, and whether national unemployment rates are unusually high or moderate.

This could be an indicator that the problems *per se* are not the main target of the solutions. While the complexity of the welfare state has no inner logic, most of the solutions can be seen as firmly rooted in an adjusted capitalistic *laissez-faire* ideology aimed at the welfare state. Part of the ideology is explicitly linked to rational economic models (e.g. 'neo-conservatism' in Sri Lanka and USA). Much of the ideology, however, is also formed through the many small and independent decisions made in response to an unidentified and incoherent crisis definition. The welfare state itself offers no answers, so the lack of alternative forces a choice between two possibilities which in fact compliment each other, namely the solutions offered in the early days of the welfare state and those of present-day neo-capitalism. Since it is also the neo-capitalistic ideology which has produced the present crisis definition, it only seems reasonable that the many small decision-making units should seek their solutions within this frame of reference.

There is little doubt that the sum of solutions offered is detrimental to the welfare state and, if carried forward with sufficient strength and intensity may be fatal, or, in our terminology, can throw the welfare state into a real crisis which will strip it of its present content and functions. These forces set into motion have been called 'recapitalization of capitalism' (Miller 1978), and are the same antagonistic forces which had initially to be overcome in order to develop a welfare state (Mishra 1981).

The welfare states respond differently to the pressure to find new solutions. In general terms it can be said that the more developed the welfare states are, the less likely they are to yield to new ideas which are counteractive to the social programmes developed. But here the content and organisation of the welfare state has a decisive influence (Øyen 1980 and 1984). Welfare states with universal benefit programmes are less subject to change because infringement of social rights challenges large segments of the population. In his analysis of the Scandinavian countries Johansen (Chapter 9) shows how these countries have been under attack because of steep increases in social expenditure and taxes. New political parties have been formed as a result of this criticism, but no major programmes have been abandoned and social expenditure has more or less kept on increasing. The vested interests in maintaining the status quo are so widespread that much of the criticism can be seen as symbolic rhetoric.

New Zealand as described by Jack (Chapter 11) and Austria as described by Busch *et al.* (Chapter 12), are other examples of stable welfare states based upon universal principles, which are resisting calls for basic changes. Welfare states which incorporate vital interest groups or have developed interest groups within the organisation of the welfare state, have defenders built into the system who are reluctant to accept change and who are in a position to defend their vested interests (Derthick 1979). The USA, as described by Piven and Cloward (Chapter 4) and West Germany, as described by Grunow (Chapter 13), can also be described as relatively stable in this sense.

Welfare states which reflect the work ethic of the country, as well as other basic norms, are also less prone to the 'new' solutions. The prime example here is Japan where it is institutionally difficult to distinguish between work and welfare, and the ethic of collectivist welfare is expressed through the work place rather than a national welfare state (Chapter 8). The demands for reform along the lines discussed above have therefore been negligible. While the fragile welfare state of Sri Lanka stands to be crushed under the weight of new reforms (Chapter 15). The stability of the well-developed Hungarian welfare state is subjected to different political forces. Interest groups and neo-conservative solutions are apparent but in principle are more effectively controlled (Chapter 10).

None the less changes are occurring in every welfare state and these changes now seem to be moving in the same direction. If allowed to continue they can profoundly alter the profile and functions of the welfare state. Two of the main trends, namely the effects of changes in redistributive patterns and the role of the state merit special attention.

The welfare state is based on the idea that distribution of individual income should not entirely be left to market forces. Through taxation, subsidies and transfers in cash and kind, social wages go through a process of redistribution. The extent and direction of redistributional measures vary from country to country as do the principles for redistribution and the groups benefiting from these transfers.

One of the pronounced aims of the welfare state is to alleviate the impact of poverty on the individual and the family; another is to provide an income for those who are excluded permanently or temporarily from the labour market. While the more superior goal is to reach a more equitable distribution of resources in the wider sense, i.e. social wages, influence, status and power. Some of the welfare states have gone quite far in securing social and economic rights for deprived and marginal groups. But in all the countries surveyed, whether they are well-developed welfare states or not, the tendency is that the redistributional patterns are changing to the detriment of the most disadvantaged and marginal groups. They are losing out both in relative and absolute terms. The decision making is done inside the traditional welfare sector as well as in other sectors and producing mainly incremental and unconnected decisions. Three key decision-making spheres can be distinguished: social policy, general fiscal policy and industrial policy.

In the area of social policy-making it can be safely said that in both developed and developing welfare states progress has come to a halt. Few new programmes are being introduced, and established programmes are being assessed with an eye to greater efficiency and cost-cutting. However, major programmes do not seem to be abandoned, although incremental changes erode the principles upon which they are built. The non-institutionalised sector is the easiest target, and paradoxical though it may be, this is also where the traditional clientele of the welfare state is found. The major part of social expenditure is bound up in institutional care, wages and universal programmes. Politically they are difficult to touch. It is easier to cut expenditure for the most marginal groups, such as the invisible poor. They are unlikely to mount a threatening protest and have least public support. But universal programmes are also under attack, and this is where the most fundamental changes can come about. Logically it can be argued that social expenditure should be directed towards those groups who are needy rather than diverting scarce resources to the population at large. Much can be said in favour of selectivity as opposed to universalism — whether the argument is based on the justice of redistribution or simply on cost saving — but the long-term effect of such a course is likely to weaken the loyalty of citizens who do not profit from it. They will turn to private solutions, while the less well off will again be left to fight for their own interests.

One of the main channels of redistribution is of course general fiscal policy, but increasing inflation rates are sapping the efficiency of this policy instrument. Inflation always hits the poor and the low-income earners the hardest because food and housing seize the main part of their available means. Kenya is the extreme example here (Chapter 14), but Britain can serve as an example just as well. Labour unions and other employees' interest groups fight to compensate for deflating wages. Organised defenders of welfare rights have also been quite successful in securing a certain inflationary compensation, while large groups of welfare beneficiaries are losing out. Some welfare programmes have been abolished or subsidies withdrawn, but more programmes have deteriorated, not because of explicit political decisions, but because of lack of compensation for increasing inflation. On the other hand, many welfare states are witnessing an explicit policy of individual tax cuts designed to boost the national economy. While taking nothing directly from the poor, this kind of (re)distribution puts the disadvantaged in a relatively worse position because tax deductions favour only those participating in the labour market and especially those with above average incomes (Townsend 1979).

On the scene of the *labour market* unemployment is, of course, the crucial variable. It is partly independent of the national economy, partly used to balance national accounts. The burden of unemployment is mainly carried by unskilled and disabled workers, married women and the aging. Retirement ages are lowered to keep down the labour supply, but at the same time retirement and unemployment benefits are cut in real terms as a result of rising inflation.

'Displacement strategies' have been successful both in West Germany and Austria to make foreign workers return to their native countries where employment opportunities are even worse. In most welfare states rights to benefits are linked to occupational welfare and those who are denied entry into the labour market are also denied welfare rights. Thus the welfare state creates new class divisions. The welfare state also defines a new non-productive class, for example, through regulation of retirement age and the number of compulsory years of schooling for the young population (Chapter 7). At the same time it more or less ignores the informal economy of the unpaid labour market where women are massively overrepresented and are the last to gain entrance to the formal economy and the welfare rights of the labour market (Chapter 6).

The second trend which can alter the profile and functions of the welfare state is the changing role of the government. Part of the ideology of the welfare state is based on the idea of government responsibility for social programmes, because government is seen — rightly or wrongly — as a guarantor of justice, a defender of the weaker groups in society, a controller of quality of service, an independent judge in conflicts, and a reliable source of funding. Underneath lies the assumption that there is a need for a dominant public sector to counteract the impact of a dominant private market sector which is crucial in creating wealth as well as poverty. Conceptually it is assumed that a distinction can be made between a public and a private economy, and a public and a private sphere of responsibility, although there are others who argue against this (e.g. van Gunsteren and Rein 1984).

There is little doubt, however, that much of the future argument about the welfare state will be over the muddled issue of state intervention. The call for 'privatisation' of public welfare services has been made world wide, and again, it makes little difference whether the country has a well- or poorly-developed welfare state, or even the extent to which the state presently intervenes. The solution offered is still less state intervention, regardless of the problems being faced. Even in Kenya where the public sector is small, and smaller yet in the welfare sector, the call is for privatisation, in spite of the widespread pressure from the population for more extensive social services and less disparity in access (Chapter 14).

Privatisation takes different forms. One is to let the private market take over welfare provisions as a commercial proposition, the idea being that a profit-oriented organisation is more efficient than a public agency. Privatisation of hospitals can serve as an example here. Another form is to subsidise voluntary agencies, through public grants, to take over welfare services. This arrangement is the basis for the functioning of the Australian and American welfare systems, whereas the proportion of such agencies in the Scandinavian countries is negligible. A third form is the introduction of fees for services which were formerly free or subsidised, such as medical treatment or home help services. A fourth means of privatisation is to decrease the capacity of institutions and return dependent elderly persons, disabled people and children to the family for care, and to encourage and financially support self-help groups. Another form is reduction of national economic responsibility and the return of nationwide programmes to local communities, to be organised and financed locally.

There is nothing new about any of these methods. They are in varying degrees part of the welfare state, and always will be. Although it is difficult to assess the impact of privatisation tendencies, there is little doubt that in all the countries surveyed trends are moving towards privatisation. In his analysis Grunow (Chapter 13) shows how these trends coincide with, and in some cases are reactions to, the shortcomings of the welfare state in providing adequate services. The development of these trends is also part of the process discussed earlier in this chapter, where capitalistic market forces are able to exploit the antagonism towards the welfare state, created through their own crisis definition of the welfare state.

Those who stand to lose in this development are those who cannot afford private hospitals, medical insurances and increased fees for services; women who are brought back into the caring role without the welfare rights of employment; former beneficiaries of welfare services which have been privatised and who are not deemed eligible by voluntary agencies; and local communities whose economy is faltering under the new financial burdens imposed by central government and who are thereby prevented from providing high quality welfare services.

Here the vicious circle is evident. Those individuals and groups who bear the social costs of privatisation are further marginalised as a result (Walker 1983), as are those who lose out due to changing redistributional patterns. While there may not be a systemic crisis of the welfare state, there is no doubt that as a result of the two major trends analysed in this chapter, large numbers of individual crises have been created and their number is increasing.

Comparing futures

The welfare states are very different in structure and function, and this will be decisive in their futures. The welfare states will continue to develop within their cultural context because human needs, except for the very basic needs, are not absolute but created within a cultural context. The processes identified above, whereby redistributional patterns are changing in disfavour of the more disadvantaged and marginal groups, and state responsibility for welfare measures is withdrawn, are trends which loom over the future of all welfare states. The core of the welfare state is the protection of deprived groups, and if these trends are carried further they will alter both the structure and the functions of the welfare state. The poorly-developed welfare states are more exposed to these changes than the better-developed welfare states, as argued earlier in this chapter. In an international context the poorly-developed welfare states take the role of the disadvantaged and marginal groups which are victimised by the worldwide restructuring of production under rapid social change.

The well-developed welfare states seem fairly stable, but they have problems of their own. Their stability is also a sign of rigidity which makes them inert as policy instruments and slow to adapt to change. Bureaucracies tend to develop an inner life where internal goal satisfaction is given priority over external expectations. The welfare bureaucracies are no exception and much criticism is directed towards the quality of service delivery. The welfare state has also become so complex that large parts of it are left outside political mechanisms of control. Nevertheless, the concept of social wages has now come on the agenda of the ordinary citizens and social rights are being extended to include also an insight into the distribution of social wages. This insight may in turn lead to a comparison of benefits across groups of beneficiaries and a re-evaluation of traditional criteria of allocation. So far the interest has been limited to discussions of selective versus universal benefits and has been confined within the arena of social policy and the crisis definition. Once the concept of social wages becomes fully linked to the labour market, the ongoing discussion of work sharing and the failure of the market to provide incomes for well skilled and able-bodied citizens, then the call for a national guaranteed income based on a wide range of temporary or permanent absence from the labour market can become salient items on political agenda. Such an 'absence income' may reduce the threatening complexity of the welfare state and absorb some of the pressures for a more equitable incomes policy to benefit those people whose incomes cannot be generated through the labour market.

It now looks as if the industrialised world is facing a new economic upswing. If this is the case it is important to ask what implications this could have for the future of the welfare state and the present crisis definition. The ideology of the welfare states was more or less created during a time of increasing poverty and economic insecurity, while the implementation of welfare states came at a time of economic growth. But few new ideas which can be channelled into new welfare state developments have been generated during the present 'crisis'. It seems as if the intellectual and political energy has concentrated on defending the present welfare state, rather than accepting its defaults and looking into the future for a welfare state which can become an even better instrument for social rights. There has been no massive resistance to the incremental changes that the welfare states are going through. The rising unemployment rates were expected to lead to unrest and attacks on respective governments, as for example in Britain. Very few co-ordinated attacks which could have led to systemic change, have been mounted. This is partly because the unemployed are marginalised, partly because further unemployment and threats about a national crisis have kept the general public from finding a common cause with the unemployed. It was also expected that the social stability which the welfare state helped create would be eroded as the welfare state marginalised deprived groups. So far this has not happened, but here the time span may be too short for any effects to be apparent yet. The question remains as to how far the marginalising process can continue and how far influential groups can go in increasing their share of the social wages before the stabilising effect of the welfare state is undermined.

The poorly-developed welfare states are fighting to survive within national economies which give low priority to welfare measures. There is also little internal agreement on the desirability of developing welfare measures. The economic crisis is a true crisis for the budding welfare states where the effect of a single increase in oil prices can be the size of a national budget for medical expenditure. From the point of view of the national economy it seems legitimate to give priority to the productive part of the population, but the social unrest is sizeable and demands for welfare rights as well as political rights are increasing everywhere. The theory is that a well-developed welfare state constitutes a stabilising environment for economic as well as cultural conflicts, and that social stability in turn increases productivity and foreign investments. Here the poorly-developed welfare states are caught in a vicious circle where there is no economic surplus to feed into either the welfare state or production; and poverty and the threat of social unrest hampers further an economy which in many of the developing countries would otherwise yield a surplus.

The relationship between the poorly-developed and the well-developed welfare states shows many resemblances to the relationship between the poor and the rich in industrialised countries prior to the development of their welfare systems. In relation to the developed countries the developing countries are now struggling for a more favourable distribution of resources, more political influence in the world community and more respect for their cultural backgrounds. Their economy has been internationalised to such a degree that they have become caught by market forces over which they have no control. Rapid social change also impedes these countries more because their poverty leaves them with few resources to counteract the impact of changing technology and changing markets. Their story on the international level is much the same as that of the deprived groups on the national level in industrialised countries prior to the existence of a well-developed welfare state. The deprived of the pre-welfare state countries fought for better incomes, protection from market exploitation, economic security, welfare rights and social rights and this resulted in what is now labelled the welfare state. History repeats itself when the developed countries are as unwilling to grant these privileges to the developing countries as were the wealthy industrialists, the bourgeoisie and the business community reluctant to relinquish privileges in the early days of the welfare state.

It is an interesting area of analysis to consider how far it is possible to draw parallels between these two developments separated by time and culture. Of particular interest is whether the relationship between the developing and developed welfare states, regardless of present circumstances, is subjected to the same kind of dependencies and forces which changed the relationship between the wealthy influentials and the poor masses in the time of the pre-welfare states. If so, it will be intriguing to follow the strategies pursued to improve international social rights and see if coalitions for self defence can be directed towards this goal. Several international organisations and agreements have been formed which can be turned into useful instruments for this purpose. The formerly forceful weapon of strike action, used in an international community with high rates of unemployment, is not likely to be very successful but an economic strike refusing to pay crippling foreign debts may be a new and powerful weapon.

The scenario of an international welfare state may never be seen, and certainly not in the near future. Some welfare rights are now slowly being extended across national boundaries, but only in symmetrical exchanges, as for example within the European community. Otherwise the well-developed welfare states are extending foreign aid as charity to meet the needs of overwhelming famine, and are keeping welfare rights strictly within their own national boundaries. In the meantime, in almost all other spheres of social life, the world is growing still more international.

References

AMPS Secretariat (1981), *What Kind of a World Tomorrow?*, Geneva: World Social Prospects Study Association.

Dahl, R.A. and Lindblom, C.E. (1976), *Politics, Economics and Welfare*, Chicago: University of Chicago Press.

Dahrendorf, R. (1958), *Class and Class Conflict in Industrial Society*, London: Routledge.

Derthick, M. (1979), *Policymaking for Social Security*, Washington, DC: The Brookings Institution.

Flora, P. and Heidenheimer, A.J. (eds) (1981), *The Development of Welfare States in Europe*, New Brunswick: Transaction Books.

Friedman, M. (1962), *Capitalism and Freedom*, Chicago: University of Chicago Press.

Gough, I. (1979), *The Political Economy of the Welfare State*, London: Macmillan.

Heidenheimer, A.J., Heclo, H. and Adams, C.T. (1975), *Comparative Public Policy. The Politics of Social Choice in Europe and America*, New York: St Martin's Press.

Korpi, W. (1978), *The Working Class in Welfare Capitalism*, London: Routledge and Kegan Paul.

March, J.G. and Olsen, J.P. (1976), *Ambiguity and Choice in Organizations*, Oslo: Universitetsforlaget.

Miller, S.M. (1978), 'The Recapitalization of Capitalism', *Social Policy*, pp. 5–12.

Mishra, R. (1981), *Society and Social Policy. Theories and Practice of Welfare*, London: Macmillan.

OECD Report (1980), *Conference on Social Policies in the 1980s*, Paris: OECD.

Øyen, E. (1974), 'Social Distance as Manipulation of Social Policy' (Sosialpolitikk som manipulering av sosial avstand), *Tidsskrift for samfunnsforskning* 15, 191–208.

Øyen, E. (1980), 'The Crisis of the So-Called Welfare State; and the So-Called Crisis of the Welfare State', paper presented at the Australian National University.

Øyen, E. (1981), *GMI. Garantert minsteinntekt i Norge*, Oslo: Universitetsforlaget.

Øyen, E. (1984), 'How to Muffle with Social Security: A Comparison of Social Security Systems and their Conflict Potential in Australia, the United States and Norway', paper presented at the conference on The Sociology of Social Security, University of Bergen, Norway.

Piven, F.F. and Cloward, R. (1971), *Regulating the Poor*, New York: Pantheon Books.

Rex, J. (1961), *Key Problems of Sociological Theory*, London: Routledge.

Sleeman, J.F. (1973), *The Welfare State. Its Aims, Benefits and Costs*, London: Unwin University Books.

Titmuss, R.M. (1958), *Essays on the Welfare State*, London: Allen and Unwin.

Townsend, P. (1979), *Poverty in the United Kingdom. A survey of household resources and standards of living*, Harmondsworth: Pelican.

van Gunsteren, H. and Rein, M. (1984), 'The Dialectic of Public and Private Pensions', paper presented at the conference on The Sociology of Social Security, University of Bergen, Norway, June.

Walker, A. (1983), 'The Future of the Welfare State: Privatisation or Sociali-sation?', paper presented at the conference on Can There Be a New Welfare State? Social Policy Options Towards Shaping an Uncertain Future, European Centre for Social Welfare and Research, Austria.

2 Social Analysis and the Welfare State: Retrospect and Prospect
Ramesh Mishra

Until recently the welfare state[1] stood for that 'golden mean' which enabled western industrial societies to balance freedom with security, enterprise with stability, and economic growth with a measure of social concern and amelioration. A mixed economy and the welfare state looked like the 'natural' evolutionary path for western industrial nations — something that was here to stay. Since the mid-1970s, however, economic problems — conveniently summarised as 'stagflation' — have precipitated a general crisis of confidence in the welfare state: it has lost a good deal of its legitimacy.

It has also become clear that although many of the current problems are manifestly economic in nature, they have no purely 'economic' solution. Economic growth, inflation, productivity, public expenditure and the like are sociopolitical phenomena *par excellence* rooted in society's institutions and attitudes. Similarly, it is clear that the future of social policy cannot be considered without regard to economic policies in so far as social policies have economic consequences and are based on economic assumptions. The crisis of the welfare state has driven home the fact that the economic, political and welfare systems are closely related, and there is an urgent need to look at the interface between the different institutional sectors. But how far has post-war social science, especially the traditions developed in the analysis of social welfare, equipped us for this task?

Analysing social welfare: a restrospect
Two broad traditions can be discerned in post-war social science as far as the analysis of social welfare is concerned (this refers primarily to English-speaking countries). First, there is the empirical or pragmatic approach focused on the study of social problems and policies. This tradition of research and the advocacy of piecemeal reform, often institutionally linked with social work education, forms the bedrock of social welfare studies in Britain and elsewhere. The second tradition may simply be described as mainstream sociological analysis. Within this orientation concern with welfare has been only indirect. Issues

germane to welfare have been raised in the context of the analysis of social institutions and processes such as the family, professions, stratification, social control and the like, or in relation to models of social structure (e.g. industrial society, modern society, etc.). The distinction between these two traditions, though 'ideal-typical', is important. To a large extent, it is also academically institutionalised. For reasons outlined below neither of these traditions is very helpful in making sense of the current crisis of the welfare state. This will become clear as we look at each of these in some detail.

The empirical study of social welfare

During the post-war decades, which saw the rise of the welfare state as a social system, social welfare has very largely been studied within an intellectual framework based on an empirical or pragmatic approach. In Britain it is known as social administration, a term used in this chapter to refer to the *ad hoc*, problem-centred study of social welfare issues. Much of the work done under this rubric centres on producing useful knowledge (for policy-makers, administrators, etc.) about the practical working of social services and social policies. This means that welfare issues are approached from the viewpoint of administrative and reformist concerns of government. Further, many teachers and researchers working within this framework are committed to 'doing good' and reject the 'value-free' positive stance of other social science disciplines. This too makes for a detailed concern with the specifics of social problems, with the here and now of social politics, and with influencing policy-making as an ongoing process. In focusing narrowly on the technicalities of social welfare policies social administration pays scant attention to the relation between welfare and other major social institutions, especially from the standpoint of unintended and unforeseen consequences (Mishra 1981: 8,25). In sum, despite its many strengths social administration seems to lack the intellectual perspectives and concerns necessary to confront the issues raised by the current difficulties of the welfare state.

Sociology and welfare

Sociology's lack of interest in the area of welfare has often been noted (Zald 1965: 1; Pinker 1971: 3—14). Yet the relevance of the discipline to current problems is also quite clear. For unlike, say, economics or politics, sociology is not confined to the study of a specific area of social life. It is concerned with the structure and functioning of the social system as a whole.

Now central to the concerns of this paper is the relevance of modern sociology to the understanding of the welfare state as a macrosocial phenomenon. As far as the macrosocial study of the welfare state is concerned the principal theoretical legacy of the post-war years is that of functionalism and its empirical counterparts — modernisation and industrialisation. These perspectives have been heavily laden with evolutionary and integrative assumptions. They have viewed change as a process involving a move from a stable and integrated social order to one subject to structural differentiation, social strain, disturbances, anomie, and the like, followed in turn by a new stable order in which integrative mechanisms appropriate to the new situation become established (Parsons 1961; Smelser 1964). Within this perspective increasing state intervention in the management of the economy and provision of social welfare has appeared as an institutional adaptation to conditions of advanced industrialism (Kerr 1960; Smelser 1963: 88). The essentials of this 'logic of industrialisation' approach as well as its critique are well known and need not be rehearsed. For the present, the main point to be made is that the assumption of functional necessity and integration underlying this approach left little room for the possibility of dysfunctions, incompatibilities, contradictions, and the like. It is obvious that a theory of this kind would be of little use in explaining what has gone wrong with the welfare state.

Apart from the bias towards harmony and integration, the model of social structure underlying this theory also fails to isolate the key components of structure and to examine their relationship adequately. In this respect there is little to choose between the technological model of, say, Kerr *et al.* (1960) or Galbraith (1967) and the modern society model of Parsons and Smelser (1956). The former tends to assimilate the economy to the technology (the economy is seen as 'industrial' or 'post-industrial') and eliminates what is distinctive about western economy, *viz.* private ownership and the orientation towards the market and profits. In the same way it reduces the political system to a mere appendage of technology — one that simply responds to the dictates of industrialism. The state and the government appear as mere instruments for promoting and managing the process of industrial development. As a result the two major institutional orders of advanced industrial society — the economic and the political — are virtually eliminated from analysis.

In this respect, the modern society version of Parsons and Smelser fares no better. True, Parsonian theory identifies the polity and the economy as two major sub-systems of society. But each is seen largely in terms of its positive functions for the social system, and the relation between the two (and other sub-systems) is seen in terms of mutually supportive exchanges (Parsons and Smelser 1956). This virtually rules out dysfunctional relationships. Moreover, in Parsons' schema the economy and the polity stand for a type of activity or function (adaptation and goal-attainment, respectively) rather than a concrete structure or institution. This leaves the economic and political systems of modern society largely formal and devoid of empirical content.

The schema becomes virtually useless for any kind of dynamic, consequential analysis of western welfare capitalism.

A somewhat different approach to the welfare state centres on the idea of citizenship (Marshall 1963: 67—127; Mishra 1981: 26—38). In this perspective, state provision of a basic minimum of economic security and social services is seen as an essential ingredient of the status of the citizen in modern society. In many ways this approach also fits into the framework of modernisation: the institution of citizenship evolves in order to create community-like conditions in the context of the modern industrial society. However, citizenship also entails conflict. Thus Marshall (1963: 87) speaks of the principle of citizenship as having been 'at war' with capitalism and class inequality. In a nutshell, since citizenship (in its civil, political and social aspects) is an egalitarian principle it is at least partly in conflict with the principle of inequality enshrined in the market economy, private property and class privilege.

What is particularly useful in Marshall's analysis is the notion that somewhat different values and 'logic' are at work within modern societies and that far from blending into a harmonious whole they might be pulling in different directions (ibid.: 281—2). In particular, the notion of a conflict between equality and democracy on the one hand (the political values), and class and inequality on the other (the economic values), takes a more realistic view of the institutional order of capitalist democracies. This is better than functionalism in that it recognises an area of conflict and choice within advanced western societies. But it is seriously flawed in its lack of a clear notion of the social structure of advanced societies and of the relation between its various components. Secondly, in restricting conflict largely to values, it pays scant attention to group interests. Even less does it consider the problems of *functional incompatibility* between various institutional sectors, e.g. the social services and the market economy. Finally, it ignores the issue of unintended consequences of social action altogether — a rather serious omission in any intellectual construct seeking to unravel the complexities of the current situation.

An alternative form of analysis of advanced societies is offered by the so-called conflict theory, associated with such writers as Coser (1956), Dahrendorf (1958) and Rex (1961). Thus, rejecting the consensus view of society altogether Rex puts group conflict at the centre of his analysis. This yields the view of the post-war welfare state as an institution encapsulating the 'truce situation' between the two warring classes — capitalists and workers — in short, as a form of class compromise (Rex 1961: 128). The idea of the welfare state as a temporary institutionalisation of class conflict (liable to change if the balance of class power changes) is a useful corrective to the evolutionary and consensual perspective of functionalism and, to a lesser extent, citizenship. For Rex, the truce situation remains precarious and 'could only become the basis of a new social order in exceptionally favourable conditions' (ibid.: 129). For example, if the balance of power between the major contenders is a long-lasting one the new social structure might come to enjoy a high degree of legitimacy and support. The Rexian analysis of change and development has the merit of grounding the Marshallian conflict between citizenship and social class in the subsoil of power and divergent group interests. Moreover, unlike Marxism, conflict theory has no difficulty in recognising contenders other than workers and capitalists, who can therefore be brought into the analysis (ibid.: 137–48). Since the competition and conflict centred on the welfare state involve a wide variety of social groups, this multiple-group analysis seems, potentially at any rate, a useful framework.

Despite these strengths, however, the Rex–Dahrendorf model is flawed in one crucial respect. It operates at the level of *group* relationships alone, and lacks the *institutional* perspective altogether. Thus the idea that despite general agreement (or compromise) among social groups about the welfare state (a situation which largely obtained in the West until recently) *institutional dysfunctions* which could undermine the social compromise can find no place within the model. As Lockwood pointed out a long while ago, in concentrating almost entirely on social groups or classes and their conflict the model ignores an important source of societal conflict and change, *viz.* the disequilibrium or contradiction between institutional parts (Lockwood 1964: 249–50). In short, the conflict model lacks adequate concepts with which to analyse the institutional orders of modern society and the disequilibrium and contradictions arising between them, which weakens its contemporary relevance seriously.

Analysing the welfare state: prospect

The argument presented above suggests that neither the empirical approach nor the sociological perspectives developed in the post-war years offer us a great deal of purchase on the contemporary problems of the welfare state. In any case academic sociology seems not to have addressed itself directly to the analysis of welfare. Partly for these reasons, but also because economic questions are at the centre of the current difficulties, the resulting gap has been filled by what has come to be known as the 'political economy' approach. Put simply, this involves looking at the economy in its wider political and social context. Using this approach Marxists (e.g. O'Connor 1973; Gough 1979), as well as liberal economists (e.g. Brittan 1977; Buchanan and Wagner 1977), have offered challenging analyses of the development and consequences of post-war welfare. For example, the liberal school (grounded in methodological individualism) has analysed the welfare state in terms of the unintended consequences of 'rational' action on the part of various actors, e.g. politicians, voters, professionals and bureaucrats. What follows is a sociology of the welfare state which incorporates some of the methods and approaches of Marxist as well as liberal political economy.

First, it is necessary to specify the nature of the western economy quite clearly. It is no use pretending, for example, that capitalism does not exist and that what we have is an 'industrial' or 'post-industrial' economy. This way of conflating the economy with the technology so that the distinctive features of the former disappear (see, for example, Bell 1973) would simply not do. Nor would it do to take the capitalist market economy entirely for granted and thus assume it out of analysis (as the social administration approach tends to do). To recognise the nature of the productive system of capitalism — in all its 'virtues' and 'vices' — is the first essential step towards understanding welfare as a part of the social structure. Thus the relationship between different aspects of the economy (e.g. unemployment, inflation, wages) as well as between economic and social welfare (and the possible trade-off between the two) has to be seen in the context of a capitalist economy.

Second, it is important to recognise that a complex social system has several major, relatively autonomous institutional parts. The two most important in modern western society are the economy and the polity. Society is a relatively coherent whole, but within it each institutional area (e.g. kinship, military, religion, etc.) may have its own distinctive principle or 'logic'. This relative autonomy of principles and institutions constitutes a fertile source of conflict and disequilibrium. The conflict between the needs of a market economy on the one hand, and the principles of entitlement and the pursuit of collective interests enshrined in a democratic pluralist polity on the other, is a case in point. As we have seen above, Marshall, in his discussion of citizenship, drew attention to such conflict in respect of the economic, political and welfare sectors. More recently Bell has recognised the same basic point in his notion of the 'disjunction of realms' (Bell 1979: 10). Both Marshall and Bell however focus on conflicting *values* or social *principles*. This is an unnecessary limitation. Analysis must include 'material' relationships between the institutional orders as well. Thus, the relationship between the private market economy, the democratic polity, and the welfare system needs to be understood in both its ideational and functional aspects. As we discuss below, the corporatist approach to the welfare state recognises these contradictory pulls within the social structure and tries to get to grips with them.

Third, analysis needs to straddle the institutional and group perspectives. True, in a theoretically unrecognised *ad hoc* manner a good deal of social analysis does utilise both these perspectives. Moreover, Marxist analysis of the welfare state manages to combine the institutional contradictions and the class struggle perspectives in a theoretically coherent model of society. But in post-war sociological models, notably structural functionalism and conflict theory, a yawning gap opened up between the institutional (functionalist) and group (conflict theory) perspectives. This gap must be closed. Thus it is important to realise that system problems (e.g. institutional integration) cannot be isolated from problems of group relationship (e.g. social integration).

Fourth, it is necessary to pay far greater attention to the unintended consequences of social action relevant to welfare. The study of social policy from a practical, problem-solving viewpoint necessarily involves focusing on the stated objectives of policy and on their realisation. But a sociology of the welfare state, which is not directly concerned with policy-making, needs to examine the interface between welfare and other social institutions from the viewpoint of unintended effects.[2]

Finally, the complex relationship between the normative and the positive aspects of welfare deserves far greater attention than it has received so far. In one sense, it is only another aspect of the problem of unintended or unanticipated social consequences. For example, with hindsight we can see that the normative model of 'moderate collectivism' underlying the Beveridge—Keynesian version of the welfare state was, in a sense, sociologically naive. Today any espousal of moderate collectivism (or similar approaches) must come to terms with the institutional dynamics of western society (connected with democratic politics as well as with the bureaucracy and the professions as vested interests) which leads to 'welfare drift'. In this respect market theorists such as Friedman and Friedman (1980: 347—53) show greater sociological realism in calling for a constitutional restriction on public spending (or other similar devices) to limit the growth of the welfare sector. An alternative approach to the same problem, more in line with the values of the post-war welfare state, is outlined below. It is based on collective national responsibility and social discipline instead of the unbridled pluralism of the political (and for that matter, economic) market place.

True, what is at issue is not simply an instrument for controlling the growth of the welfare sector. The problem of a durable consensus over the level of social expenditure, i.e. over the rationale of the welfare sector as a mixed economy, is also important (Hirsch 1978: 132—58; Bell 1979: 251—82). But given that the private market economy and a pluralist interest-group polity are essential features of western society consensus over social justice, including distribution, may be difficult, if not impossible, to achieve. Today any attempt to put forward a viable normative approach to welfare must come to terms with this wider, social-structural context of welfare. However, as we shall see below, political *practice*, in the form of corporatism, has at least evolved an institutional device that seeks to build a working consensus over distribution and other issues and goes some way towards meeting these problems.

To conclude: a sociology of the welfare state, along the lines outlined above, could be useful in making sense of the society—welfare relationship in the 1980s and beyond. The political-economy approach (liberal as well as Marxist) on the one hand, and the empirical study of social policies on the other, has left a sizeable gap in the social analysis of contemporary issues, especially as seen from the value standpoint of the welfare state. What we have done so far is to suggest the nature of the gap to be filled.

The corporatist welfare state: the way ahead
This section speculates on the future of the welfare state, drawing upon the analytical propositions advanced above. Very briefly, it outlines a model of the welfare state which seems capable of dealing effectively with some of the major problems of welfare capitalism that have arisen in recent years. In this sense the model seems relevant to the conditions of the 1980s and beyond in so far as they can be foreseen. What is offered here is more an illustration and extension of the general ideas presented above (e.g. system and social integration) than an attempt to address practical problems of welfare (e.g. institution-building).[3]

Following a well-established tradition in social thought, an ideal-type or model is outlined to which historical reality may only approximate but whose elements are present in contemporary society. This model may be described as the corporatist welfare state (CWS) as distinct from the post-war, Keynes—Beveridge configuration which may be called the pluralist welfare state (PWS). Table 2.1 presents an ideal-type of the CWS contrasted with a similar construct of the PWS in order to highlight what is most distinctive about the corporatist approach to welfare.

Briefly, corporatism[4] differs from the post-war welfare state in two respects. First, it sees economic and social policy as closely interrelated and therefore in need of coordination. The Keynes—Beveridge approach was based largely on the notion of 'correcting' the tendencies of a market economy through judicious state intervention and limited forms of social policy. The corporatist view, by contrast, is more systemic and recognises the need to 'harmonise' the economic and the social within society as a whole, i.e. within the social economy of capitalism. To put it in another form, the 'feedback' of the social on the economic, and vice versa, is recognised and an attempt made to come to terms with it. For example, issues of distribution are seen as inseparable from those concerning production (a Marxian insight by and large ignored in the 'social engineering' approach of the post-war welfare state). The upshot is that, unlike the PWS, the economic implications of social policy are not shirked while, on the other hand, social policy objectives are introduced quite explicitly into economic policies. Second, the system integration implicit in the institutions of the welfare

Table 2.1   The pluralist versus the corporatist welfare state

Pluralist welfare state[a] (Keynes–Beveridge formula)	Corporatist welfare state[b] (beyond Keynes)
Economy – regulation of the economy from the *demand* side. Government measures, e.g. pump-priming, deficit financing, fiscal and monetary policies to stimulate or inhibit demand. Little explicit consensus-building, limited to a few key objectives, *viz.* full employment and provision of social welfare.	Economy – regulation of the economy from both *demand* and *supply* side, e.g. concern with profits, investments, wage levels, labour-market conditions, and the like. Regulation and consensus-building across wide-ranging economic issues.
Social welfare – relatively autonomous realm seen as distinct from the economy. State provision of services seen as 'socially' oriented, with little explicit link with reference to the economy.	Social welfare – not a realm autonomous of the economy and economic policy. Interrelationship, including inter-dependence, between the social and economic recognised and institutionalised (e.g. Labour Market Board in Sweden, Social Partnership in Austria). Functional relations and trade-offs between the economic and the social (e.g. between wage restraint and social expenditure) clearly recognised.
Polity: interest group pluralism – a free-for-all or market model of the polity and societal decision-making process. Free collective bargaining in the industrial area and the pursuit of sectional interests generally, with little concern for the overall consequences. Exercise of economic power without social responsibility.	Polity: centralised pluralism – bargain between peak asso-ciations/representatives of major economic interests over a broad range of economic and social policies (e.g. voluntary incomes and prices restraint). Interdependence of economic groups recognised and institutionalised by way of class co-operation and social consensus (e.g. Social Partnership in Austria, Labour Market Board and centralised wage agree-ments in Sweden). Major economic powers assume social responsibility.

Notes:

[a] A good example of this model is Britain, c.1945–75.

[b] Examples of this model are post-war Austria and Sweden.

state is seen as related to social or group integration. In short, the functional integration between the economy and social welfare is seen as connected with the relationship between major economic groupings, *viz.* capital and labour. This implies that a productive market economy and a highly developed system of social welfare (system integration) cannot be sustained in the long run without the cooperation and agreement of major social groupings. (This 'systemic' or 'holistic' approach to problems of integration differs from the 'piecemeal social engineering' or 'process' approach implicit in the Keynes—Beveridge notion of the welfare state.) Thus owners of capital as well as workers in their organised capacity (i.e. employers' and workers' associations) are recognised as major partners within the national system of production and distribution. They are expected to assume appropriate responsibility for making the system work. This means for example that, as in Austria and Sweden, employers recognise full employment as a social objective, while workers accept the need for wage moderation and higher productivity as a prerequisite for economic growth and social welfare (Shonfield 1969: 201—11; Jones 1976: 16, 39, 63—6, 80; OECD 1981: 43, 49). Thus the relative autonomy ('disjunction of realms') of the economic and the social within the system is recognised, and an attempt made to harmonise them. In contrast with the Hobbesian view of an unremitting conflict of interests at work in the economic as well as the political market-place, and the Marxian view of a class war, society is seen as a web of interdependent functions as well as interests which therefore requires compromise and cooperation.

Looking at it from another viewpoint we might say that the CWS carries the logic of collective responsibility for the social economy beyond Keynes. In this respect, just as the welfare state (PWS) was a step forward from a largely *laissez-faire* economy and residual welfare, the CWS may be described as another step forward on the road to collective responsibility for the economy and society. Not only management of demand but also the supply of productive resources and motivation are issues that have to be addressed collectively. It should be noted that this does not necessarily imply an enlarged *scope* of the state in economic and social life. It is rather that the *approach* to social management is different, that is, based on a more integrated view of the social system. Thus corporatism does not mean state ownership or control of industry (Sweden, for example, has a very small nationalised industrial sector). Nor does it imply a *statutory* incomes policy (neither Sweden nor Austria has one). Indeed the very opposite, for corporatism implies 'voluntary' cooperation among major economic groups in maintaining basic societal objectives — economic and social — albeit in close collaboration with the state. What is true of the economy is also true of social welfare. The corporatist approach does not imply a change in the ideology or scope of state welfare. The CWS is quite compatible with, for instance, an enhanced role of occupational (work-related) and voluntary welfare instead of the state provision of services. The main point is that collective responsibility for the well-being of the population is maintained (e.g. through commitment to full employment) and a broad consensus arrived at in respect of economic efficiency and social protection (the exact nature of the mix between public, quasi-public and voluntary welfare is not directly relevant to the question of corporatism *per se*). In any case the essence of corporatism lies not so much in specific institutional patterns as in an integrated approach to welfare based on a working consensus among the major economic partners. Perhaps the CWS is best seen as an institutional framework and a set of attitudes (in sum, an effective device) for maintaining the post-war commitment to full employment and social welfare in the context of a liberal market society — something that the Keynes—Beveridge model seems incapable of doing.[5]

Let us remind ourselves, at the risk of repetition, of what this involves. First, it means recognising the importance of production for distribution and also of the trade-offs between such socioeconomic phenomena as inflation, economic wage, unemployment and social welfare. In this sense the CWS recognises the interdependence of the Keynesian and Beveridgian aspects of welfare much more clearly than the welfare state (PWS). Second, it recognises that in order to harmonise economic and social objectives (i.e. to maintain system integration) institutionalised cooperation between major economic interests in society becomes essential. This is the essence, for example, of the Austrian 'social partnership'[6] between labour and capital. Admittedly, such a compromise and general understanding about economic questions between organised interests involves some curtailment of a 'free-for-all' pluralism, whether in respect of wage bargaining or social welfare. And what we have is a kind of centralised pluralism which recognises the reality of economic power and its relevance for achieving societal goals. Undoubtedly the tripartite structure of decision-making, which involves the state, employers and workers, implied in corporatist problem-solving also means that the formal political order — parliament and political parties — is to some extent bypassed and even downgraded. But this is perhaps a small price to pay for harmonising the 'axial' principles of the market economy with those of a plural polity, a potential source of disequilibrium responsible for some of the current difficulties of capitalism.

We have outlined the PWS and the CWS as ideal-types. They are however no more than points on a continuum. And it is not surprising that some European countries (e.g. Austria and Sweden) have been closer to the ideal-type of CWS or at any rate have developed elements of a corporatist approach. However, the conditions which favour the emergence of corporatism (see Schmitter and Lehmbruch 1979), though an important issue, is not our concern here. Our main concern is the viability of this particular model of the welfare state, the fact that it possesses distinct advantages over the PWS and that it may well represent the next stage in the evolution of welfare capitalism.

Notes

1. By welfare state I mean a state which assumes responsibility for citizen welfare in the context of a private market economy and a plural polity. The reference here is both to the *idea* of collective responsibility for welfare as well as to the appropriate *institutions*, i.e. the social welfare services.
2. Janowitz (1976) offers a good example of an exploration of this kind. See also Wilensky (1976).
3. This chapter presents the *idea* of a corporatist welfare state. It does not consider the kind of institutions needed to make it work which are likely to vary from country to country, since the same thing can be done in many different ways.
4. The literature on corporatism, as a form of modern political system, is quite extensive. Schmitter and Lehmbruch (1979) provide a useful overview. For a welfare state perspective, see Wilensky (1976) and Cawson (1982). In this chapter corporatism refers primarily to the corporatist welfare state, presented as an ideal-type.
5. Austria in particular is a success story so far. Its corporate structures have stood up to the strains and stresses of the 1970s quite well, cf. Chapter 12.
6. Refers to the mode of voluntary cooperation and collective decision-making, involving major economic interests, institutionalised in post-war Austria. See OECD (1981: 29—40).

References

Bell, Daniel (1973), *The Coming of Post-Industrial Society*, New York: Basic Books.

Bell, Daniel (1979), *The Cultural Contradictions of Capitalism*, London: Heinemann (1st edn 1976).

Brittan, Samuel (1977), *The Economic Consequences of Democracy*, London: Temple Smith.

Buchanan, James M. and Wagner, Richard E. (1977), *Democracy in Deficit*, New York: Academic Press.

Cawson, Alan (1982), *Corporatism and Welfare*, London: Heinemann.

Coser, Lewis A. (1956), *The Functions of Social Conflict*, London: Routledge.

Dahrendorf, Ralph (1958), *Class and Class Conflict in Industrial Society*, London: Routledge.

Friedman, Milton and Friedman, Rose (1980), *Free to Choose*, Harmondsworth: Penguin Books.

Galbraith, J.K. (1967), *The New Industrial State*, London: Hamish Hamilton.

Gough, Ian (1979), *The Political Economy of the Welfare State*, London: Macmillan.

Hirsch, Fred (1978), *Social Limits to Growth*, London: Routledge (1st edn 1977).

Janowitz, Morris (1976), *Social Control of the Welfare State*, New York and Amsterdam: Elsevier.

Jones, H.G. (1976), *Planning and Productivity in Sweden*, London: Croom Helm.

Kerr, Clark, Dunlop, John T., Harbison, Frederick and Myers, C.A. (1960), *Industrialism and Industrial Man*, Cambridge, Mass.: Harvard University Press.

Lockwood, David (1964), 'Social Integration and System Integration', in George K. Zollschan and Walter Hirsch (eds), *Explorations in Social Change*, London: Routledge, 244—57.

Marshall, T.H. (1963), *Sociology at the Crossroads and other Essays*, London: Heinemann.

Mishra, Ramesh (1981), *Society and Social Policy*, 2nd edn, London: Macmillan.
Mishra, Ramesh (1984), *The Welfare State in Crisis*, Brighton: Harvester Press/ New York: St Martin's Press.
O'Connor, James (1973), *The Fiscal Crisis of the State*, New York: St Martin's Press.
OECD (1981), *Integrated Social Policy: A Review of the Austrian Experience*, Paris: OECD.
OECD (1982), *Economic Surveys: Austria*, Paris: OECD.
Parsons, Talcott (1961), 'Some Considerations on the Theory of Social Change', *Rural Sociology*, XXVI(3), 219—39.
Parsons, Talcott and Smelser, Neil J. (1956), *Economy and Society*, London: Routledge.
Pinker, Robert (1971), *Social Theory and Social Policy*, London: Heinemann.
Rex, John (1961), *Key Problems of Sociological Theory*, London: Routledge.
Schmitter, Phillipe C. and Lehmbruch, Gerhard (1979), *Trends Toward Corporatist Intermediation*, London and Beverly Hills: Sage.
Shonfield, Andrew (1969), *Modern Capitalism*, New York: Oxford University Press.
Smelser, Neil, J. (1963), *The Sociology of Economic Life*, Englewood Cliffs, N.J.: Prentice-Hall.
Smelser, Neil, J. (1964), 'Toward a Theory of Modernization', in Amitai Etzioni and Eva Etzioni (eds), *Social Change*, New York: Basic Books, 258—74.
Wilensky, Harold (1976), *The 'New Corporatism', Centralization and the Welfare State*, London and Beverly Hills: Sage.
Zald, Mayer N. (ed.) (1965), *Social Welfare Institutions: A Sociological Reader*, New York: John Wiley.

3 The Future of the Welfare State. A Question of Holistic Diagnosis and Structural Reforms
Ulf Himmelstrand

We are told that the welfare state is facing a crisis: the state can no longer raise the taxes needed to maintain and develop it. The so-called fiscal crisis is seen, not as a conjunctural and passing phenomenon, but as a structural reality. However, it is not only on the input side that the welfare state is in trouble; the quality of its output is also called into question. Economies of scale, and labour-saving rationalisations seem to be depriving welfare services of compassion and human content.

Furthermore it has been predicted that the reformist labour movement, which has played such an important political role in shaping the welfare system in collaboration with progressive social-liberal forces, will inevitably be weakened in the 1980s and 1990s as a result of the diminishing size of the industrial working class. The welfare state is thus weakened, both internally, as a result of its own internal contradictions; and externally, as a result of the diminishing numerical and political strength of its most significant proponent and supporters: the working class and the reformist labour movement.

Ironically, the alleged deterioration of the internal structure and external support for the welfare state is taking place at the same time as our highly industrialised and bureaucratised societies are creating an increasing number of people in need of welfare services: the (traditional) unemployed, addicts and criminals, but also an increasing number of elderly, who are exposed to the problems of health and handicap in old age. We need to ask whether these tendencies are indicators of a crisis of the *welfare state* rather than of the wider socioeconomic system of which the welfare state is a part.

Not only theoretically but also in practical political terms, it makes a difference whether we are dealing with a crisis of mature welfare capitalism, or a crisis of the welfare state. In the latter case it would not seem illogical to demand significant cutbacks in welfare services. If the crisis is seen as being due to the contradictions of mature capitalism, then it would seem more sensible to dismantle the capitalist relations of production than to dismantle the welfare system. But neither of these two options seem feasible. Both require and generate political and industrial conflict, adding to the structural pressures on the welfare state (or on mature capitalism, choosing whichever seems most appropriate) and polarising political action.

This is the kind of dilemma confronted today by social-liberalism as well as by the reformist labour movement in many European countries. In this chapter I shall first attempt to analyse this dilemma in more detail, and second, propose a number of alternative solutions.

Too often the programmes offered by a particular welfare system are judged without considering the origin of the problems which the system is trying to solve. Only by taking this larger nexus into account can we evaluate how effective the system is and whether the focus might not better be turned to the elimination or at least the reduction of the problems themselves.

The problems of mature capitalism

First, in mature capitalism there is a growing discrepancy between the increasingly intense concentration of capitalists and management on capital accumulation,[1] and the increasing societal implications and repercussions of their business decisions: in Marxist terms, the contradiction between the private character of social relations of production, and the increasingly societal character of productive forces.

Second, on the micro-level of the single firm, this contradiction manifests itself as the internal contradiction between the limited range of value judgements involved in making business decisions, and the much wider spectrum of social and productive incentives for employees of the firm. In other words, the narrower the spectrum of incentives with regard to industrial production, the greater the power over the direction and management of that production.

Third, as a result of these increasing contradictions (which manifest themselves as 'non-decisions' concerning 'non-issues') a growing number of 'external effects' of capitalist production obtains. No one would have taken responsibility for these so-called negative externalities if the interventionist welfare state had not been promoted by concerned pressure groups and by voters in democratic elections. However, over time, a conflict emerges between the fiscal requirements of the interventionist welfare state and the financial requirements of private capitalism. The second contradiction generates the third.

Even though some of the welfare measures undertaken by the state, and a great deal of the infrastructural investment of the state, are needed to reproduce labour power for capitalism and to maintain the capitalist system as a whole, it can be argued that this state investment is not *altogether* necessary for the capitalist system. Quite obviously the business community dislikes the high taxes levied on it to enable the state to meet its welfare expenditures. But since welfare services are demanded in order to cope with the negative effects of the capitalist system itself, they cannot be considered an external nuisance; they are rather a manifestation of an internal contradiction of mature capitalism.

Fourth, due to the processes of capital concentration the sheer size of enterprises in financial crisis makes it too costly politically and too destructive economically to allow the completely free play of the classic market mechanisms for long-term productivity — bankruptcies, unemployment, devaluation of capital, etc. — and therefore the state is forced to intervene by subsidising ailing companies and also attempting to control and discipline individual capitalists as well as the working class. But by exceeding the limits of 'market conformity'[2] and by disrupting the 'optimal' allocating mechanisms of the free market, the interventionist state can scarcely create a viable and dynamic alternative. What renders this an internal structural contradiction of capitalism is the extent to which these 'disruptive' interventions have been generated by market processes — namely, a combination of capital concentration and economic recession or crises.

Fifth, marginalisation of labour with large numbers of permanently unemployed as a result of mechanisation and computerisation has generated new and unfamiliar economic and political problems for which neither the present capitalist order nor traditional socialist programmes have any satisfactory solutions. Rather than a class struggle between labour and capital, we may be approaching a situation of conflict between the working class and a class of non-workers, or as Andre Gorz has suggested more succinctly, between a non-class of unemployed and marginalised labour on one side, and employed labour, capital and the state on the other.[3] This prospect should also be included when we speak of the contradictions of mature capitalism.

Sixth, while capital is becoming increasingly internationalised, the processes of consensus-creation, political legitimisation and social reproduction remain nationally or locally based. While international capital may need to maintain some aspects of these national bases for its own operations, nation states are becoming increasingly powerless in relation to international capital.

These six contradictions of mature capitalism could be reduced to a smaller number by reference to a more abstract terminology. Here our main effort will rather be to look for various ways of resolving them. Often a closer look at the elements involved in a contradiction, and at the possibilities of changing them, suggests a solution.

Resolving the contradictions of mature capitalism
A contradiction can only be resolved by effectively removing or changing one or other of the elements involved in the contradiction.

The contradiction between the societal implications and repercussions of capitalist production on the one hand, and the narrow range of considerations involved in business decisions on the other, cannot be resolved simply by limiting the impact of capitalist production on society. This is a *contradictio in adiecto*. Mature capitalism is by definition wide-ranging and highly societal in character. However, some of the more radical 'New Age' alternatives with their battle cry 'Small is Beautiful!' imagine that this is both a logical and a viable possibility. But these 'New-Age' alternatives imply a complete break with modern capitalism. Can the prophets of the 'New Age' achieve such a change without the support of progressive factions in the 'Old Left'?

If it is impossible to bring about a better fit between the narrow focus of capitalist business decisions and the wide-ranging negative social effects of capitalist production by limiting those effects, then the focus of capitalist business decisions must be widened to include considerations of the social costs of business decision-making. But is that realistically possible?

Whatever vestiges of paternalistic responsibility remained in early capitalism, it seems to me that mature European and US capitalism, as we know it, is now wholly concentrated on capital accumulation; social responsibility is token, rhetorical and in fact left to whatever kind of national welfare state exists. If mature capitalism could develop some kind of functional equivalent to the welfare state, by making the delivery of various welfare services profitable, and if furthermore this could be combined with a wages policy which enabled everybody to pay for these welfare provisions (which are theirs by right in the welfare state) then at least part of the contradictions of mature capitalism could be resolved within the capitalist system itself. But such a system would not be capable of *preventing* the adverse effects of capitalist production in the first place. Such a system would both profit from neglecting these effects, and also profit from curing or ameliorating these previously neglected effects! We must look for other less costly ways — in terms of human costs — of resolving the basic contradiction of mature capitalism.

The only other alternative is to widen the focus of capitalist decision-making to consider the wide-ranging ramifications of modern production processes, not only after the fact, but prospectively. A broader focus can be created in one of two ways. The first is to introduce a degree of political planning and direction in production which is based on the wider considerations of societal effects and human needs. The political basis for this sort of planning would consist of the central committee and the executive branches of one political party monopolising interpretations of what is good for the population as a whole. This is the system prevailing in the Soviet Union today. However, it should be possible to adopt a similar scheme through representative bodies elected by universal suffrage within a multi-party democracy.

The experiences of Eastern Europe have been cited to 'prove' that central planning and direction of industry are incompatible with pluralistic democracy. However, the historical experiences of Eastern Europe are not relevant to Western Europe today. East European socialism was first introduced in a country without any democratic tradition. The Bolshevik revolutionaries had to overthrow a Tsarist oligarchy, and faced external and internal counter-revolutionary forces during the formative years of the new Soviet state.

None of these conditions would be present if a Western European nation decided, with majority support, to take significant steps on the road to some kind of centralised socialism. In the West, according to this view, state socialism could be combined with civil liberties and humanitarian values.

Once the political control of industry and business has been made constitutional, it could be argued, this kind of economic democracy or democratic socialism would cease to be controversial, just as political democracy today is no longer questioned in stable pluralist democracies. The political parties would organise around issues other than the pros and cons of democratic socialism, just as they stopped arguing about the advantages and disadvantages of political democracy after the introduction of universal suffrage. Thus a multi-party democratic system could be incorporated with a system which maintained centralised political control over business.

Such a scenario would undoubtedly be hotly contested by some. I find it quite reasonable, but at the same time somewhat problematic. Even if pluralist democracy and a civil society were left intact after the introduction of a representative system of control over industry and business, there are other reasons for questioning it. A centralised economy would probably become rather bureaucratic, and leave little room for decentralised creativity and worker participation. Over time such a bureaucracy, like bureaucracies in all kinds of societies, might well become inflexible, weak, and passively obstructive. Alternatively, a socialist bureaucracy might become too powerful, vital and demanding, producing a new class of economic power-holders occupying much the same positions as monopoly capitalists hold today, while the multi-party parliament and cabinet would be left to struggle over more or less peripheral issues.

There may, however, be another way of resolving the contradictions of mature capitalism. On paper this solution may not look quite as acceptable as centralised democratic socialism — at least not to observers committed to traditional socialist ideology. This alternative implies a broadening of the range of entrepreneurial decisions, to mitigate the wide-ranging societal implications of modern industry, not through a *centralised* system of democratic political representation, but locally through a change in the main actors responding to market forces in single enterprises. We assume that there are people at this level who, if given enough power over entrepreneurial decisions, would respond to market forces with a more multi-dimensional kind of satisficing than the private capitalist by virtue of their broader productive and social concerns. In this way the content of decentralised business decisions would be given serious advance consideration. As a result some of the adverse effects of businesses, which today are so widespread, would be overcome.

But do such people exist with 'broader productive and social concerns', and with a greater capacity for 'multi-dimensional satisficing'? Elsewhere, I have argued that the incentive structure of labour comes closer to such requirements. It might therefore be instructive to consider this matter from the point of view of the ordinary worker.

From the worker's perspective there are fewer options and more risks within the capitalist system than for the private capitalist — the term 'risk-assuming capital' is quite misleading as seen from the perspective of the worker. Most fundamentally, the worker can never part company with the one commodity he has at his disposal — his labour power. While the private capitalist can sell his shares and move his money elsewhere, the worker selling his labour power is attached both to that commodity and to the capitalist who buys it, in a relationship of subordination, until he is fired or otherwise found dispensable. In moving to a new job, he is not transferring any profit. Unlike owners of capital the worker cannot spread his risks but must commit all that he controls — his labour power — to one enterprise. Capital-owners can not only spread their risks, they can easily move their capital from less profitable to more profitable companies without physically uprooting themselves. This may be difficult or impossible for the worker — unless he is young, or still geographically or socially mobile. So-called human capital is less mobile than financial capital.

Closely related to the smaller number of options open to the worker in comparison with the private capitalist, is the greater number of incentives which attach the worker to 'his' workplace. In addition to the profitability of the enterprise, seen as a precondition for paying reasonable wages, workers are naturally concerned with stable and continued employment, with reasonable prices for food and housing, and with decent working conditions. On the other hand, the main incentive of capital-owners and speculators is capital accumulation. Thus it would seem that workers are subject to a wider range of incentives than private owners of capital, in relationship to a given enterprise. For these structural reasons the rationality of labour becomes a multi-dimensional rationality, in contrast to the uni-dimensional rationality of private capitalists.[4]

Substituting the private capitalist with actors committed to a broader, multi-dimensional rationality and incentive structure at the enterprise level where decentralised market-responsive decisions are taken, is obviously a very different method of resolving some of the basic contradictions of mature capitalism than that of national democratic representation discussed above. This approach has more in common with the traditional model of entrepreneurial, decentralised responses to market forces than with that of political democracy. Yet this model, in so far as it involves collective labour rather than private capital in appointing management, is more democratic at the local level than the current mode of private capitalism: workers — both manual and non-manual — will be fully represented in board decisions. It might be called a system of democratic collective capitalism with workers' self-management, responding to market forces.[5]

Lindblom has reminded us that, analytically, we can separate 'two institutional components of capitalism: market system and private enterprise system'.[6] A competitive consumer market, where the consumer has a good chance of influencing the direction of production in a decentralised manner, according to Lindblom, does not require the existence of private enterprise, and is not even guaranteed by private enterprise.

Nevertheless, we are still only at a conjectural level in asserting that the multi-dimensional rationality of workers and self-management meets the multi-dimensional reality of contemporary societies better than does the unidimensional rationality of the private capitalist. This topic offers much scope for further theoretical analysis as well as empirical research. So far I have advanced no more than a theoretical argument, the essence of which rests on the fact that the workforce are dependent for the maintenance and development of their way of life on several different aspects of industrial production (e.g. profitability, wages, job security, the quality of the working environment, the relationship between work and leisure, etc.) while the private capitalist is principally concerned with profit and capital accumulation, and is therefore likely to neglect other aspects of industrial production in decision-making except when they appear as constraints on capital accumulation. Per-Olov Edin and Anna Hedborg, two Swedish trade union economists, have recently described this difference between the incentive structures of workers in a system of workers' self-management and of private capitalists in the following way. For private capitalists profit is a goal, and the demands of labour and of consumers on the market are constraints on their attempts to attain that goal. For the workforce the opposite prevails: realising the demands of labour and consumption are goals, and the need to make profit is a constraint on the attainment of these goals.[7]

Our argument so far about the contradictions of mature capitalism, and their resolution, can be summarised as follows. The present capitalist system (1) creates different incentives between the two sides of industry namely, capital and labour; (2) allocates most power to capitalists, who have the least number of incentives; and consequently (3) requires state intervention to rectify the imbalances and negative externalities which result from the effects of these limited incentives.

Workers' self-management operating within a system of democratic collective capitalism and competitive commodity markets implies a shift of power and style in the production for such markets. Most power is given to those actors who exhibit the least limited range of productive and social incentives: that is, workers. Within this relatively wide range, many incentives remain incompatible, but in this kind of system these various incentives are integrated within the multi-dimensional satisficing process of a *single* collective actor. This approach can be compared with current arrangements in which we have non-integrated separate processes of satisficing, with *different* categories of actors responding to different and partly contradictory incentives. This is a characteristic of private capitalism, and it is one which calls for constant and expensive remedies after more or less irreversible damage has already been caused by the processes of non-integrated satisficing which are dominated by those least capable of multi-dimensional satisficing, namely private capitalists.

All the solutions proposed so far for dealing with the contradictions of mature welfare capitalism deal with problems which are evident today. Now we must look at new kinds of problems: namely, mechanisation and the consequent marginalisation of labour, not as a 'reserve army' but as permanently unemployed.

Workers' self-management centres on the predicament and the role of the workforce. However the greatest coming challenge to the welfare state comes from the fact that we are rapidly approaching a new industrial revolution where increasingly workers are becoming replaced by robots and computers. So-called unmanned factories will become more common. Under these circumstances, what sense will it make to talk of workers' self-management? Several different ways have been suggested for resolving these new problems and these include:

(1)   A negative income tax or a guaranteed minimum wage irrespective of work status could be introduced so that the unemployed are able to maintain a reasonable standard of living. These proposals have come from conservative as well as radical sides of the political spectrum. If these proposals were implemented their effects would depend on the ideological context and political framework within which they were introduced. When suggested by more progressive political forces, the guaranteed minimum income (GMI) is intended to simplify and improve an established but highly complex and not always equitable system of welfare subsidies of the Scandinavian type while, at the same time, retaining the role and services of the welfare state. In this form, GMI appears principally as a programme of administrative

rationalisation, designed to achieve a greater degree of equality and universality.[8]

When a conservative like Milton Friedman recommends the introduction of a negative income tax, his proposal is combined with the demand for the dismantling of the welfare state, and the total privatisation of welfare services which consequently have to be purchased on the commercial welfare market. If the income distribution is inegalitarian as it would be, for example in the USA, firms offering welfare services after the introduction of Friedman's proposed negative income tax, would cater primarily for the well-to-do, who alone would be able to pay for them. Inequality would be both preserved and reinforced. The optimistic Friedmanite prospect of broad masses of unemployed consumers 'free to choose' in a competitive consumer market with the help of their negative income tax, while enjoying their leisure and reaping the benefits of free enterprise, would, in reality, probably turn out rather differently. What this opportunistic approach overlooks is the emergence of a new class structure, which is characterised by broad masses of consumers who lack adequate protection from the concentration of capital, and inequality of service provision which seem to be inevitable trends in market processes. Friedman also overlooks the possible emergence of a growing number of people who become so dissatisfied with being nothing more than poor consumers that they protest in 'irrational' as well as 'rational' ways, and thereby provoke harsh and repressive state measures, acting in the name of individual freedom and free enterprise.

(2)   Another way to resolve the problems created by automation and the consequent marginalisation of labour would be for the state to transfer to the public sector an increasing share of the profits generated by the efficiency and productivity of unmanned factories. In this way employment opportunities in the public sector could be increased as the need for paid workers continued to decline in the private sector. If private ownership of automated industries prevails, and if private owners fail to appreciate the need for such fiscal transfers in the interest of the maintenance of a stable social order, then these industries may have to be nationalised to ensure that such transfers take place. It seems likely that further scientific and technological revolutions in industrial production along these lines will intensify demands for the transfer of these industries to the public sector as an alternative to the free enterprise model favoured by Friedman.

(3)   The two alternatives suggested above were relatively easy to outline because they follow ideological 'blueprints' which have already been put into practice. But those who are more sympathetic to the general idea of self-management might prefer other solutions which, although largely untried, could prove both feasible and attractive.

André Gorz, for example, has pointed out that the trend towards computerisation and automation holds the prospect of promise as well as threat.[9] If the pursuit of capital accumulation is gradually replaced by the production of use-value related to social and human needs in the context of a growing non-industrial sector, financially supported by transfers from automated production, it is possible that the quantitative and qualitative use of leisure could be enhanced in ways which have not yet been recognised by the European reformist labour movement. Such changes, however, are not without their problems.

First of all, it will be necessary to secure the transfer of the profits of automated industry to the social and human needs sector. The socialisation or nationalisation of automated industry may be a precondition of such a transfer.

Secondly, from the perspective of a holistic philosophy, it will be necessary to prevent the division of society into two quite separate populations — the highly skilled minority of designers, managers and service personnel, in the highly automated industries, and the non-productive with no responsibility for anything but the management of their own free time. Such a separation might be overcome by introducing some kind of rotational system, in which everybody is expected, and expects, to devote part of their working life in the automated industrial sector, while enjoying some degree of choice regarding the period of their life spent there.[10]

Thirdly, from the perspective of self-management, most of the infrastructural and reproductive functions, and some smaller-scale, labour-intensive industrial production remaining outside the automated sector, could be taken as self-managed, local producers' cooperatives working in close contact with local automated industries. A kind of local or regional system of 'vertical integration' between infrastructural, reproductive component-part-productive and automated units is conceivable. It would be necessary to create self-management directorates able to negotiate problems of coordination between the different levels of the vertically-integrated overall unit. These larger work-and-life units could include housing and child day-care centres, as well as health, educational, cultural and leisure services. It might seem difficult, if not impossible, to maintain the mechanisms of a competitive market within this kind of vertically-integrated and negotiated conglomerate. Nevertheless there are lessons to be learned from our present system which exhibits many examples of the principle of vertical integration. This principle has also influenced some aspects of the well-known Basque cooperative community of Mondragon.[11]

Some of the units described as integrated parts of the vertical structures of production would provide welfare services financed by a corporation tax on industry. The term 'vertical' implies that some units would be subordinate to others. In the vertical structures found in present-day conglomerates, subordinate units provide infrastructural or reproductive services, or component parts, to the main unit of production at the top. It is conceivable that this vertical rank order will in the future be turned upside down. What is today considered to be the mere reproduction of human capital for industry — education, health services, recreation etc. — may in the future occupy the central or top position in a vertical structure, while the robots in industrial production are the 'slaves' who furnish the socially necessary work needed to maintain activities in the free and the public sectors.

The three different types of solution which have been suggested are ways of coping with the problems possibly generated by the proliferation of highly automated production. The third seems to fit best with the kind of arrangements mentioned earlier as superior ways of resolving the various contradictions of mature capitalism. In summary, the preferred arrangement would be one which is characterised by democratic collective capitalism with workers' self-management, and a vertical integration of infrastructural and reproductive functions with highly automated industry fulfilling maintenance functions in a vertically-integrated unit. A considerable amount of local and regional decentralisation might prove possible within such structures.

There are, however, more questions to be answered. Is it not contradictory and unrealistic to design systems with such a large measure of local and regional decentralisation and self-management when the *inter*nationalisation of production and business is the order of the day? And what is the role of the state in all these activities? These two questions are connected.

It can be argued that while the nation state is becoming increasingly powerless in relation to international capital, 'the state must continue to sustain the basic socio-political conditions necessary for that economy'.[12] But if international capital depends on sustaining the national bases of the international economy, then it is conceivable that perceptive leaders of international capital will, in the future, devote more time and resources than they do now to finding solutions which make it possible to maintain these national bases. For example, the fact that industrial automation is likely to exclude ever-increasing numbers of national populations from gainful industrial employment poses a threat to domestic stability. This threat can only be reduced if the business community refrains from opposing measures which create new employment in the public sector, or in an integrated sector of work and life units along the lines suggested above.

It is an empirical question as to whether or not leaders of international capital are intelligent and informed enough to understand that no economy — not even the international economy — can be run and managed as if human needs, local demands and labour movements did not exist. To understand this is a necessary but not sufficient basis for meeting the challenge. More detailed analytic studies must be devoted to the kind of solutions needed to cope with the interplay of national and international forces.

As for the state, in the various kinds of solution outlined in this chapter which might help resolve the contradictions of mature capitalism, the state has played an important but limited role. Within the terms of the main arguments advanced here the following limited, but crucial, tasks for the state can be isolated: (1) As a prelude to the decentralisation of the highly concentrated and centralised capitalist economy, it may prove necessary to nationalise key sectors of industry. These nationalised industries could then be placed under the control of workers in a system of self-management. Alternatively, such a system of workers' self-management — which may be partial or wholesale — could be directly legislated without nationalisation. In either case the central authority of parliamentary legislation would be needed to effect this decentralisation. (2) Securing the transfer of resources from the productive sector to the non-productive sector, or to what I have called work and life units in a highly automated industrial society, requires the intervention of the state. (3) In a complex and fluctuating economy there is always a need for corrective redistribution, counter-cyclical intervention, coordination, and some degree of overall planning. These are residual tasks which enterprises cannot individually handle and which therefore must be left to central authority. The state could meet some of these needs by defining the parameters of decentralised economic activity rather than by detailed regulation.[13]

However, whenever welfare measures are concerned there is an additional factor which has not been considered so far. In the modern welfare state of the Scandinavian type it is not only the material substance of welfare services that matter; it is also the fact that citizens are legally entitled to those services. It is beyond negotiation, means-testing, or the relations of selling and buying. It is a right which is vested in the status of citizenship. This legal entitlement is increasingly being questioned by conservative forces who wish to privatise the welfare services — which means selling them in a competitive market with a view to reducing government expenditure.

In my view it is vitally important to preserve this statutory entitlement even if the administration and delivery of welfare services is decentralised and integrated within the self-managed work and life units I have proposed. A statutory entitlement implies that welfare benefits cannot be negotiated away. Complaints about the provision of the services to which citizens are entitled should be addressed, in the final instance, to the state.

The role of the democratic state is thus largely defined as the residual tasks which other actors cannot perform.[14] Whether the welfare state will 'wither away' or simply change its form depends entirely on the results of a holistic analysis, which includes an evaluation of what other actors are doing with reference to the satisfaction of democratically-defined welfare requirements, what other tasks they could or could not undertake.

From this very brief and tentative discussion we have concluded that a guaranteed minimum income for all, including the unemployed, combined with welfare services for sale in a capitalist welfare market, would leave too many welfare problems unresolved. In addition it would maintain and perhaps increase existing social inequalities. A system of workers' self-management should be able to do a better job, although it could not assure basic welfare services as a statutory entitlement without centralised back-up. Only the democratic state can offer such an assurance. That, at least, is the minimum 'residual task' which the democratic state can fulfil. Furthermore, in order to make this entitlement viable, the state must also be vested with responsibility for redistributive measures through taxation and other allocative powers.

Summary and conclusions

In this chapter we have not attempted a detailed analysis of the characteristics of particular welfare systems. Other chapters in this volume undertake this task. My task has been to look at current and possible future developments within the larger socioeconomic system which generate the problems requiring a welfare response and which are frequently left unresolved owing to 'lack of resources'. Why are the resources lacking? Again we must look to the larger socioeconomic context to find an answer.

The welfare state and the significance of specific welfare policies and proposals need to be assessed as solutions to social problems. There is a quite broad consensus today that the various so-called mixed economies (which are all basically capitalist) are fraught with contradictions. These are the problems. Such problems can be solved, in principle, by studying in more detail the logic of the contradictions which are involved. In this chapter, therefore, I have attempted to identify the basic elements of six distinct, but interrelated contradictions which seem inherent in mature capitalism.

There is a limited number of ways in which a contradiction can be resolved: the elements involved in the contradiction can be eliminated or changed. In some cases it may be possible to find a trade-off, a compromise, or perhaps even a new and less contradictory synthesis of the elements. I have suggested that it may be possible to allocate a number of welfare tasks to decentralised and self-managed work and life units, linked at the local level to industry within a framework of vertical integration, with the state serving the vital function of authoritative guarantor that welfare services provisions to which all citizens are statutorily entitled is delivered within these work and life units. No other agency can serve this function.

Notes

1. It is reasonable to assume that a growing number of investment companies (i.e. companies which do not produce but which buy shares in profitable production companies) help in increasing the mobility of capital in the interests of profitability and capital accumulation but to the neglect of broader social considerations. Whereas the individual owner in industry is likely to have a personal involvement in the production of his company, and will want to keep his capital in the company as long as possible, institutional owners, including investment companies, can be expected to use their greater freedom of action by moving capital to where it secures maximum profitability, even if such a move implies a destruction of capital at the point of exit. Therefore the trend toward an increasing number of investment companies would seem to imply a narrowing of social responsibility within capitalism.

2. For a discussion of the concept of 'market conformity', see Mayntz, R. and Scharpf, F.W. (1975), *Policy-Making in the German Federal Bureaucracy*, Amsterdam: Elsevier, pp. 15ff.

3. André Gorz (1980), *Adieu au Prolétariat. Au delà de Socialisme*, Paris: Edition Galilée.

4. See Himmelstrand, Ahrne *et al.* (1981), *Beyond Welfare Capitalism*, London: Heinemann, pp. 132ff; also pp. 300ff.

5. This label has been suggested by Bo Gustafsson in his interesting article 'Kapitalismens kris — och vägen framåt' (1978), *Socionomen*, no. 17.

6. Charles Lindblom (1982), 'Epilogue', in Makler, H., Martinelli, A. and Smelser, N. (eds), *The New International Economy*, Beverly Hills and London: Sage.

7. Edin, P.O. and Hedborg, A. (1980), *Det nya uppdraget*, Stockholm: Tidens Förlag.

8. See Øyen, Else (1981), 'Hva er garantert minsteinntekt?', in Else Øyen (ed.), *Garantert Minsteinntekt i Norge*, Oslo: Universitetsforlaget.

9. Gorz, op.cit.

10. Gösta Rehn, a Swedish economist, has suggested a scheme of life-long 'drawing rights', allowing employees a free choice in timing the vacations, further education, sabbaticals, etc. to which they are legally entitled ('Towards a Society of Free Choice' (1977), in Jerzy Wiatr (ed.), *Comparing Public Policies*, Wroclaw: Ossolineum, pp. 121–57). Such 'drawing rights' could also be used for the rotation of jobs in the highly automated industrial sector, and activities in other sectors.

11. For a comment on recent developments in the Mondragon cooperative community, see Young, Michael (1981), 'How Large a Future for Cooperatives? Some Personal Reflections on the OECD Seminar of 12–14 September 1980', in *Economic Analysis and Workers' Management*, XV, pp. 409–11.

12. Makler, H., Martinelli, A. and Smelser, N. (1982), *The New International Economy*, Beverly Hills and London: Sage, p. 8.

13. Wlodsimierz Brus has discussed this type of state intervention on the market in his *The Market in a Socialist Economy* (1972), London: Routledge and Kegan Paul, p. 132ff.

14. Esping-Andersen, G. Friedland, R. and Wright, E.O. (1976), 'Modes of Class Struggle and the Capitalist State', *Kapitalistate* nos. 4–5, p. 189, proposes that the capitalist state be 'residually defined by the functions capital units cannot perform'.

4 The New Class War in the United States
Frances Fox Piven and Richard A. Cloward

In response to the economic crisis in the United States, the Reagan administration and its big business allies have declared a new class war. To cope with a stagnant economy, the federal tax structure has been reorganised to promote a massive upward redistribution of income. The Reagan administration also set out to save business and industry billions of dollars by undoing the regulatory apparatus through which government exerted some control over environmental pollution, health and safety at work, monopoly practices and discriminatory employment. At the same time, the programmes that provide for a national minimum income are being cut back. This is part of the larger strategy of enhancing business profits. By the summer of 1981, congressional approval had been obtained to slash $140 billion from the social programmes over the years 1982—85, more than half of it from the income-maintenance programmes that provide low-income groups with cash, food, health care and low-cost housing. Nor was this all. The administration announced that further social programme reductions of $45 billion and $30 billion would be necessary, in 1983 and 1984, respectively, in order to achieve a balanced budget by 1984.

Part of the reason for slashing welfare services is to pay for tax cuts, as well as to finance the massive increases in the defence budget. But direct redistribution upward is not the whole reason. The income-maintenance programmes are also coming under assault because they act as a brake on company profits by strengthening the bargaining power of workers. Analysts of different political persuasions now recognise that social welfare programmes in the US have grown sufficiently to disrupt the traditional trade-off between unemployment and wage inflation (Fabricant 1975; Fiedler 1975, 1979; Haveman 1978; Bosworth 1980; Danziger, Haveman and Plotnick 1981; Schor 1981; Bowles and Gintis 1982).

This disruption first began to occur in the late 1960s when, despite periodic recessions, wage levels did not fall. The reason is obvious. If the desperation of the unemployed is moderated by eligibility to various welfare benefits, they will be less eager to take any job on any terms. In other words, an industrial reserve army with unemployment benefits and food stamps is a less effective instrument with which to deflate wage and workplace demands. Slashing the social programmes therefore raises profits by generating greater economic insecurity in a broad stratum of the working class.

The major question posed by this momentous effort to roll back the income protection embodied in the welfare state is whether it will succeed. Is it possible, in the late twentieth century, to restore the kind of economic insecurity which prevailed before the emergence of the welfare state?

This is not the first time that capitalists have combined to strip away the state programmes on which the unemployed, the unemployable and the working poor depend for their subsistence. In the late nineteenth century, for example, industrialists mobilised to stop public relief in order to drive down wages by leaving the unemployed no option but to take any job at any wage. This mobilisation was prompted by the instabilities of the period. The rapid industrial expansion of the post-civil war period was characterised by ferocious competition and over-production, and industrialists responded in part by forcing more work at lower wages from their employees. Intensifying economic insecurity was essential to this strategy. Corporate leaders called for and obtained 'open immigration' policies and so flooded the labour market. They also made regular use of the state to help maintain labour discipline by breaking strikes with armed force, and by prosecuting strike leaders through the courts. Not least, public relief was abolished in most major industrial centres. In this period, as in other periods, employers understood that relief interferes with the terms of wage labour, and they mobilised successfully to abolish it.

However, we are doubtful that American capital can use the stratagems of the nineteenth century in the twentieth. It seems unlikely that the range of protections afforded working people through the state can be significantly reduced, much less abolished, as profound ideological and structural changes have occurred since the late nineteenth century. These changes helped bring the welfare state into being, and they will help sustain it.[2]

Ideology and state structure in the nineteenth century

The *laissez-faire* ideology which dominated America in the nineteenth century treated economic life as governed by market 'laws' which could brook no interference by government, except on penalty of inhibiting the market processes that generated wealth, and perhaps on penalty of creating economic disaster. *Economic issues were thus defined as beyond the ambit of state intervention, and therefore beyond the reach of the democratic majorities that participated in the state.* In the fully developed form they acquired in the United States, these ideas made

economic questions unthinkable as politics. This ideological development was remarkable on several counts. First, the doctrine of the
separation of the economic and political was wholly new. The immigrant masses who populated the United States brought with them a
world view which reflected a feudal past in which political and
economic roles and relationships had not been separated actually or
ideologically. The prince's revenues came from his estates, where he was
both landlord and ruler, the peasant both tenant and subject, and the
rents owed by the peasant to the landlord were also the dues owed to
the ruler. In such a world, most of what we understand as political
rights — the right to speak freely, to assemble, to vote — did not exist.
The main political rights of the common people pertained to their
economic situation, to their struggle for subsistence. Their justifiable
claims on political authority had to do with their right to use the land
or the forest, to ply a particular trade, to buy bread and grain at a fair
price, and to receive charity in times of distress. The significance of the
new doctrine of separation is that these subsistence rights were denied.

This was the more remarkable because subsistence rights were being
denied even while democratic rights were being won. Nor was this
victory without meaning. The economic élites who set out to create a
new government in the aftermath of the revolutionary war were
apprehensive about the threat to property posed by mass enfranchise-
ment. But their situation was tenuous and unstable, and their ability
to withhold the franchise weak. They set out to build a nation state in
the aftermath of a revolution fought by the common people. The
support of the farmers, artisans and urban poor who made up the
troops of the revolutionary army had been earned with the promise
of the democratic idea — the most powerful idea of its time. Moreover,
these people were still armed and still insurgent. Nor did these
American property-owners have the enormous advantange of an
existing state structure with which to eradicate revolutionary zeal and
quell public disorder. They were not shielded by the panoply of
traditional authority of an established state, or by the monopoly of
legitimate force of an established state.

As a result, white working-class men gained the franchise virtually
at the beginnings of the Republic. They were party to the spellbinding
idea that the state belongs to the people. To be sure, the common
people of Europe and America who fought for democratic rights
wanted protection from coercion by the state; but they also wanted
protection from coercion by the propertied rich. And while something
of the one vision was realised, nothing of the other was, for ordinary
people participated in government even as that participation left them
helpless in economic contests. They could not even prevent government
from sending troops against them to crush their strikes, or their demon-
strations for poor relief.

Finally, the triumph of *laissez-faire* ideology was remarkable because it was so at odds with the American reality. The post-revolutionary state-builders wanted and gained national policies to protect and enhance their propery (Beard 1965). The new constitution provided for the establishment of a national currency, and prohibited the states from enacting laws creating inter-state trade barriers or impairing the obligation of contract, in order to facilitate business dealings among the former colonies. The establishment of a national currency also precluded state legislatures from issuing cheap money in response to the demands of indebted farmers, thus securing the interests of bankers. The large landholdings of this élite were made secure by the establishment of a standing army, and their shipping interests by a navy. These and the subsequent history of state policies developed over the course of the nineteenth century — from the financing of canal-building to the construction of transcontinental railroad systems to imperial conquest — were indisputably economic interventions by government. They were part of the framework of state policy without which a large-scale market economy cannot exist. *Laissez-faire* was thus ideology in the old-fashioned sense of the term: it concealed rather than revealed this social reality.

No doctrine can be communicated and imposed by words alone. The interpretations people make of the world around them are, without question, influenced by the ideas that the dominant class propagates. Even so, people do not merely believe what they are told to believe. Ideas take root only if they are consistent with social life as people experience it, and they can be sustained only if they continue to be confirmed by social experience. Ideology, in other words, is bound up with structure, an insight that is one of the great contributions of Marxist thought. How, then, did the doctrine of *laissez-faire*, whose prescriptions were so at odds with the pattern of collusion between state and property, come to have such force and durability?

The answer is that the experience which nourishes ideology is itself a social construct. The experience of politics which was available to most Americans throughout the nineteenth century was organised by particular and elaborate institutional arrangements that concealed the alliance of state and property, while simultaneously creating a concrete and visible arena of politics in which democratic rights seemed to matter. Even as the economic activities of government on behalf of property were rendered almost invisible, other activities of government became the locus of popular participation. The ideology of separation seemed credible, in short, because the institutions that organised American politics made it credible.

One such institutional arrangement was constitutionalism. The constitution defended the propertied against popular demands by embedding the rights of property in the basic legal structure of the nation. Of course, the interpretations given the constitution were modified over time to serve changing economic and political purposes. But the process of reinterpretation was itself protected from popular influences by constitutionally-defined procedures which gave ultimate authority in determining the meaning of the constitution to the judiciary who were shielded from electoral influence by lifetime appointment. Consequently, the sanctity of property came to be taken for granted as a first premise of the new polity. And because the protection of property constituted a fundamental structural element of the new polity, it became difficult to perceive it as an arrangement contrived by some men to dominate other men, and women. A judicial tradition that gave constitutional protection to property thus defined the true and natural boundaries of the political world. It was as if these boundaries represented a new natural law, linked to and supporting the natural law of the market.

Other institutional arrangements that stemmed from the legal structure created by the constitution, but whose full realisation was not determined by the constitution, were also important in breathing life into this doctrine that insulated the economy from politics and government. One was the creation of a national government with powers that overarched the powers of town and state legislatures. The immediate impetus for the creation of a national government in the 1780s seems clear: the political action of ordinary people had always of necessity been local, for their ability to communicate and act was bounded by the organisation of their everyday life on the farms and in the towns. The wealthy, by contrast, were linked to one another across great distances by their business and social networks. A national government was, in short, a government that could be less influenced by popular opinion if only because of its inaccessibility to the majority and its accessibility to the minority.

This insight also helps make sense of the superficially chaotic pattern of centralisation and decentralisation that has marked American history (Friedland, Piven and Alford 1977; Piven and Friedland 1984). Underlying the appearance of chaos were two strong tendencies. One was toward the centralisation of policies critical to property whenever these policies were jeopardised by popular political mobilisation at the local level. The other and opposite tendency was that policies less critical to property remained decentralised, or were even deliberately localised. As a result, local government was exceptionally vigorous in the United States, and its vigour resulted from the fact that localities did indeed do many things. They administered the schools, organised community services, policed the streets, raised the taxes and distributed the patronage associated with these activities. And because local governments did things, an intense local politics developed, a school politics, a property tax politics, and a patronage politics. In other words, there was a level and a realm of government in which democratic rights mattered, but it was a different level and a different realm from that in which policies to protect and promote property figured large. The variable centralisation and decentralisation of government policies, by thus stratifying the politics of property and the politics of democratic rights, helped give credibility to the doctrine that politics had little to do with economic matters.

The political machine also contributed to the insulation of issues important to property from electoral politics. The wide extension of the franchise and the availability of patronage from decentralised government, combined with a system of territorial electoral representation, helped create circumstances favourable to the development in nineteenth-century American cities of pervasive clientelist relations between working people and the political system. Through a politics of favours and symbols doled out to sustain individual, ethnic and neighbourhood loyalties, class-consciousness weakened. However, a politics of favours and symbols was only the public face of the electoral machine. Most patronage was neither so visible nor so benign. The control of the votes of the largely immigrant wards enabled the machine to win political office. But the authority of those offices was used in another and far more private and important exchange with business. It was the graft proffered by the traction, utility, insurance and banking firms in return for the franchises, contracts and interest-free deposits of the nineteenth-century municipalities that greased the wheels of the political machine. The achievement, then, was the ability to nurture a politics of individualism, ethnicity and neighbourhood among working people, even while sustaining in another and hidden sphere the big-time politics of big-time profit.

The machine ultimately collapsed, undermined by decades of reform manoeuvres by the large numbers of businessmen who were not profiting from it. Even before it collapsed, however, these business reformers were creating new structural arrangements to take its place to continue the insulation of the politics of property from popular politics. This was done by locating the municipal functions critical to property in separate agencies, in commissions, boards and authorities with mandated powers to control capital infrastructure investments in such areas as transport and construction. These agencies were legally insulated from electoral politics. Their officials were appointed (usually from lists drawn up by business-oriented civic groups), and once appointed were typically secured by law against political removal. Meanwhile, the elaborate language and rationales generated by such agencies simultaneously shielded them from political scrutiny and gave the appearance that the issues with which they dealt were technical, and thus fit only for experts rather than politicians to decide.

In combination, these various institutional arrangements created a realm of actual experience that confirmed the doctrine of separation. People saw and participated in a politics: it was a visible and a vigorous politics, but it was not a politics of property.

Government intervention in the twentieth century

In the course of the twentieth century, capitalism itself contributed to the demystification of *laissez-faire* ideology. As the economy expanded and changed, so did the demands by capital, with results that progressively exposed its reliance on the state. Moreover, economic concentration and change altered the form and extent of popular resistance. Taken together, these developments led to pressures for new kinds of state intervention in the economy, and thus for a greatly enlarged state role in the economy. As this happened, the institutional walls constructed around the world of popular politics began to give way, overwhelmed by the sheer scale of state action on behalf of property.

Industrialists themselves were key political actors in forcing state expansion into the economy (Kolko 1977). The process was sometimes circuitous. Toward the end of the nineteenth century, as economic concentration increased, protests against the 'trusts and combinations' mounted, especially among farmers who were being bankrupted by the pricing practices of granaries and the railroads. The solution was the first introduction of a federal regulatory apparatus that appeased popular clamour while working closely with capital.

If the immediate impetus was to appease public clamour, federal regulation also suggested a solution to the problems of competition and over-production that plagued nineteenth-century American capitalism. From the Interstate Commerce Commission and the Sherman Anti-Trust Act of the late nineteenth century, to the mechanisms created for the regulation of the meat-packing, rail transportation and communications industries under Theodore Roosevelt, to the establishment of the Federal Reserve Board and the Federal Power Commission under Woodrow Wilson, the leaders of industry and finance learned, if they did not already know, the usefulness of government in ensuring a measure of stability and predictability for their ever more concentrated industrial and financial empires.

While federal regulation failed to curb corporate excesses — and even served corporate purposes — it nevertheless initiated the long process through which popular economic demands emerged to affect state policy. Again and again, as corporate leaders conceded legislation to placate inflamed public opinion, and promoted it to secure a measure of industrial stability, they prepared the way for the idea that government had something to do with the economy after all.

Government intervention to solve the problems of capital accelerated with the Great Crash of 1929. Given the rapid advance of economic concentration, economic collapse was more widespread and its effects more pervasive. Not even the moguls of the corporate world were spared, and it was 'uneconomic competition' (in Bernard Baruch's words) from which they asked government to protect them. Under Franklyn Delano Roosevelt, the National Industrial Recovery Act created the mechanisms that industrialists had been calling for: industry-wide boards dominated by industry representatives who would regulate production and fix prices, with government authority. Farmers gained the Agricultural Adjustment Act, which established price supports and cheap credit. Public works programmes were funded by the federal government on a huge scale, and were used to build the highways, airports and bridges needed by business and industry that states and localities could no longer afford to construct. In 1934, the Securities and Exchange Commission was established to stabilise the financial markets; and the Interstate Oil and Gas Compact set price levels for a generation in the high-technology industries.

But if business was demanding government action to restore the economy, so by this time were working people (Piven and Cloward 1977). The 1932 election showed that voters had become activated over the economic issue. Massive waves of popular insurgency followed among the unemployed and among industrial workers. The scale of these movements was made possible by increasing economic concentration that brought more and more people closer together in factory and city where they were exposed to common experiences. It was also made possible by the increasing scale of economic instability, which subjected so many people to the same joblessness, the same wage cuts, the same speed-ups. These movements, in other words, arose from the new capacities for collective action afforded people by the evolution of economic development.

In this climate of breakdown and insurgency, *laissez-faire* doctrines could not remain credible, and the idea of economic rights as political rights began to emerge. Indeed, by its very demands on the state for stabilising interventions in the economy, the leaders of business and industry themselves gave the lie to *laissez-faire* in visible and dramatic ways. Economic issues, in short, had entered the realm of democratic politics.

The victories for working people are familiar enough. Politics and economics fused in the granting of federal emergency relief to the unemployed, in collective-bargaining legislation, in wages and hours laws, in unemployment insurance, in pensions for the aged and disabled, in the enactment of public welfare subsidies for the unemployable, and in low-cost housing for workers. These developments were of great significance: the doctrine of separation had begun to collapse, and as it did, political rights became the means by which ordinary people could and did act on the most pressing issues in their lives.

The second world war greatly strengthened the links between government and capital because of the enormous productive demands generated by war contracts. It also enlarged the means through which state and capital together attempted economic regulation, including the wartime regulation of labour. None of this was remarkable or exceptional; wars have always been the occasion for state expansion into the economy, and the second world war was no exception. What was significant, however, is that federal intervention continued after the war, mainly in the form of Keynesian policies to subsidise investment and maintain aggregate demand. The instruments of this new and fully-fledged political economy included high levels of military and defence spending; subsidies and tax credits for the construction and real estate industries; infrastructure subsidies in the form of highway, water and sewer grants; farm subsidies; and, somewhat later, the use of investment tax credits as a strategy for economic stimulus. Corporate leaders also obtained tax and tariff policies favourable to overseas investment, and used developments such as the Bretton Woods Agreement and the International Monetary Fund to facilitate overseas expansion.

These developments transformed the economy and polity. The state's role in the economy expanded in ways that overwhelmed the institutional barriers that had shielded earlier forms of intervention from public view. The sheer scope of the problems and the opportunities business confronted during and after the war, and the scale of government intervention which was demanded, exposed the national state as a principal as well as a public actor in the economy. Not only was the economy becoming intensely politicised, managed as it was by an alliance of state and capital, but at least some of the institutional arrangements that had once obscured the politics of property were crumbling. And it was business that was wielding the wrecking bar.

Once again, however, there were other hands on the wrecking bar. The end of the depression did not signal the end of the politicisation of popular economic demands, although these demands were subdued and countered by appeals to patriotism during the war. Immediately after the war, with strikes by industrial workers spreading once again, the federal government moved to appease the widespread fear that post-war demobilisation would precipitate the high levels of unemployment that prevailed in the 1930s. The Employment Act 1946 proclaimed that 'creating and maintaining . . . useful employment opportunities' was 'the continuing policy and responsibility of the Federal Government'. Moreover, the Act created a Council of Economic Advisors charged with the responsibility of promoting the economic stability and growth that would ensure full employment. As a practical matter, this was no guarantee of full employment, and in the succeeding decades average unemployment levels inched steadily upwards. It was nevertheless one more small step in the politicising of economic grievances.

A more significant step was taken as a result of the emergence of another insurgent movement, this time among the urban blacks who had been displaced from agriculture by mechanisation (Piven and Cloward 1977). Blacks were able to act together in the protest movement of the 1950s and 1960s because migration and subsequent segregation had brought them together in greatly expanded ghettos. They were able to make economic demands political issues because the old doctrine of separation had weakened, its institutional supports broken by the combined and continuing claims of both property and democracy. And they could hope that these demands would be effective because migration to the cities had given them voting rights.

The federal government responded because it was vulnerable. The southern civil rights movement made it the object of black rage, and the northern black movement soon followed suit. The Democratic administrations of the 1960s could not ignore intensifying conflict in the older cities that local governments were incapable of containing, for the New Deal realignment had made these cities the urban strongholds of the party.

The immediate result was the battery of legislative measures known as the Great Society, launched on a wave of rhetoric about poverty and injustice. These new federal resources, and the heightened awareness of federal responsibility they implied, combined with the smouldering anger of the ghettos, created enough political pressure to force a much enlarged flow of benefits from the social welfare programmes created in the 1930s, and to force the creation of new programmes too. The Aid to Families with Dependent Children (AFDC) rolls quadrupled after 1965, and expenditures rose from $4.7 billion to $14 billion. The Medicare and Medicaid programmes were enacted, and a food stamp programme was introduced which rapidly expanded to include 20 million recipients. The elderly gained too as social security benefits increased sharply, partly because the black movement had politicised the issue of poverty and partly because the electoral instabilities that the black movement generated gave the votes of the aged greater leverage. Overall — after adjusting for inflation and deducting administrative costs — cash, benefits in kind and service provision rose at a rate of about 8 per cent each year between 1965 and 1972.

The movements of the 1960s subsided, as had the movements of the 1930s before them. But those movements left a changed reality; they had transformed the state. If the rise of popular struggles over economic issues was made possible by the erosion of institutional arrangements that had shielded state economic activity from democratic influence, popular victories in turn created new institutional arrangements that helped expose the state to democratic influence in a continuing way. The programmes won in the 1930s and 1960s produced pervasive new linkages between the state and democratic publics that paralleled older linkages between state and capital. The structure of state bureaucracies linked to capital facilitated the federal role in subsidising investment, maintaining aggregate demand, and smoothing the way for overseas investment. The agencies established to administer the new benefit programmes, services and regulations represent another set of linkages — not with capital, but with the unemployed, the poor, women, ethnic minorities, the elderly, the disabled, unions and environmental groups. By incorporating so wide a range of an enfranchised population, the state has become partially democratised.

The dimensions of this structural change enlarge the vulnerability of the state to democratic influence. The social programmes constitute a large and intricate apparatus of governmental and quasi-governmental organisations and personnel that is linked to and dependent on popular constituencies. This apparatus includes public agencies that administer pensions, unemployment benefit, social security, the food stamp scheme, Medicare and Medicaid, and housing subsidies. It includes the organisations that operate the job creation programmes and job-training programmes, provide counselling or rehabilitation services, and enforce environmental or affirmative action regulations. It also includes the programmes that reach into older and larger institutions, such as the enormous public education system, the voluntary social agencies, the hospitals, nursing homes and other parts of the health system, and even into sectors of private enterprise such as the construction, real estate and the retail food industries. In other words, this apparatus is lodged in all levels of government, and in non-governmental institutions as well. It is staffed by millions of people who are civil servants, social workers, construction workers, teachers, doctors and mental health workers. And this entire unwieldy structure, along with the people who staff it, is firmly linked and exposed to broad popular constituencies by the benefits and services provided, or by the regulations enforced. Finally, and most fundamentally, this vast apparatus with its millions of personnel exists by virtue of popular demand. It is dependent, in short, on democracy. The result is not the well-organised and well-articulated interest-group politics that characterises the relations between industry and government, but, nevertheless, is an institutional arrangement that tends to articulate and focus popular demands on state entities that are susceptible to those demands.

The probable outcome of the new class war
The emergence of the state as the principal arena of class conflict confronts big business with a crisis of power the dimensions of which are

comparable to the earlier struggle by capital to win control of the state from an alliance of monarchy and landed classes. From this perspective, the Reagan administration's efforts to reverse the policies through which people have finally been able to compel the state to protect them in market-place relations is only the surface manifestation of an evolving conflict of profound importance. The deeper expression of this conflict will take form over efforts to reverse the ideological and structural developments that now make the state susceptible to popular influence. Unless capital is able to restore the vitality of old doctrines and, more important, unless it is able to reconstruct the institutional arrangements that once helped sustain those doctrines, its current success in dismantling or reducing the array of twentieth-century social programmes will be short-lived. Worsening economic conditions will once again bring to power national administrations committed to acting upon popular economic grievances by rebuilding the welfare state, and even enlarging it. The critical analytical problem, then, is to evaluate the likelihood that this administration, or any future administration, can succeed in reversing the ideological and structural developments that made popular mobilisations over economic issues possible in the first place.

The ideological side of the struggle is evident in the corporate campaign to revive the doctrine of the separation of the political and economic worlds by warning of the dire consequences of 'big government'. These *laissez-faire* arguments about the perils of political interference in the workings of the market still retain some influence. Nevertheless, the popular ideology of the twentieth century − the view that economic rights are also political rights − is by now more deeply rooted, and it has been continually confirmed by twentieth-century experience. In any case, words alone have never been powerful enough to transform popular interpretations of the world in a lasting way.

The present national administration is also moving to reconstruct some of the institutional arrangements that once breathed life into the doctrine of separation. One way is to decentralise authority over programmes inaugurated in response to popular demands through 'block grants' (the successor to Nixon's 'revenue-sharing' scheme), and thus to restrict popular political influence to the local level. The new administration may also couple this transfer of programme authority with a shift in funding responsibilities, perhaps with some federal taxes earmarked for the states and localities to ease the way.

If decentralisation succeeds, the effects would be many. National organisations and national constituencies that formed to press popular economic demands would tend to become fragmented as political energies now focused on the federal government were diffused among the states and localities. At the same time, intense competition would develop among these localised fragments for the reduced funds available. Popular economic demands would thus be deflected from the national political arena and channelled into an increasingly competitive state and local politics, sparing the national government not only the reverberations of current discontent, but the reverberations of future discontent generated by the effects on working people of federal policies favourable to capital.

It should also be pointed out that state and local governments have little influence over the economic conditions that generate wealth and poverty. They are also much more vulnerable than the national government to mobile capital. Investors can and do bargain for favourable tax and policy concessions as the price of putting their money to work in a particular state or locality. That considerable form of pressure could well be used by investors to limit social programmes so as to curb their labour-market effects. One consequence would be to reverse the pattern, apparent since the 1930s, by which nationally-administered programmes created something approaching a national minimum wage, and therefore a national floor under wages. Decentralisation would remove this national equalising effect and expose state-administered programmes to the threats of investors who can decide to go elsewhere in search of lower taxes and cheaper labour. The result for the country generally would be to drag benefit levels and eligibility criteria down to the levels prevailing in the lowest wage states and localities. And since it would then be the states that were restricting eligibility and lowering benefits, the national administration could avoid the onus of slashing those programmes directly.

Other structural reforms are being instituted within the federal government. One is to make the federal agencies less accessible to popularly-based interest groups, but very accessible indeed to business groups. Many of the new regulatory and benefit agencies inaugurated in response to popular protest were staffed by people drawn from these same movements. But no more. The Reagan administration is restoring an older pattern of exclusive industry representation. It is as if the new administration were trying to insulate not only parts of the federal government from the sight and sound of democratic influence, but rather the whole federal apparatus.

Sweeping tax cuts represent another significant structural change, for they will be exceedingly difficult to reverse. The revenue-extracting capacity of the federal government was built up gradually over a long period of time. Moreover, the major increases in this power were made possible only by wartime mobilisation: the initial shift to income tax as a major source of federal revenue took place during the first world war, and the major expansion of taxing authority was made possible only by the second world war. Now that so much revenue has been forfeited, it will be difficult for a future national administration to reclaim lost resources except in the event of another war, or in the event of a popular mobilisation that creates a crisis of comparable national proportions.

The structural significance of the tax cuts is that, by sharply reducing revenue, they place limits on future government expenditures, including expenditures on social programmes, and that is one goal. Thus the tax cuts narrow the parameters within which future political struggles will be fought, because the prospect of large annual deficits will make social expenditures seem impractical. Under these circumstances, fiscal austerity will not appear to be politics; rather it will appear to be the inevitable adaptation of a responsible government to the constraint imposed by limited resources. The tax cuts, then, are for the time being a genuine achievement for corporate mobilisation.

But will corporate mobilisation against the social welfare state succeed in the longer run? Can the nineteenth-century doctrine that economic activities are regulated by the laws of the market-place rather than by the laws of the state be revived? And can people be persuaded of it? More to the point, is it still possible to so alter the structure of the state as to make this doctrine appear credible?

Despite the Reagan administration's propaganda and attempts at structural reforms, we believe the effort will fail. Propaganda alone will not suffice for very long; and the particular structural reforms that are being attempted are puny compared with the far larger structural changes that have accumulated and transformed American society over the past century. It was these structural changes that promoted the widespread politicisation of economic issues in the first place, and neither the Reagan administration nor anyone else is proposing to undo them. No one is proposing to reverse the pattern of intricate interdependency that has evolved between American capital and the state. Neither the decentralisation of a few popularly-oriented programmes nor the restructuring of the regulatory agencies will suffice to obscure the range of interdependencies between state and economy. Consequently, the scale and visibility of the state's penetration of the economy will continue to nourish popular belief that government has a great deal to do with the people's economic circumstances. It was just this 'transparency of the connections between the causes and the consequences of the "class situation"' to which Weber particularly attributed outbreaks of mass action (1946: 184). If government is the connection, then the democratic right to participate is likely to continue to produce demands that government enact policies of economic reform.

It must also be emphasised that capital is mobilising against the gains made by democracy at a time when the state itself has been transformed in ways that make it far more susceptible to popular pressure. This transformation, as we noted earlier, resulted from an accumulated history of democratic victories institutionalised within government.

Left-wing analysts have tended to view these victories as new systems of social control. They are that to be sure, but that is not all they are. Social control is never complete, and never enduring. The very mechanisms that effect such control at one historical moment generate the possibilities for political mobilisation at another. If that were not true, the history of insurgency from below would have ended long ago.

The contemporary welfare state affords new opportunities for mobilisation. There now exists an enormous array of agencies and programmes oriented to popular grievances against property. Of course, the Reagan administration is cutting budgets and even abolishing some programmes. It is also dismissing some federal civil servants and no doubt intimidating a good many others into silence. But for all its zeal, it cannot simply eliminate the huge and intricate state apparatus created in response to a history of popular demands. Nor can that apparatus be effectively disciplined either, for much of it lies beyond federal reach. The historical pattern of fragmentation and decentralisation thus has an ironic contemporary significance, for it resulted in many popularly-oriented programmes being lodged in state and local government, and in private institutions that receive government contracts or are reimbursed by government for services. This large and intricate apparatus, together with the millions who staff it, stands as a source of internal bureaucratic opposition.

These state and local agencies and staff have already been hurt by the budget cutbacks and the new federal constraints, and the prospect of larger and larger cutbacks means that more and more of these agencies and their staff are at risk in the future, and that will be a cause for opposition. This opposition can assume enormous importance because local agency staff are directly linked to the far greater numbers of people who will lose benefits, services or regulatory protections. The millions of teachers, health workers, social workers, and state, county and municipal civil servants all interact with tens of millions of parents and patients, clients and citizens. Together, they constitute a veritable electoral host. O'Connor makes the same point this way: 'The social democracy built into the . . . bureaucratic structure is perhaps the main domestic problem facing big capital' (1981: 54).

Under these circumstances, federalism itself will be turned against the national administration. Governors, county supervisors and mayors, attempting to cope with the explosive pressures generated by the new federal policies, will try to deflect popular anger upwards. That was their strategy during earlier periods of popular unrest and insurgency. The Conference of Mayors, for example, was formed in the early 1930s to demand federal help in dealing with a turbulent unemployed, and in the 1960s it was again a vehicle for pressure on the federal government to respond to urban unrest. When political leaders thus lend their prestige to the legitimation of popular grievances, as de Tocqueville and others have long since instructed us, the climate of denunciation becomes far more intense. In eighteenth-century France, it was mainly the *philosophes* who denounced the regime for its oppression of the people. In late twentieth-century United States the *philosophes* will be joined by a federalism divided against itself.

Notes

1. This chapter has been adapted from the authors' *The New Class War: Reagan's Attack on the Welfare State and its Consequences* (1982), New York: Pantheon Books.
2. This conclusion is not implicit in our past writings on the relations between the state, labour markets and public relief. In *Regulating the Poor* (1971), we argued that relief-giving was cyclical. Relief was sometimes inaugurated or expanded in response to the protests provoked by mass unemployment. But then, when protest subsided, relief was cut back, thus restoring the economic insecurity that has been the driving-force in the operation of labour markets. Contemporary developments in American public relief seem to confirm this pattern. Once the protests of the 1960s began to wane, real benefits began to fall. But public relief, once the sole form of state intervention to ameliorate destitution, has come to be embedded in a complex structure of income-support programmes for a range of constituencies. The changes in American society that gave rise to this development, which are the subject of this chapter, lead us to the conclusion that the cyclical pattern is not likely to be restored.

References

Beard, Charles A. (1965), *An Economic Interpretation of the Constitution of the United States*, New York: The Free Press.

Bosworth, Barry (1980), 'Re-establishing an Economic Consensus: An Impossible Agenda?', *Daedalus*, 109, no. 3, Summer, 5–70.

Bowles, Samuel and Gintis, Herbert (1982), 'The Crisis of Liberal Capitalism: The Case of the United States', *Politics and Society*, 11, no. 1, 51–93.

Danziger, Sheldon, Haveman, Robert and Plotnick, Robert (1981), 'How Income Transfer Programs Affect Work, Savings, and the Income Distribution: A Critical Review', *Journal of Economic Literature*, 19, September, 975–1028.

Fabricant, Solomon (1975), 'The Problem of Controlling Inflation', in C. Lowell Harriss (ed.), *Inflation: Long-term Problems, Proceedings of the Academy of Political Science*, 31, no. 4, 156–68.

Fiedler, Edgar R. (1975), 'Economic Policies to Control Stagflation', in C. Lowell Harriss (ed.), *op.cit.*, 169–78.

Fiedler, Edgar R. (1979), 'Inflation and Economic Policy', in Clarence C. Walton (ed.), *Inflation and National Survival, Proceedings of the Academy of Political Science*, 33, no. 3, 113–33.

Friedland, Roger, Piven, Frances Fox and Alford, Robert R. (1977), 'Political Conflict, Urban Structure, and the Fiscal Crisis', *International Journal of Urban and Regional Research*, 1, no. 3, 447–71.

Haveman, Robert H. (1978), 'Unemployment in Western Europe and the United States: A Problem of Demand, Structure, or Measurement', *American Economic Review*, 68, no. 2, 44–50.

Kolko, Gabriel (1977), *The Triumph of Conservatism*, New York: The Free Press.

O'Connor, James (1981), 'The Fiscal Crisis of the State Revisited: A Look at Economic Crisis and Reagan's Budget Policy', *Kapitalistate*, 9, 41–62.

Piven, Frances Fox and Cloward, Richard A. (1971), *Regulating the Poor*, New York: Pantheon Books.

Piven, Frances Fox and Cloward, Richard A. (1977), *Poor People's Movements*, New York: Pantheon Books.

Piven, Frances Fox and Cloward, Richard A. (1982), *The New Class War*, New York: Pantheon Books.

Piven, Frances Fox and Friedland, Roger (1984), 'Public Choice and Private Power: A Theory of Fiscal Crisis', in Andrew Kirby, Paul Knox and Steven Pinch (eds), *Public Service Provision and Urban Development*, New York: St Martin's Press.

Schor, Juliet B. (1981), 'The Citizen's Wage: An Analysis of the Influence of Social Welfare Expenditures on the Wage Inflation—Employment Trade-off', unpublished manuscript.

Weber, Max (1946), *Essays in Sociology*, trans. and ed., and with an introduction by H.H. Gerth and C. Wright Mills, New York: Oxford University Press.

5 The Institutional Crisis of a Welfare State. The Case of Germany[1]

Rolf G. Heinze, Karl Hinrichs and Thomas Olk

Introduction

Among students of the modern welfare state three causal explanations for the coming crisis are put forward. In broad terms, supporters of the first approach argue that there is an economic crisis as an input, a crisis of the welfare state as an output, and a 'black box' in between. Economic problems arising in the private sector are looked on as exogenous factors which affect the 'black box', and the welfare state is not capable of modifying this input autonomously. The second argument is that the welfare state itself represents the problem. It creates ever-rising expectations and demands, lowers the incentives for achievement, and extracts too many resources from the private sector. According to this view, the welfare state is causing or at least exacerbating economic problems. Disturbances in the economy increasingly become endogenous to the welfare state the more it expands. The third diagnosis centres on the decreasing efficiency of the welfare state. Although an ever-increasing share of GNP is spent on welfare, poverty is far from being abolished, public health has not improved significantly and psycho-social deprivation has not been remedied by the highly bureaucratic and efficiency-oriented measures the welfare state has taken. Furthermore, proponents of this approach refer to the negative side-effects engendered by welfare state procedures, which disable its clientele through powerful experts, destroy traditional social networks and support systems, and make the welfare recipients increasingly dependent on central bureaucracies.

Common to all three arguments is the insight that we are dealing with problems within the *structure* of the welfare state which might grow into a crisis *of* the welfare state. However, none is adequate in its analysis.

In this chapter we shall focus on those aspects of crisis resulting from reciprocal relationships between the economy and the welfare state's institutional system. In this respect, we are not interested in examining the question of how governmental control affects the functioning of the capitalist economy, but rather in analysing how capitalism affects the welfare state.

Our starting point is the present economic crisis, but unlike the second approach above, we do not hold it to be caused by the welfare state, nor do we treat it as a totally exogenous dimension as does the first approach. We also differ from the third position by not viewing bureaucratisation, centralisation and professionalism as evils altogether. In our view the welfare state is a concomitant of the modernisation of democratic and capitalist societies. It protects the individual against economic risks caused by modernisation based on private ownership of the means of production. Thus it is confined to coping with the negative consequences of market failures. But by its expansion it also gives rise to problems. It was and is a contradictory creation (cf. Giddens 1983; Offe 1984), and we shall therefore study how the malfunctioning of the economic sub-system, via imbalances in the labour market, endangers the balance of the welfare state's institutional system. The dependency of the welfare state on an unimpaired working of the economy is based on two interrelated processes: only a buoyant economy generates sufficient resources which can finance the welfare state; equally only economic growth enables individuals to ensure their subsistence by participation in the labour market and thus staying independent of public support. Economic growth alone, however, does not lead to an equilibrium of revenue and expenditure in the welfare state, there must also be sufficient demand for labour in proportion to total supply. Economic growth without demand for labour ('jobless growth') constitutes no adequate contribution to the maintenance of a balanced welfare state.

Whereas idle capital does not necessarily pose a problem to the welfare state, it does if the potential labour force is also kept idle. The reason for this is that on the one hand, social security benefits, for example, are largely financed from taxes and social security contributions levied on employed workers and employers. On the other hand, most entitlements to social security benefits are related to length of participation in the labour market. As the economy deteriorates and unemployment rises, increasing demands are made on the social security system, while at the same time the funds to meet these demands decrease. Therefore, economic growth sufficient to achieve a balance in the labour market might postpone the crisis *within* the welfare state, but continuous imbalances make this crisis *within* manifest and increase the risk that these processes will result in an overall crisis *of* the welfare state. In short, as the tax base shrinks, so demands for benefits increase. The most obvious solution to this dilemma is to improve the efficiency and effectiveness of problem-solving mechanisms in the welfare state. Structural barriers to such a strategy create another dilemma: the broad consensus, a precondition for innovation of the political administrative system, dwindles precisely during those periods when the need for rational policy-making is strongest. The institutional structures of the German welfare state are likely to be confronted with both dilemmas, resulting in a vicious circle by which increasing demands for political activity and decreasing capacity for problem-solving end up in a paralysing non-action.

The major consequence of this situation is dwindling support for the welfare state. To tackle the dilemmas requires flexibility but this is prevented by dissent within the political élite on how to cope with the changed conditions. So far, there has been a relatively high consensus about the ideology of the welfare state, and widespread support for the welfare state as a 'peace formula' between conflicting socioeconomic groups. Overcoming the problems of a turbulent society requires co-ordinated action in the fragmented institutional system of the West German welfare state, which provides welfare benefits from a number of different agencies. Foremost are the social insurance systems (unemployment, health and pensions), central government (with two legislative chambers), the states and the local governments, each with their own legislative rights, revenues and budgets. This complex network generates considerable coordination and cooperation costs, the result of budget specifications, dual responsibilities and overlapping jurisdictions.

This overriding need for a continuing high level of consensus is a barrier to innovation. The separation of the political—administrative systems fosters particular interests along the vertical line of institutions (central, state and local) as well as among the agencies placed on the horizontal level (e.g. the different social insurance systems). In the decision-making process it is often more effective for an institution to pursue solutions with a positive effect on its own performance, while ignoring the negative effects on other agencies in the system. Thus, comprehensive solutions overcoming departmental self-interest can be prevented by a single agency. As conflicts approach a zero-sum game this tendency increases. Under such conditions *negative coordination* seems to be the main outcome of the bargaining process within the political—administrative network. The pattern is enforced by every agent avoiding collaboration as far as possible, because they fail to realise a cooperative allocation of resources (Fürst and Hesse 1978), and the initial problem (in this case, unemployment) is aggravated or at least no substantial improvement takes place.

We shall look more closely in this chapter at how the crisis in the labour market is reflected in the social security system of the Federal Republic of Germany and how the welfare state has responded so far.

We then present three strategies which different sections of the political élites consider appropriate for solving these urgent problems. None of these strategies is able to win enough support to be realised as proposed. Accordingly, the future development of the German welfare state will be shaped by compromise in the attempt to cope with the crisis as it affects different parts of the welfare state, or the system itself.

The German labour market

The situation of the German labour market and its development is illustrated in Figure 5.1. Unemployment is a function of two factors: production and labour supply. Therefore, each of these is a potential lever for adjustment. The third relevant factor is the increase in productivity which is assumed to be 3–3.5 per cent per year. Keeping productivity rates down is out of the question. On the contrary, increasing production is looked on as the main goal. But it seems to be quite impossible to stimulate growth rates sufficiently to restore full employment — whether by adopting a Keynesian strategy, or by following neoclassical formulae under present conditions. Annual growth rates higher than 2–2.5 per cent seem to be unrealistic considering the state of the world economy.

Strategies to reduce labour supply have been quite successful so far. Displacement strategies have affected the so-called 'marginal workers' (e.g. women, older and handicapped workers, foreigners) — displacement is considered legitimate, and acceptance in the population is expected (cf. Offe and Hinrichs 1984). Since 1973 almost half a million foreign workers have returned to their native countries, and nearly as many older workers have taken early retirement (partly legislated for this purpose). The participation rate of gainfully employed males between 55 and 60 years of age fell from 86 per cent in 1973 to 82 per cent in 1982, and in the 60 to 65 years age group from 67 per cent to 45 per cent. The 'hidden' labour force also grew as young people postponed their entry into the labour market by staying longer in school or university, or withdrawing into informal work, interrupted by periods of temporary employment in the formal sector. The 'hidden' pool also grew as (married) women dropped out of the (official) labour force after a period of unemployment, and as other women interested in employment were discouraged after a fruitless search. The secular trend towards a higher female labour-force participation would have been stronger under more favourable labour-market conditions.

But the displacement of these marginal groups in their roles outside the labour market has reached its limits. Fewer foreign workers and their families are leaving, since the employment opportunities in their home countries are also becoming ever more reduced. On the contrary,

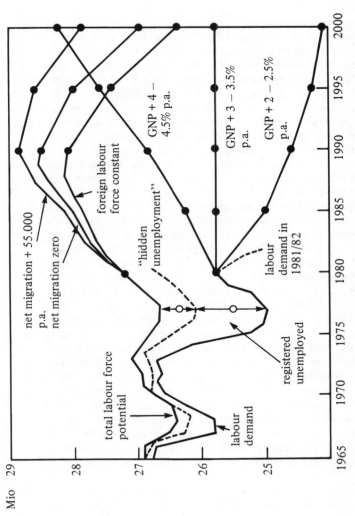

Source: **Klauder, W., Schnur, P. and Thon, M. (1982),** *Perspektiven 1980–2000. Neue Alternativrechnungen zur Arbeitsmarktentwicklung* 2, Nachtrag zu QuintAB 1, Nürnberg.

Figure 5.1   German labour market 1965–2000

the second generation of foreign workers is starting to search for jobs in Germany. Therefore, the upper line in Figure 5.1 indicating the development of the labour supply seems most realistic. Women are staying in the labour force for extended periods and further increase in the female participation rate is likely. Unfavourable labour market conditions should not be expected to reverse this trend. Furthermore, periods of occupational training for younger people to delay their entering the labour market are now seen as suspect custodial measures and are therefore increasingly rejected. A further lowering of the retirement age without any complementary financial measures would cripple the pension system, apart from the demographic fact that fewer persons will reach retirement age in the course of the coming years. Even a reduction in retirement age (to 58 years) is not expected to release more than 520,000 workers, not all of whom will be replaced by unemployed persons. Forcing ever-younger cohorts out of their jobs will be met with growing resistance. In sum, the potential labour force is expected to increase, at least until 1988 (see Figure 5.1).

Another way of reducing the labour supply is by shorter working hours. But the long-term downward trend of annual working hours (about 1 per cent per year) has diminished since 1973, at the same time as labour-market problems have been aggravated. Attempts to redistribute work by reducing working hours per person are vehemently opposed by employers and their associations, who regard them as unsuitable and even harmful for economic recovery at the national level. Despite their weak bargaining power, most unions are firmly determined to negotiate on this subject. Even if successful, substantial improvement of the employment situation will depend on the pace and the specific application of such reductions. It is impossible to foresee what mix of outcomes (e.g. increased substitution of capital for labour, more overtime, lower production or additional employment) will emerge in the end. In the short run, results other than preventing further dismissals are unlikely. Employers are offering an extension of flexible working hours (e.g. part-time work, flexible distribution of an agreed number of contracted hours within a year) as an alternative to collective reductions. Since employees are not willing both to forgo income for extended leisure and bear the associated productivity increases, effects are expected to be poor (cf. Engfer *et al.* 1983; Hinrichs and Wiesenthal 1984).

Non-adaptive structures of social policy

The main welfare institutions are the insurance systems tied to employment.[2] These are based on contributions related to earnings, although the federal government subsidises some benefits and covers the budget deficit on unemployment insurance. Approximately 60 per cent of all social expenditure is channelled through these systems. Most affected by the worsened employment situation are the pension and unemployment insurance systems since fewer employees are paying contributions while more unemployed and (early) retired persons are claiming benefits.

That non-adaptive institutional structures of the German welfare state can foster a crisis can be exemplified by looking at the problem-solving attempts in these two systems. Here a regression in the level of policy rationality can be demonstrated in the shift from a *long-term-oriented, active* to a *reactive* policy pattern with an ever *shorter* time-horizon. During the annual deliberations on the budget, deficits are transferred between the different social insurance branches, the federal government being the superior agency of distribution. These transactions are accompanied either by a cutback in benefits (i.e. an impairment of the claimants' position) or an increase in the contributions paid by employees. A vicious circle is set in motion which aggravates the initial problem: unemployment. To tackle this problem requires an increased level of consensus within the fragmented system.

The enactment of the Employment Promotion Act (*Arbeits-förderungsgesetz*) was a departure from 'reactive' policy towards 'active', long-term, future-oriented policy (cf. Schmid 1976; Kühl 1982; Webber 1982). The dominant concern was no longer to provide income maintenance after unemployment had already occurred. Rather, unemployment was to be prevented by promoting geographical and occupational mobility (retraining, further education, relocation grants etc.), job-creation schemes, settling-in allowances, short-time compensation (to prevent dismissals), etc. All these programmes were to favour steady growth (and hence a high level of employment) and to enhance the life-chances of individual workers. This type of 'active' ('preventive') policy had taken place in other areas too (e.g. industrial and technology policy) by the end of the 1960s when Keynesianism (i.e. the manageability of the economy by interventionistic policies) became the quasi-official doctrine of the FRG. There were no serious problems in financing the active policy measures as well as the reactive unemployment benefits in the early 1970s when full employment still prevailed. But when unemployment figures began to rise in 1974, the accumulated funds dwindled away and in 1975 the federal government had to subsidise the unemployment insurance budget for the first time. Only after increasing the contribution rate by 50 per cent (from 2 to 3 per cent of gross earnings), and by curtailing some elements of active labour market policy could a balanced budget be restored in 1977. Further cutbacks occurred in the following years so that the absolute and relative share of expenditures for active policy declined. In short, these policies proved to be fine weather policies (cf. Heinze *et al.* 1982).

During periods when labour is scarce a smoothing of the labour force corresponding to the needs of the demand side happens anyway through the efforts of the employers. The improved position of specific groups (e.g. the disabled, women, unskilled labourers) in the labour market is not due to the effects of an active policy, although it may appear to be. However, when the labour market situation worsens and social policy measures are really needed, the proclaimed objectives of this policy and the measures taken are considered unnecessary and inefficient. The abandonment of policy goals is due to the 'deficit exposure' of the social insurance system. As the federal government itself suffers from problems with its budget, it is tempted to cut back active policy measures in order to reduce the additional and unexpected expenditures it has to bear from subsidising the unemployment insurance budget. Therefore, how funds for active policy are raised is also decisive for a regression in the level of policy rationality. Wilensky's argument (1981: 192), that the better performance of some corporatist democracies depends on the decision to stick to active labour market policy, does not hold true for the FRG.

The growing proportion of the population aged 60 years and over is becoming a serious problem for the pension insurance fund, but in the long run it also faces severe financial restrictions resulting from the crisis in the labour market and the way the different budgets are balanced. Since the federal government has more freedom to determine the level of subsidies to pension insurance fund than to unemployment insurance it tries to limit subsidies as far as possible in order to minimise federal budget deficits (cf. Mackscheidt *et al.* 1979; Adamy and Koeppinghoff 1983). The pension insurance fund has therefore dwindled to almost nothing.

Before 1980 only transfers between the two insurance systems in question took place. We are now also witnessing an increase in contributions paid by employees, and a change for the worse for those receiving benefits — the annual increase in the pension is to be postponed, and is to be kept below the rate of inflation, periods of eligibility for unemployment benefits are to be reduced, etc. The focus here is not simply on the effects of these reductions on aggregate consumer demand — and hence on production and employment — but rather that all attempts to reduce the level of social insurance benefits as well as curtailments of universal benefits (e.g. child allowances) affect the last safety net, viz. the welfare system itself (*Sozialhilfe*). A good part of the increase in dependency on welfare assistance is due to the worsened labour market situation. The proportion of long-term unemployed is rising and with it the number of those unable to meet their daily needs through unemployment assistance (*Arbeitslosenhilfe*), which is 58 per cent of former *net* income. Although the share of welfare assistance amounts to only 3 per cent of all welfare expenditure, it represents an increasing part of the welfare budget of the municipal governments as they have to bear the financial consequences of cutbacks agreed elsewhere in the welfare system.

To illustrate the thesis that institutional fragmentation aggravates unemployment and thus endangers the working of the welfare state, it is important to look closer at the relationship between the different government levels: federal, state and municipal.

The federal level is held responsible for 'full employment'. Since the beginning of the employment crisis (1973—74) the federal government has tried to meet this requirement by an anti-cyclical budget policy. However, the *states and the municipal governments* reacted in a more procyclical way, and thus destroyed in part the possible positive employment effects the federal government made. Worse, local governments even misused federal job-creation programmes by cutting regular local government staff, and using the job-creation funds to replace them. Nobody denies that there have been some real positive employment effects, but the main deficit relief has been not on the federal but on the local government budgets (Scharpf 1983).

So far agreement between the public institutions engaged in providing welfare has not been achieved so as to manage a way out of the growing crisis. At the moment these institutions pursue their own interests in balancing their separate budgets rather than seeking an overall balance (flexible comprehensiveness). This obstructs concerted efforts to make better use of the *DM 55 billion* — the total cost of unemployment expenditures in 1983 (including benefits and forgone contributions and taxes). The defensive 'administration' of unemployment leads to a progressive 'institutional sclerosis'. The problem — as Scharpf (1981) puts it — is the extent to which the institutions concerned with employment and welfare policy are able to adapt themselves to the structural breakdown in the economic development we are observing.

Future perspectives of the West German welfare state

The welfare state in West Germany, and elsewhere, is confronted with the problem of increasing demands upon the social services on the one hand, and insufficient fiscal, political and organisational resources on the other. In developed capitalist societies individual wages are the primary source of income for the population as well as for financing the social security system. If the responsibility of the welfare state is to guarantee a minimum standard of living then the stability of the state depends on a high level of employment and on fiscal and organisational means to meet demands. Therefore, crisis management of the welfare state is directed towards two goals: (1) restoring financial freedom to act and reducing demands resulting from the under-utilisation of labour supply by realising a type of economic intervention oriented towards the labour market; (2) implementing a social policy capable of balancing demands and rising expectations with the capacity to meet these demands.

There are several development paths the welfare state in the FRG may take. These can be derived from the alternative strategic options we shall propose. These alternatives constitute no sophisticated devices. We only focus on those which are most likely to be implemented, given the existing political and institutional structure on the one hand, and the relative chances of success of conflicting vested interests on the other.

Let us first consider the possibility that a policy of 'more of the same' be pursued. The strong fragmentation of the West German institutional system, and the need to mobilise broad political support in order to achieve institutional change, appears to favour this possibility. The barrier to political innovation might even prevail in the presence of narrowing redistributive margins. Any attempt at redistribution might then assume the character of a zero-sum game (Thurow 1981) and, as a result, is bound to provoke the vehement opposition of the interest groups adversely affected.

In the domain of economic policy, this variant is a departure from Keynesian control of the economy in favour of a moderate supply-oriented strategy. By relieving firms of costs and by shifting governmental spending from social consumption expenditures to expenditures on investment, the goal here is to launch a new expansion of economic activity in order to create jobs. Such a policy, which might be labelled a half-hearted defence of the welfare state, would centre on the settlement of financial deficits in one area (e.g. unemployment insurance, pension insurance, etc.) by temporary shifts of deficits to other areas, and/or by increasing social security contributions, and/or gradually reducing benefits. Provided the forecast middle-range trend of the economy and the labour market proves correct, this strategy entails that ever-increasing financial deficits be filled within ever shorter time-intervals. Thus, it becomes more and more difficult to manage the crisis without eliminating the underlying causes.

This solution caused the fall of the Social–Liberal coalition in 1982. It was initially pursued by the new Conservative–Liberal coalition, but because it did not show success rates, the Conservative–Liberal government abandoned it after gaining a comfortable majority in the national elections in March 1983. Since then the coalition has tried to break up the rigidity of 'institutional sclerosis' by removing 'bureaucratic' obstacles and by strengthening the self-correcting capacities of the market.

This response stems from the diagnosis that the main contributory factor to the present crisis is the welfare state itself. It is assumed that the welfare state imposes a burden of taxation and regulations upon capital which leads to a disincentive to invest. Moreover, the expansion of the welfare state strengthens the power of organised labour and at the same time, via a weakened morale, constitutes a disincentive to work. Consequently, the proposed strategy aims at radically reducing legal and bureaucratic interventions into the free play of market forces, with a parallel reduction in taxation and a dismantling of welfare provisions. Cuts in social expenditures, which worsen the situation of the beneficiaries, are not merely intended to contribute to the 'recovery' of the national budget. Rather, they are aimed at restoring the work ethic and thus facilitating the adjustment of the potential labour supply to the decreased demand for labour. Such a strategy entails the consequent withdrawal from an active human capital-oriented social and employment policy in favour of a closer linkage of social security entitlements to individual labour market contributions (equivalence principle). The state is no longer seen as the primary guarantor against the risks of everyday life; the onus for this is returned to the citizen him/herself.

While the Liberal wing of the ruling Conservative—Liberal coalition praises the principle of economic success, the Social—Conservative wing stresses the principle of 'subsidarity'. This principle originates in a Catholic—Social doctrine which suggests that higher-level institutions should not take over functions that can be fulfilled just as well by lower-level institutions. Accordingly, the public provision of welfare should yield to self-help and self-reliance within the family, neighbourhood, parish and voluntary associations. In this way, it is hoped that the rising expectations, as seen from a conservative point of view, can be controlled, and the increase in social benefits and welfare expenditures halted. In the event of 'neo-liberal' forces withdrawing from the welfare consensus, a revival of class conflicts could certainly be expected and, at the same time, the cooperative relationship between management and labour would be at stake.

Even if one accepts that this strategy might improve business profitability, it cannot guarantee job-creating investment. It is just as likely that job-*saving* rationalisation measures will be taken, especially if employers take a medium-term view of profitability and consider the future expansion of production as uncertain. But even if this possibility is ignored, a substantial risk cannot be excluded: the immediate advantages resulting from this strategy might very well be outweighed in the long term by the costs incurred by denouncing 'social peace'. In the long run, a concerted action of *all* actors could prove to be more effective than a hard-boiled policy of austerity which always involves the risk of social conflict.

In the FRG public support for the welfare state has been much broader and more deep-rooted than in less developed welfare states like the United States. Furthermore, there are two influential groups which take advantage of the institutional systems of welfare: the producers, and the consumers of social benefits (cf. Klein 1981). Problems of legitimacy which result from a strategy of dismantling the welfare state must not be underestimated, especially if universal benefits are threatened. Nevertheless, policies already adopted in Britain and the United States are being followed: in 1984 drastic cuts in social security expenditure will affect the elderly, handicapped, unemployed and the poor.

The electoral success of the Conservative–Liberal coalition in 1983 was partly due to a distrust in the competence of the Social-Democratic Party to cope with the economic crisis. But it is far from certain that neo-Conservative therapy will justify the trust given at the polls.

A second alternative is represented by the new social movement which entered parliament for the first time (*Die Grünen* – the Green Party). So far, they have not presented a coherent plan for the future of the welfare state. What remains is the Social-Democrat proposal for an *innovative reorganisation* of the structural elements of the welfare state. The main thrust of their strategy is to increase the level of rationality in policy-making. Concerning labour-market policy, two lines of action have been proposed to increase employment: one is to qualify and mobilise the labour supply according to demand and to channel the demand for labour into areas for *qualitative* growth; the other is to reduce working hours and create attractive alternatives to work. Both proposals aim at fitting labour supply more closely to demand.

Without new areas for economic growth, combined with corresponding positive effects on labour demand, the welfare state will not be able to generate enough resources to survive. The strategy of qualitative growth looks for potential investment where social needs are not met, e.g. energy-saving measures, urban renewal, improving the quality of the environment, suburban traffic systems, development of district heating systems, new energy sources, and so on (Krupp and Edler 1981).

Another strand in this strategy is a *counter-cyclical labour market policy*, i.e. a reorganisation of the institutions involved in labour-market policy, which at present contribute to the institutional inflexibility we have described. The current method of financing active labour-market policy normally leads to cuts of just these elements due to the 'deficit-proneness' of the unemployment insurance system. Since the expenditures are not concerned with ensuring the reproduction of unemployment, they are supposed to be negligible. Policies aimed at increasing the level of rationality need to adopt a total cost-benefit analysis of measures combating unemployment. These costs appear in different budgets as forgone taxes, contributions and increased expenditure. The cost incurred in relocating the unemployed, which accrue to *all* in terms of additional revenues or reduced expenditures, are shared among all benefiting sub-units of the network in the form of a set-off of the different budgets. From this perspective the expenditure on an active labour-market policy cannot be considered as 'lost' since, in the long run, the stock of human capital is improved.

As for the question of shorter working-hours, it is insufficient to rely solely on the willingness of the employed to cooperate, or to over-emphasise the ability of firms to bear the costs of maintaining real incomes when working hours are reduced. Proposals have been made to improve the implementation of a successful working hours' policy: by sharing the costs of this policy the state would alleviate the burden of collective bargaining on this subject for both sides. A reform of the legal framework regulating working hours is considered indispensable in order to increase employment. In 1983 the Social-Democratic members tried unsuccessfully to enact such a law, primarily aimed at restricting the amount of overtime.

Attempts at increasing the level of rationality require greater con-sensus by further developing the modes of interest conciliation. This goal can be achieved by persuading powerful interest organisation to use adequate procedures to contribute to public welfare and not always to pursue their particular interests. Previous experience (*Konzertierte Aktion*) shows that the outcome of these neo-corporatist arrangements depends on the policy area and the characteristics of the participating organisations (cf. in the area of wage policy, Heinze 1981; for the health care system, Wiesenthal 1981).

Even if all these measures and institutional reforms can be realised, it is doubtful whether full employment could be restored and maintained in the long run. One can expect that rising productivity will reduce the number of permanently employed workers even as production is growing. As a result public debate on the mode of financing social security has arisen. It has been suggested that contributions to the social insurance system be based not only on wages, but also on cash flow (profits and depreciations). By taking into account capital for-mation, the flow of resources would become more stable in the longer run when growth without job-creation occurs. Another result might be that the substitution of capital for labour would be delayed when investment in new technology becomes costly in relative terms.

In almost all western countries proposals for a guaranteed minimum wage independent of former labour market participation has been dis-cussed (Øyen 1981; WRR 1981; Freedman 1983). Because of the danger that an ever-growing proportion of the population will draw its livelihood *not* from a market income, this discussion has been taken up in the FRG. Although there are many unresolved questions — such as the level of the minimum wage, how to maintain the incentive to work, and the compatibility of other systems providing benefits — this kind of policy might contribute to relieving the situation on the labour market:

a standardised basis income reduces the pressure to sell one's labour on the market. It could also lead to a reduction in working hours and might motivate people to interrupt their labour-market participation.

Conclusion

The three options outlined in this chapter are analytical proposals only. In the real world of policy-making none of these is pursued in a pure form. All have their specific enforcement problems, and uncompromising attempts at implementation would be most unlikely.

The market-oriented strategy, which includes a partial dismantling of the welfare state, is applauded by the public in so far as it promises to reduce the public debt, which is a highly sensitive issue in the FRG. The Liberal—Conservative coalition succeeded in discrediting the expansion of the welfare state during the Social-Democratic reform era by indicting it as a superfluous (waste of money) 'free ride' for unneedy groups. On the other hand, a drastic reduction in social benefits would provoke growing resistance from the beneficiaries of the welfare state (consumers as well as producers). A 're-activation' of policy which would come close to the third option might probably reduce the internal problems of the welfare state in the long run, but in the short run it would be more costly and also increase public debt. In addition, it would run against the criteria of rationality of vested interests.

However, these interests differ from those which would be adversely affected if the market-oriented strategy was implemented. Besides the interests of the administrative sub-units, which in the course of an integrative policy would lose some of their autonomy, the interests of private investors would be mostly impaired — by higher taxes, constraints on their autonomy, etc. Because of the importance of investment and the provision of jobs by private business both for public revenues and the level of demand in the economy, the resistance by business groups must be considered seriously. These groups are quite capable of portraying their particular interests as a common interest.

An example of this asymmetrical interest constellation is the conflict over reduction of working hours to 35 a week. Using the argument that the increase in the wages bill resulting from such a reduction would strangle the expected economic upswing, the employers are not only influencing the decisions of politicians, but also undermining support for this demand among workers in general. Even a change in government under the prevailing economic zero-sum conditions would not lead to an alteration of the barriers to innovation. Thus, the realisation of an active type of policy (option 3) in its strict sense is most unlikely. We conclude from this that the continuing prevalence of the strategy of 'muddling through' (option 1) is the most realistic. The pursuit of this strategy means a swing towards a market-oriented *or* an active type of policy depending on the composition of the federal government.

This means that in an historical situation where the need for restructuring the welfare state is at stake, incrementalism oriented towards solving short-term problems has the best chance of being put into practice.

Notes

1. We received helpful comments on an earlier draft of this chapter from Klaus Gretschmann, Nils Jacobsen, Stephan Leibfried and Claus Offe.
2. For an overview on the German welfare system, especially the different social security branches, see Eska (1980).

References

Adamy, W. and Koeppinghoff, S. (1983), 'Zur Krisenanfälligkeit der Rentenversicherung. Arbeitsmarktbedingte Finanzierungsprobleme in theoretischer und empirischer Sicht', *Konjunkturpolitik* 29, 285—313.
Autorengemeinschaft (1983), 'Der Arbeitsmarkt in der Bundesrupublik Deutschland im Jahre 1983 — insgesamt und regional', *Mitteilungen aus der Arbeitsmarkt- und Berufsfeldforschung* 16, 5—16.
Engfer, U., Hinrichs, K., Offe, C. and Wiesenthal, H. (1983), 'Arbeitszeitsituation und Arbeitszeitverkürzung in der Sicht der Beschäftigten. Ergebnisse einer Arbeitnehmerbefragung', *Mitteilungen aus der Arbeitsmarkt- und Berufsforschung* 16, 91—105.
Eska, B. (1980), 'The Social Security System of the Federal Republic of Germany', *Social Service Review* 54, 108—23.
Freedman, D.H. (1983), 'Seeking a Broader Approach to Employment and Worklife in Industrialised Market-Economy Countries', *Labour and Society* 8, 107—22.
Fürst, D. and Hesse, J.J. (1978), 'Zentralisierung oder Dezentralisierung politischer Problemverarbeitung?', in Hesse, J.J. (ed.), *Politikverflechtung im föderativen Staat*, Baden-Baden: Nomos, 191—204.
Giddens, A. (1983), 'Klassenspaltung, Klassenkonflikt und Bürgerrechte — Gesellschaft in Europa der achtziger Jahre', in Kreckel, R. (ed.), *Soziale Ungleichheiten. Soziale Welt, Sonderband 2*, Göttingen: Schwartz, 15—33.
Heinze, R.G. (1981), *Verbändepolitik und 'Neokorporatismus'*, Opladen: Westdeutscher Verlag.
Heinze, R.G., Hinrichs, K. and Olk, T. (1982), 'Produktion und Regulierung defizitärer Soziallagen. Zur Situation von Behinderten und Leistungsgeminderten im Sozialstaat', in Heinze, R.G. and Runde, P. (eds), *Lebensbedingungen Behinderter im Sozialstaat*, Opladen: Westdeutscher Verlag, 79—112.
Hinrichs, K. and Wiesenthal, H. (1984), 'Die Erfolgschancen der 35-Stunden-Woche-Bewegung. Eine vorläufige Analyse der Auseinandersetzung', *Sozialer Fortschritt* 33, 34—6.
Klein, R. (1981), 'Values, Power and Policies', in OECD, op. cit., 166—78.
Krupp, H.-J. and Edler, D. (1982), 'Fehleinschätzungen und Vorurteile blockieren die Beschäftigungspolitik', *Mitteilungen aus der Arbeitsmarkt- und Berufsforschung* 15, 225—31.
Kühl, J. (1982), 'Das Arbeitsförderungsgesetz (AFG) von 1969. Grundzüge seiner arbeitsmarkt- und beschäftigungspolitischen Konzeption', *Mitteilungen aus der Arbeitsmarkt- und Berufsforschung* 15, 251—66.
Mackscheidt, K., Böttger, G. and Gretschmann, K. (1981), 'Der Finanzausgleich zwischen dem Bund und der Rentenversicherung', *Finanzarchiv* 39, 383—407.
OECD (1981), *The Welfare State in Crisis. An Account of the Conference on Social Policies in the 1980s, Paris, 20—23 October 1980*, Paris: OECD.
Offe, C. (1984), *Contradictions of the Welfare State*, London: Hutchinson.
Offe, C. and Hinrichs, K. (1984), 'Sozialökonomie des Arbeitsmarktes: primäres und sekundäres Machtgefälle', in Offe, C., *'Arbeitsgesellschaft'. Struktur-*

probleme und Zukunftsperspektiven, Frankfurt-am-Main/New York: Campus, 44—86.

Øyen, E. (1981), *GMI. Garantert minsteinntekt i Norge*, Oslo: Universitets-forlaget.

Scharpf, F.W. (1981), *The Political Economy of Inflation and Unemployment in Western Europe: An Outline*, Wissenschaftszentrum Berlin IIM/LMP 81—21, Berlin.

Scharpf, F.W. (1983), 'Institutionelle Bedingungen der Arbeitsmarkt- und Beschäftigungspolitik', *Aus Politik und Zeitgeschichte* 33, no. 6, 3—15.

Schmid, G. (1976), 'Zur Konzeption einer aktiven Arbeitsmarktpolitik', in Bolle, M. (ed.), *Arbeitsmarkttheorie und Arbeitsmarktpolitik*, Opladen: Westdeutscher Verlag, 165—85.

Thurow, L.C. (1980), *The Zero-Sum Society. Distribution and the Possibilities for Economic Change*, New York: Basic Books.

Webber, D. (1982), 'Zwischen programmatischem Anspruch und politischer Praxis. Die Entwicklung der Arbeitsmarktpolitik in der Bundesrepublik Deutschland von 1974 bis 1982', *Mitteilungen aus der Arbeitsmarkt- und Berufsforschung* 15, 261—75.

Wiesenthal, H. (1981), *Die Konzertierte Aktion im Gesundheitswesen*, Frankfurt-am-Main/New York: Campus.

Wilensky, H.L. (1981), 'Democratic Corporatism, Consensus and Social Policy: Reflections on Changing Values and the "Crisis" of the Welfare State', in OECD, *op.cit.*, 185—95.

WRR (1981), *Vernieuwingen in het arbeidsbestel, Rapporten aan de Regering No. 21/1981*, 's-Gravenhage: Staatsuitgeveij.

6 Women and the Restructuring of the Welfare State
Hilary Rose

The problem for women is that, despite continuous assaults by feminists and their allies, the debate about poverty and the future of the welfare state has been primarily couched in gender-free terms. Yet the deepening crisis is borne particularly sharply by women both nationally and internationally. Women carry the burden of poverty, the exhausting labour of the micro-administration of insufficient resources, for their families and themselves, both in the decaying deindustrialising cities of the developed First World and also in the unevenly modernising nations of the Third World. In the developed world, the dominant ideology still declares that a woman's place is in the home, but punishes her economically and socially for being there. In the Third World it has become an economic necessity for young women to work in the New World market factories with little or no health regulations, and where they may be the objects of super-exploitation.

The feminisation of poverty
At the 1980 Copenhagen Conference of the UN Decade for Women, the empirical reality of world poverty for women was set out plainly enough:

> We heard that although women make up half the world's population, they account for only one-third of the recognised labour force, although they put in more than 60 per cent of the world's working hours, they receive only 10 per cent of the wages and salaries paid in the world as a whole, and own less than 1 per cent of the world's wealth measured in terms of land and property, capital and means of production.[1]

At a global level, women are massively over-represented among the poor. Development moving, for example, beyond subsistence farming towards cash crops has all too often been associated with the appropriation of the cash by the men, so that the women and their children find their conditions are worsened rather than improved by development. Within the old advanced capitalist societies we can also see an increasing feminisation of poverty, even though it is the United States that gives us its most dramatic expression (Pearce 1978).

It may not be immediately obvious why it is important to bring this worldwide phenomenon to the forefront of our discussions about the future of the welfare state. The answer must remain that it is theoretically and politically inadequate to constrain the debate about the welfare state within the experience of one country, when the reasons for the major problems of the welfare state are located within the global crisis of capitalist society. What is presently taking place is a massive restructuring of production, not simply within the different First World nations but between them and the newly-industrialising societies of the Third World.

Within this process, the restructuring of the paid and unpaid labour of women is central. Because participation in economic activity (the term being used not in the economist's sense, but in the more profound sense of participation in the production of the material necessities for existence) is the first guarantee of welfare, then the changing structure of the new international division of labour is of central significance (Fröbel *et al.* 1980). This capital-directed restructuring seeks to limit both the welfare state of the old metropolitan countries which are presently deindustrialising, and the future development of welfare in newly-industrialising societies.

This restructuring of capitalism is interwoven with that older structure of patriarchy, which has historically pre-dated capitalist society and lives on, in new ways, within it. It is in this context that we can see that the historic achievement of the welfare state — an accommodation between capital and a male-dominated labour movement — reached its maturity in the post-war years in North-Western Europe, more slowly in Southern Europe, and rather debatably within the United States. As such, the welfare state has constituted a specific phase of capitalist development. Feminist scholarship has pointed out how this particular achievement, which offered substantial gains for the working class, none the less did so at the price of the continued subordination and dependency of women (Land 1976; Wilson 1976). At the same time, this now visible alliance between the logic of capitalism and the logic of patriarchy made women the majority of paid workers within the expanding welfare services, and also the main dependants of the welfare state. The dominating class and gender are thus faced with the contradiction that women, having been called into existence as political subjects through the welfare state, cannot once more be returned to being mere objects of history, to be represented by male others claiming to defend their interests.

Thus the very existence of the massive provision of public welfare, through which market capitalism became welfare capitalism, means that women have been at the centre of a rising tide of expectations. These new expectations, in which women increasingly and effectively articulate their own needs and their own demands, are thus brought into existence by a state which cannot by its nature adequately meet them. The old welfare state simultaneously turns on the enforced dependency of women and their subordination within the home, the labour market and in political life and, at the same time provides the preconditions through which women increasingly challenge both its form and content. The contradiction of the welfare state is precisely that it has created the conditions in which women have become political subjects, with their own needs and desires which are no longer subsumable to those of men. In voting patterns and opinion polls, the gender gap is increasingly evident. For instance, women are significantly more favourable towards welfare services and more hostile towards military expenditure (Piven and Cloward 1982).

To speak of the strength of the demands of women, and the sense in which at the present stage of social development they become political subjects, is not to diminish either the struggles or conscious- ness of earlier generations of women. It is rather to argue that in large measure male-organised labour had through its practices become able to represent women's interests as identical with its own and thus to establish new patriarchal structures in the name of the achievements of the entire working class.

In *Three Guineas* Virginia Woolf wrote that women 'have no country'. In the sense that women have not been political subjects and thus created any country, it is perhaps easier for feminists to respond to the inner connections for women within the present crisis, even while we recognise the immense diversity of women's experience within and between different societies. Thus, despite the difficulties of trying to connect the arguments about what is happening at an international level to the arguments about the prospects of the industrialised welfare state, the perspective of feminism has an advantage over the more masculinist and nationalistic construction of the welfare state debate.[2]

The transnational restructuring of production

It is true that discussions of the future of the welfare state increasingly recognise the position of women, none the less, few acknowledge the centrality of women in the current crisis.[3] The spread of industrial production in the developing and newly-industrialising regions of the world and the predominantly female new production workers, is intimately connected with the future of the old welfare states. The new structures of production are organised transnationally, so that different stages in the production process are carried out in different low-wage countries. These new structures are made possible by the micro-chip and a sophisticated transport system, together with the economic and political power of the multinational corporations. This change began even in the long post-war boom with the development of free trade zones, and now accelerates, so that while industrial production stagnates or declines in the old centres, it advances in the new. The relations between the Third World periphery and the metropolitan countries are undergoing changes which carry with them not only a new international division of labour but also a new sexual and age division. For it is women, particularly young women aged between 14 and 25, who labour in the New World factories (Elson and Pearson 1981a, 1981b; Safa 1981).

In the earlier phase of capitalism and imperialism the metropolitan countries produced manufactured goods, and the periphery raw materials. Production work — particularly that which was defined as skilled production work — became, through protective legislation, almost exclusively the province of men. The seeming atomisation of the workforce at the inception of capitalism, in which the child, the man and the woman competed for work, has slowly changed through the central device of the family wage and its accompanying powerful ideology into a system of men's privileged access into what was to become the primary labour market (Land 1980).

The old locations of production are collapsing with increasing speed. As full employment is the precondition of the Keynes-Beveridge model of the welfare state, unemployment becomes a central social problem for the old industrialised countries. In some countries, notably Britain which has been in gentle industrial decline for a century, there has been a rapid nose-dive towards deindustrialisation — a process aided by monetarist economies — towards mass unemployment of some 3—4 million, with little foreseeable prospects of improvement. In so far as the welfare state has been defined as 'redistribution between the productive and non-productive sectors' (Kaufman and Leisering, Chapter 7, this volume) a 'surplus population' develops, now consisting not only of those who through age or disability are defined as dependants, but a substantial proportion, excluded by the failure of the labour market, of the potential workforce. Thus unemployment, in a situation where increased life-expectancy has led to more older dependants, creates too large a burden for the reduced population of employed workers to carry. While this definition of the problem as one of 'surplus population' flows out of a specifically capitalist conception of the welfare state, it is none the less both a compelling ideology and rooted in material practices of rejection, exclusion and humiliation accorded to substantial numbers of enforced dependants.

Even the hitherto much stronger economies of the United States, Germany and Japan are not immune to the restructuring process. The difficulty of ensuring profitability within the high-wage economies has led increasing numbers of firms to search for new sites of production in low-wage economies with abundant labour supplies. The very special case of Japan (see Pinker, Chapter 8), in which welfare is primarily allocated through the occupational sector, is particularly significant.

Welfare is thus very sharply dependent on the man's participation in the employment and welfare structures of the corporation. As employment is increasingly located outside Japan, the situation of both the male worker and his dependants in a context of few state benefits is potentially daunting.

The first phase of post-war expansion

The transnational reorganisation of production has not been a sudden process. At first, in a very traditional way, private firms — and for that matter, public services — sought to resolve their labour problems by attracting low-cost migrant labour and indigenous married women into the labour market of the advanced industrial countries (Kahn and Kammerman 1978). The mix of migrant labour and married women was not evenly handled by the different Western European societies: West Germany and the Netherlands, for example, were relatively slow to admit married women into the labour market. In the present situation of extremely high unemployment in the Netherlands this means that a rather small proportion of the adult population is actually engaged in the labour market. The chances in this situation for women to influence the outcome in the welfare state debate is likely to be much weaker than in those societies where they have gained better access.

The reasons behind the different national mixes of migrant labourers and married women lie in the cultural domain. Yet, the solution chosen by each country in the years of expansion of the labour market in western society is important for the present struggle. The migrant labourer, above all the *Gastarbeiter* who was to find that the invitation to be a 'guest' was to be withdrawn as employment contracted, offered two great advantages. First, the migrant worker was returnable if and when the boom economy ceased;[4] second, the society which employed the migrant worker did not have to meet the full costs of reproduction. Not only was the migrant worker typically reared in his home country, but children left behind to be cared for by relatives were often not acknowledged — certainly not in Britain — as legitimate beneficiaries of income-maintenance programmes devoted to children's welfare. In that the first wave of migrant workers was substantially male, the voice of women and their needs has been heard[5] even more slowly.

As married indigenous women and migrant workers became located within the labour market, it became clear that both were almost entirely within the secondary sector — paid lower wages, and for the main part enjoying poorer working conditions. During the years of expansion while women gained access to the labour market, it was substantially the service sector, above all the welfare state itself, which was to become the chief employer of female labour.

Phase 2 — Changing the locus of production and the gender of the workforce

Production during this earlier phase still remained largely in the hands of men. It is the present phase, in which production is being relocated in entirely new regions of the world, which so sharply affects women. Industrial production oriented towards export and world markets is rapidly expanding not only in Asia but also South America, Central Africa and, in a particular way, Eastern Europe.

Fröbel *et al.* (1980) examine in detail the development of the West German textile and garment industry, and demonstrate the links between the collapse of production in West Germany and the expansion of production in the low-wage countries of Asia, which chiefly employ young female labour. Some 43 per cent of this external labour force is under 20, and over 90 per cent are women. In 1975—76 West German garment and textile industry alone employed some 80,000 young women workers in low-wage economies.

The racist and sexist stereotyping of Asian women indicates why they are viewed with such favour by the multinationals:

> the manual dexterity of the oriental female is famous the world over. Her hands are small and she works fast with extreme care. Who, therefore, is better qualified by nature and inheritance to contribute to the efficiency of a bench assembly line than an oriental girl? (Grossman 1979)

But the genetic argument of this Malaysian brochure ignores the previous social training of such girls and young women in fine needle-work. In a very practical way such young women have already acquired, as part of their gender experience, the skills which fit them for the new world factories (Elson and Pearson 1981b). Here they are employed to work long hours bonding hair-fine wires to circuit-boards the size of a child's fingernail. Often such work is carried out with microscopes, but careful selection amongst the potential labour force means that, in Mexico for example, firms find it possible to hire young workers who for a while are able to carry out such work without the aid of a microscope or even glasses (Baerresen 1971). Not surprisingly in these conditions, as Grossman (1979) reports, 'a worker's vision begins to blur so that she can no longer meet her production quota'. At this point — perhaps no older than 25 — she is likely to be replaced by fresh labour with the perfect vision the first has had destroyed.

There are similar hazards in working with the chemicals involved in bonding. The *South East Asia Chronicle* reports:

> Workers who dip components in acids and rub them with solvents frequently experience serious burns, dizziness, nausea, sometimes even losing their fingers in accidents . . . . It will be 10 or 15 years before the possible carcinogenic effects begin to show up in women who work with them now. (Grossman 1979)

Where similar work is carried out in the advanced capitalist societies, such as the so-called Silicon Valley in the US, women workers have begun to protest at the teratogenic effect of working with these chemicals. Stillbirths and deformed babies appear to be the hidden hazards of working in the new electronics firms.[6]

Not only are these young women in the Third World the victims of super-exploitation — literally and formally unable to renew themselves (to say nothing of any dependants) — they are also excluded from further employment at a very early age, unable to play any further part in the making of super-profits. They must, therefore, seek re-employment in economies where agriculture has been modernised, and where traditional labour-intensive subsistence farming has virtually ceased, expelling unemployed peasants to the cities. In the crowded cities there is desperate competition for work in which all, including children, join: Hong Kong, for example, has a particularly large number of child workers. In South Korea, one of the most rapidly indus-trialising countries, girls of 12 and 13 work an 18-hour day, seven days a week. Eventually, excluded from the factory, yet separated from traditional family life by their participation in factory work, these still very young women are left with few alternatives other than joining the growing number of prostitutes, a process facilitated by the growing industry of sex-packaged holidays for foreign businessmen to the 'exotic' Orient.

Despite the support of the United Nations for the development of free trade zones, few commentators on development see much prospect of social development, especially in a form which benefits women, accompanying the new industrialisation.[7] In the context of an in-exhaustible local and international labour supply, local labour lacks the conditions for sustained collective self-defence. Wild-cat strikes can and do occur, but the prospects for trade union development and sustained industrial struggle are weak. That these new production workers are young women, constrained by the patriarchal relations of pre-capitalist society — often skilfully maintained within the factory to preserve social stability and docility — weakens such possibilities further. Ruling masculine élites constitute the main local beneficiaries of the new industrialisation. They work to facilitate the presence of the new factories, to sustain the gender relations of the old society, to guarantee tax havens, and to prohibit through repression the possi-bility of trade unions. Feminists and others wishing to defend the interests of all exploited people will have to do rather better than come up with pleas for protectionism, whether as legislation or as 'Buy British/American', etc. campaigns. There is evidence that European garment workers have grasped this, and are pressing for barriers specifi-cally against those countries tolerating super-exploitation.

The history of this new industrialisation is qualitatively different from the original development of capitalism (Sivanandum 1982). Then the very process of production, with its insatiable demand for relatively localised labour, called into existence great masses of workers, and at the same moment the possibility of their collective self-defence. The improvement of workers' conditions, their political participation in the democratic forms of liberal capitalism, and the establishment of public welfare services were thus made possible by the needs of accumulation and legitimacy within the framework of the nation state. We now understand that the entry of workers into public life through their trade unions and their political parties was paralleled by the exclusion of women and their interests from the public. But even this view of the welfare state as being about the gains of the male working class and the sacrifice of women — a history of partial progress at best — is precluded by the new forms of industrialisation.

The original development of capitalism, because of its need to produce at one site — so markedly contrasting with the multi-site production of today — depended during periods of boom on a finite labour supply. This was so even with labour recruitment through migration, whether internally through agricultural modernisation or externally from low-income countries; or even by the lowering of barriers against the participation of married women and ethnic minorities in the labour force. In this past situation, the interests of organised labour and those of capital coincided in their recognition of the need to intervene and guarantee social reproduction.

The old capitalism and state intervention in social reproduction

The scattered interventions of the nineteenth and early twentieth centuries in sanitation, housing, health, education, social security and town planning were to be consolidated as mature welfare states in the post-war era in the northern countries of Western Europe. Britain's history was a little different: the 1939—45 war itself gave a sharp push towards the welfare state, as the military necessity of a struggle for national survival demanded that the old antagonisms of class and gender be laid to one side. The new military technology, above all the air war, put the civilian population at risk.[8] The rules for the successful conduct of war were transformed. In the past, deaths had been largely confined to the young men directly engaged in the conflict. Now the new aerial bombardment threatened women, children and elderly people of both sexes. The conduct of the Home Front (as domestic policies were termed) became intrinsic to the overall conduct of the war (Titmuss 1950; Calder 1969). The embryonic welfare state which emerged under these conditions was much more favourable to the interests of women than the consolidation of the welfare state proposed by Beveridge, and was substantially realised in the post-war period.

Thus, where the struggle for national survival had demanded that various aspects of Poor Law thinking were laid to one side, it had also required the access of women into the labour market and supported their economic participation through the provision of child-care facilities. The anticipatory construction of the welfare state contained in Beveridge's Report implicitly regarded this as a temporary aberration. The post-war development of the services initiated during the war years turned on the renaturalisation of women; and the gains for women made during the war years by the embryonic welfare state were systematically negated. If war had, not for the first time, acknowledged women as subjects, peace was to restore women, through the welfare state, to objects.

At its core, the Beveridge model required — and contributed to — the maintenance of full employment made possible by the application of the Keynesian theory of demand management. It sought to extend and systematise the range of state-provided social services funded by social insurance. Contributing to social insurance was the guarantee for participating as a full citizen within the welfare state. Thus all men (and single women) were full citizens, but their dependants — above all the wife/mother and her children — were to benefit in a secondary and indirect way through the husband/father's contribution. Indeed, what was termed the national insurance principle might have with equal justice been termed the husband/fatherhood principle. Married women had no place (except when husbands were too unfit to work) in employment; they were not political subjects within Beveridge's welfare state; they were rather the secondary and dependent Other.

The ideology of complementary roles between men and women was successfully restored: woman the carer, man the provider. Such an ideology facilitated the exclusion, and self-exclusion, of women from participation in paid work, and helped secure — or seem to secure — the political objectives of Beveridge's full employment, even if the society which it secured was less than free for women.

The return of married women to the kitchen sink, and of single women to a female sector of the labour market were necessary to make space for the demobbed military within the occupational structure. Thus, in the first phase of post-war reconstruction the provisions of the welfare state, organised around patriarchal principles, facilitated the functioning of the labour market. That we know from alternative accounts by women, such as those of 'Rosie the Riveter' that not all women contentedly returned to caring and service activities, was for the most part politically ignored. Social and economic policies recognised women's 'best interests' as located within the home, and sought to ensure it by inducement and exclusion.

In so far as this early period (say up to the mid-1950s when the economy began to pick up, and the fit between welfare state provisions and labour market requirements and family structure began to come unstuck) reflected the high point of the Beveridge model, it is important to acknowledge the massive and unpaid contribution by women to social reproduction which was built into the model (Land 1976). This caring labour was extracted from almost all women as their primary task, and they were denied even the moderate choice between occupations open to men. As such, the category of wife/mother as worker belongs to the formal definition of unfree labour, that status which we had believed was abandoned with the development of capitalism (Corrigan 1977). It is a reflection of the deeply ideological thinking of both liberals and socialists alike that this labour was not seen as part of the social division of labour, but as an extension of womanliness itself. Beveridge's political and economic project of *Full Employment in a Free Society*, which commanded widespread popular support in a society sickened by the memory of the distress of the inter-war years, turned on the unfree — as well as unpaid — labour of women.

The economic activity of women

Although the concept of 'economic activity' as it is conventionally used is a grossly inadequate and sexist category in which most of women's work is deemed to have no economic significance, it none the less offers an indicator of the increased participation of women in the recognised and paid labour force. It has incidentally taken the present crisis for the masculine preoccupation with the informal economy to emerge (Gershuny 1983). Women's economic coping has long run the gamut from cleaning other people's homes, homeworking, taking in lodgers, making clothes, to prostitution — typically over and above their primary labour of making a home and caring for children and men. The theoretical significance for the analysis of the economy of these intermediate activities located between family work and the external workplace is increasingly recovered through feminist historical work on, for example, prostitution as an essentially economic activity rather than the expression of some individual psychological malfunctioning or moral inadequacy. Women — above all poor women — have been coping within the 'informal' economy for a very long time, suffering intolerable hours of work. Denied time (Rose and Ward 1984), that crucial factor necessary for reflection and theorisation, separated from one another by the conditions of their work, it is scarcely surprising that while women coped, men made theory.

The Beveridge model and the changing reality: the labour market

However, the development and recognition of the informal economy apart, what is clear is that over the past 30 years there has been a significant expansion of women's participation in the labour market.

After running at around 30 per cent in Britain for almost a century, the proportion of women in the acknowledged labour force began to grow during the growth years of the 1950s. As the economy changed and new opportunities opened up in the service and tertiary sector, women's participation rates increased both as full and part-time workers. The process continued throughout the next decade and, even in the 1970s when unemployment for women suddenly increased, new jobs continued to open up, particularly on a part-time basis. At present some 40 per cent of the total workforce is female.

The relationship between employment and marriage has also changed. Whereas in the past on marriage or soon after women left paid employment, 60 per cent of married women now work. Choice and the lack of support facilities — above all adequate child-care provision — mean that many women will withdraw from participation in the labour force during the pre-school years of a child's life. However, the smaller size of families means that this entails a relatively short period of some seven years outside formal employment. The necessity, in a period when more lip-service than pratical support has been paid to the family (Land 1978), together with the real if circumscribed freedom which stems from an independent income for the woman, has led to the need for the two-wage family. The plight of the low-income single-wage household, and above all that internationally growing category of the single-parent family, is increasingly evident.[10]

At the same time, it is important to stress the very narrow range of occupations to which women have had access. Census evidence for Britain gathered by Hakim (1979) points to the existence of an increasingly tightly-defined labour market developing over the century so that labour market segregation by sex was more marked in 1971 than in 1911. In the space of 60 years women had, despite their overall greater participation in the labour market, been eased out of their share of the 'skilled' jobs. It is important to write 'skilled' as the concept of skill is constructed with a powerful gender bias, so that when women enter occupations they do so as bearers of inferior labour (Phillips and Taylor 1980). None the less, even within the existing definitions, women seem to have lost out. While in 1911 they held 24 per cent of the more skilled jobs, in 1971 they held only 13.5 per cent. Their share of unskilled jobs correspondingly grew: in 1911 women held 15.5 per cent of all the unskilled jobs, by 1971 they held 37.2 per cent (Hakim 1979). Not surprisingly, the presence of low pay is associated with women. Of the 7 million workers earning some two-thirds of male average earnings, the great majority are women (Bassett and Weir 1983). But while these statistics are derived from British experience, the evidence on labour market segregation is international, with women systematically relegated to the worst-paid sector, despite the equal pay legislation which has been enacted in some form by most advanced industrial countries with varying levels of success. Statistics from the Common Market suggest, for example, that with the exception of Italy and France, where it is claimed that women receive 80 per cent of the hourly average earnings of men (in the case of the former a function of the official and the unofficial labour market), in most countries the rate has levelled off at around 70—75 per cent. The Nordic countries do rather better, with the Swedish women's movement able to issue a badge saying '87%' — their present rate — and demanding equality from that position; which from the rest of Europe in itself looks enviable.

The future of 'work' debate
Because of the importance of participation in the labour market for access to the growing sectors of occupational and fiscal welfare, the debate about the future of work — or employment as it should more accurately be termed — is of special significance for women. For while there are everywhere struggles and grudging accommodation to the demands of employed women, there is at the same time a profound anxiety about the future. It is clear to all that the heavy manufacturing industries (almost entirely the preserve of men) are rapidly declining. Production is moving away from the old deindustrialising societies, to the new sites in the developing countries, where the disorganic development of capital appears to preclude — at least in any straightforward way — the development of a new form of welfare capitalism (Sivanandum 1982). Thus, while there can be few hopes that capitalist economic development has a positive message for social development in the industrialising societies, few feel tranquil about the prospects for either women or men in the process of deindustrialisation. There is little difficulty in dispensing with the illusions of the utopian technocrats who preach that boring work is to be abolished simply as a result of the new technology and that the future of creativity and leisure is at hand. For women, the realistic options seem to be whether further fragmentation and deskilling will ensue, so that the work remains women's, or whether the job (or the more highly skilled work that remains) will be redefined upwards so that it is only suitable for men.

Few projections of the levels of unemployment in the old industrial societies whether they adopt an optimistic or a pessimistic scenario, give rise to anything other than concern at the prospects over at least the next decade. The more pessimistic reading sees a level of unemployment at around 10—15 per cent, with an increasing contrast between the high-skilled, high-waged and predominantly white male sector of the labour market and a low-waged, part-time, excluded sector below, where women, unskilled men, youth and members of ethnic minority groups compete for too few jobs.

The growth of women's part-time employment has been a conspicuous feature of the labour market within the welfare state, and nowhere more so than in Britain. For the individual woman part-time employment may be experienced as choice, so offering a human means of managing the double day, above all when she has children or elderly relatives dependent on her for care. Many feminists are none the less concerned at the way part-time employment serves to facilitate those mechanisms which locate women in a poorly-paid female ghetto with low prospects of advance. The attractions of such a flexible low-cost labour force are not lost on employers, and although there are few western governments (whether Social-Democratic or Conservative) who have not had at least one spokesperson who has articulated the masculinist wish that the problem of unemployment could be solved if only women would go home,[11] there are few possibilities that either employers or the women themselves will do other than resist this solution.

Theoretical and political responses to the crisis

There is increasing public recognition that the costs of the welfare state crisis are disproportionately borne by women. They stand to lose their occupations as the paid workers within welfare and to lose the crucial support services which make possible their unpaid caring within the family. While the costs are evident, it is rather less clear how well theories of the crisis either explain the situation or offer effective means of contesting it. Mainly written from within Marxist and neo-Marxist perspectives, male theory has focused on the growing fiscal crisis of the state. It has spoken of the twin projects of accumulation and legitimation, and has argued that the welfare state, by guaranteeing social reproduction, has facilitated both. Such theory has two main weaknesses. First, it is silent on the international dimensions of the crisis, in which production work is being moved out of the old societies, throwing into question the extent of the state's commitment to guarantee social reproduction. Secondly, it is silent on the centrality of women within the crisis, both within the deindustrialising and the industrialising societies.[12]

The main contribution of the new political economy of welfare was the innovation against the view which saw only the 'real' proletariat (males engaged in manufacture, mining, etc.) as the harbingers of revolution through class struggle, of looking much more favourably at trade union struggles within welfare. While there was little explicit analysis of the class position of, say, social workers as against home-helps or ambulance drivers, there was an expectation that these groups within the welfare services and the working class would act as one coherent whole. In this model (Gough 1979) struggles by users, consumers and dependants on welfare, while not unwelcome, were seen as peripheral to the main struggle, which was around the point of social reproduction as well as that of production. By contrast, US scholarship was more open to considering the collective actions of recipients as integral to the struggle and welfare. Thus Piven and Cloward (1971) made a persuasive argument for the power of disruption by both the poor and their allies. O'Connor (1973) too made space for the collective action of recipients in a way precluded by European Marxism with its pre-occupation with the employed worker. Indeed, the focus on the welfare state employee as an ungendered 'worker' inhibited the new political economy from recognising that most of these were in fact women who thus had a double relationship to the welfare state. They worked within the formal economy of care as welfare state employees, but at the same time worked on an unpaid basis within the informal system of care, a task which was critically dependent on the services of the welfare state. Unable to see either the gender of the worker or this double relation-ship, the new political economy welcomed the unmodified transfer of forms of struggle appropriate to production to the expanding realm of social reproduction.

While this criticism of the new political economy of welfare should not be read as suggesting that the employees of the welfare state are mere sheep to follow the vagaries of social theorists, it is reasonable to argue that an engendered analysis of welfare work as embracing both paid and unpaid labour would have probably searched for more com-plex forms of resistance appropriate to the more complex conditions in which the largely female labour force found itself.

This chapter marks a way-station in the theoretical debate con-cerning the future of the welfare state. It is relatively easy to criticise the shortcomings both of the old welfare state and of the present theoretical proposals for moving beyond it. Even while we grasp at the need for an engendered theory of welfare, it is difficult to propose a coherent theoretical and strategic way forward. None the less, it is the struggles both against the erosion of the old welfare state and for new forms of welfare which offer the base from which new and trans-formative theory and practices will come.

Notes

1. This was derived from Margaret McKintosh's 1980 report on the UN Con-ference for Women published in *Signs: Journal of Women in Culture and Society*, but the substance has been seized on by badges and postcards in the feminist movement bringing a new international awareness to the discussion of women and poverty.
2. Maintaining the perspective of women's needs in practice is extremely diffi-cult. Irene Tinker's report of the UN Conference on women, observes how the New International Economic Order (NIEO) discussion works in this respect. She writes: 'the issue is no longer women's needs but rather nationalistic demands and the desire of women as citizens.' She argues that, for this to be rectified, the discussion of women's needs must be given 'effective space with-in all the fora where the NIEO is debated'. *Signs: Journal of Women in Culture and Society* (1981), 6(3), 534.
3. Both the new Fabian collection ed. Howard Glennister (1983), *The Future of*

the *Welfare State*, London: Heinemann, which includes the now obligatory feminist piece — and it is a good piece — and also the important text by Ulf Himmelstrand *et al.* (1981), *Beyond Welfare Capitalism*, London: Heinemann, are examples of this.

4. The notion of 'returnability' was always most clearly formulated within the West German concept of *Gastarbeiter*. In 1973—75 no less than 25 per cent of the foreign workers were returned. Others such as Britain, which guaranteed citizenship to members of the Commonwealth in 1948, have, through a series of immigration measures widely criticised as racist as they have been directed most sharply at black and Asian potential immigrants, sought to achieve the economic and social advantages of the *Gastarbeiter* status.

5. Thus John Berger and Jean Mohr's influential study *The Seventh Man*, London: Allen Lane, documented the plight of the male foreign worker in Europe. Accounts of women, such as that of Amrit Wilson (1978), *Finding a Voice*, London: Virago, were to emerge more slowly.

6. *Sunday Times*, 31 July 1983.

7. See, for example, the special issue of *Signs: Journal of Women in Culture and Society: Development and the Sexual Division of Labour* 7(2), Winter 1981.

8. The air defence committees in the period leading up to the outbreak of war were preoccupied with trying to estimate the ratio of the weight of explosives to the numbers likely to be killed. In this history of social policy propelled by considerations of military technology there are some parallels with the present nuclear age about which social policy is distressingly silent.

9. The work of the new feminist history has been very important in recovering such activities, both demonstrating them as work, and simultaneously pointing to the false dichotomy between the two domains of 'work' and the 'home' so far as women's working lives are concerned. See, for example, Leonore Davidoff (1979), 'The Separation of Home and Work? Landladies and Lodgers in Nineteenth- and Twentieth-Century England', in Sandra Berman (ed.), *Fit Work for Women*, London: Croom Helm.

10. In the USA, '100,000 additional women with children fell below the poverty line each year from 1969 to 1978. In 1979 the number surged to 150,000 and was matched in 1980. Households headed by women — now 15 per cent of all households — are the fastest growing type of family in this country.' Kavin Stallard, Barbara Ehrenreich and Holly Sklar (1983), *Poverty in the American Dream*, Institute of New Communications, Cambridge, Mass.: South End Press.

11. For Britain it was Patrick Jenkin, then Secretary of State for the Department of Health and Social Security, who said in a television programme: 'Quite frankly I don't think mothers have the same right to work as fathers. If the Lord has intended us to have equal rights to work, he wouldn't have created men and women. These are biological facts, young children do depend on their mothers.'

12. See, for example, James O'Connor (1973), *The Fiscal Crisis of the State*, St James Press; Ian Gough (1979), *The Political Economy of Welfare*, London: Macmillan; W. Korpi (1978), *The Working Class in Welfare Capitalism*, London: Routledge; J.E. Stephens (1981), *The Transition from Capitalism to Socialism*, London: Heinemann; U. Himmelstrand, G. Ahrne, L. Lundberg and L. Lundberg (1981), *Beyond Welfare Capitalism*, London: Heinemann; G. Esping Anderson (1980), *Social Class, Social Democracy and State Policy*, Copenhagen.

References

Baerresen, D.B. (1971), *The Border Industrialisation Programme of Mexico*, Lexington, cited in F. Fröbel *et al.* (1980).

Bassett, Liz and Weir, Stuart (1983), 'Ending Low Pay', *New Socialist*, May—June.

Calder, Angus (1969), *The People's War*, Harmondsworth: Allen Lane.

Corrigan, Philip (1977), 'Feudal Relic or Capitalist Movement?', *Sociology* 11(3), 411−63.

Elson, Diane and Pearson, Ruth (1981a), 'The Subordination of Women and the Internationalisation of Factory Production', in Kate Young, Carol Wolkowitz and Roslyn McCullagh (eds), *Of Marriage and the Market*, London: Conference of Socialist Economists Books.

Elson, Diane and Pearson, Ruth (1981b), 'Nimble Fingers make Cheap Workers: An Analysis of Women's Employment in Third World Export Manufacturing', *Feminist Review* 7, Spring, 87−101.

Fröbel, Folker, Heinrichs, Jürgen and Kreye, Otto (1980), *The New International Division of Labour: Structural Unemployment in Industrialised Countries and Industrialisation in Developing Countries*, Cambridge: Cambridge University Press.

Gershuny, Jay (1983), *Social Innovation and the Division of Labour*, Oxford: Oxford University Press.

Glennister, Howard (ed.) (1983), *The Future of the Welfare State*, London: Heinemann.

Gough, Ian (1979), *The Political Economy of Welfare*, London: Macmillan.

Grossman, Rachel (1979), 'Women's Place in the Integrated Circuit', *Southeast Asia Chronicle* 66, 2−17.

Hakim, Catherine (1979), 'Occupational Segregation', Research Paper no. 9, London: Department of Employment.

Kahn, Alfred and Kammermann, Sheila (eds) (1978), *Family Policy*, New York: Columbia University Press.

Kaufman, Franz-Xaver and Leisering, Lutz (1983), 'Demographic Challenges to the Welfare State', paper given at a meeting at Bielefeld.

Land, Hilary (1976), 'Women: Supporters or Supported?', in D. Leonard Barker and S. Allen (eds), *Sexual Divisions in Society*, London: Tavistock.

Land, Hilary (1978), 'Who Cares for the Family?', *Journal of Social Policy* 7(3), 257−84.

Land, Hilary (1980), 'The Family Wage', *Feminist Review* 6.

O'Connor, James (1973), *The Fiscal Crisis of the State*, St James Press.

Pearce, Diana (1978), 'The Feminization of Poverty: Women, Work and Welfare', *Urban and Social Change Review*, February.

Phillips, Anne and Taylor, Barbara (1980), 'Sex and Skill: Notes Towards Feminist Economics', *Feminist Review* 6.

Piven, Frances and Cloward, Richard (1971), *Regulating the Poor*, New York: Pantheon.

Piven, Frances and Cloward, Richard (1982), 'The Moral Economy and the Welfare State', in D. Robbins, L. Cauldwell, G. Day and H. Rose (eds), *Rethinking Social Inequality*, London: Gower.

Rose, Hilary (1976), 'Participation: the Icing on the Welfare Cake', in S. Baldwin and K. Jones (eds), *Yearbook of Social Policy*.

Rose, Hilary and Ward, Sue (1984), 'Time, Gentlemen, Please: the Politics of Time', *New Socialist*, May, 16−19.

Safa, Helen I. (1981), 'Runaway Shops and Female Employment: The Search for Cheap Labour', *Signs: Journal of Women in Culture and Society* 7(2), 418−33.

Sivanandum, A.N. (1982), 'The Silicon Chip in an Imperial Age', in A.N. Sivanandum (ed.), *A Different Hunger*, London: Pluto.

Titmuss, R.M. (1950), *Problems of Social Policy*, London: HMSO.;

Wilson, Elizabeth (1976), *Women and the Welfare State*, London: Tavistock.

7 Demographic Challenges in the Welfare State
Franz-Xaver Kaufmann and Lutz Leisering

This chapter deals with a basic issue of welfare state theory that has been overlooked in recent years, but was quite obvious to the intellectual founders of the welfare state: the relationship between demographic change and the managing of social welfare. Current discussions have concentrated on *internal* causes for a 'crisis of the welfare state'. Demographic change, however, is *external* to the economic as well as to the political system (cf. Alber 1982: 203–7). But given the fact that eligibility to benefits and services is dependent on age, sex, employment and marital status, it is quite obvious that demographic changes in size or composition of the population affect the growth and the distribution of productive as well as of reproductive activities in society.

The following argument is based on the assumption that changes in the age structure of western (and also East European) societies in the next 50 years will act as a decisive factor on growth and change in welfare needs. We shall then try to illuminate the relationship between the population problem and the functioning of the welfare state.

Demographic changes and challenges

The demographic evolution of western societies has followed similar patterns in the last two centuries. Demographers speak of a period of 'demographic transition' in order to characterise these common features. Pre-industrial populations grew slowly as a consequence of high fertility and high mortality. The improvement of living conditions during the industrial revolution first led to a continuous decline in mortality and consequently to a great increase in population growth. After some time the social changes induced by technical and economic progress also influenced fertility rates, which similarly decreased. In recent years, since approximately 1965, a new decline in the birth rate has been observed in nearly all European countries (East and West) as well as in North America. The starting levels and the speed of the decline have shown differences, but the trends are comparable and seem to remain at below population maintenance level.

Let us first look at some of the consequences of these demographic variations for expenditures in two basic welfare state provisions: old age pensions and the health service. The analysis will be given for the West German case which is particularly dramatic. Tendencies in other countries, however, vary only in scope not in direction.

At present almost 1 in 6 persons in the Federal Republic of Germany is 65 years of age or more. In 1961 and 1910 the figures for the same age group were 1 in 9 and 1 in 20, respectively. According to population projections the *ageing* of the population will continue in the future, interrupted only by a slight decrease in the percentage of old people during the 1980s. At the same time fertility has been declining rapidly since 1963/64, going down by half until 1978 (from 87 live born children per 1000 women in the 15–45 age group to 44) and remaining since at a low level, with slight oscillations. Since today's children will be the economically active part of the population of tomorrow, a declining working population will have to support a growing number of old people. In fact, the dependency ratio (i.e. the number of economically inactive persons in relation to the number of economically active persons) is likely to rise considerably in the future. Population projections point out that the old age component of the dependency ratio will rise in the 1990s and peak in the year 2030, only falling off slightly and remaining at a high level thereafter (Figure 7.1).[1] Thus, the process of demographic transition has not led to a harmonious, almost stationary development of the population (Kaufmann 1975: 46). These new developments are caused by changes in fertility rather than mortality since drastic changes in life-expectancy are out of sight for the near future.[2] The recent decline in fertility appears to be the basis of a new far-reaching 'wave' in the future demographic process.

In the field of social policy the ongoing change in the structure of the population has given rise to lively and sometimes anxious discussions in the mass media and political arenas. Referring to the so-called 'pensioner mountain', some people fear that the social security of future pensioners and the overall welfare of the nation might not be maintained. It has been claimed that the present fertile generation is to blame for increasing its own standard of living at the expense of future generations by not providing enough children.

In which ways do the trends in population development outlined above really constitute a challenge to the welfare state? Mere figures such as dependency ratios, birth rates and proportions of old people in the population do not tell us the *real* burden of dependence society has to face. In order to assess the impact of changes in the population on

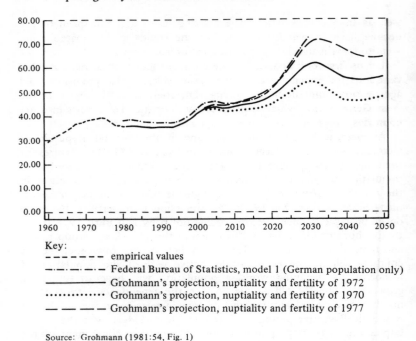

Key:
------- empirical values
—·—·—·— Federal Bureau of Statistics, model 1 (German population only)
——————— Grohmann's projection, nuptiality and fertility of 1972
·············· Grohmann's projection, nuptiality and fertility of 1970
— — — — Grohmann's projection, nuptiality and fertility of 1977

Source: Grohmann (1981:54, Fig. 1)

Figure 7.1   Projected dependency ratio of the elderly (%), 1960–2050

the institution of social security we have to examine the allocation systems which provide benefits, services and other resources for the elderly.

The bulk of old people receive the major part of their income from the social security system. Their dependency on the welfare state has largely increased in the course of the last 100 years, though private provisions as well as family and local support systems still play an important role. Old age pensions and the health service constitute the two biggest single items in social expenditure, accounting for more than two-thirds of the total.

The German *old age insurance* of today dates back to 1957 and is organised according to the so-called *Umlageverfahren*, that is to say, the insurance contributions paid by the economically active part of the population are immediately transferred to the recipients of old age pensions; and hence no reserve funds or capital assets are established. That is the reason why the pensioner ratio is so crucial to the operation of the system. In a population with a stable age structure the system will function at a constant rate of contributions to be raised, assuming no government subsidies, with the level of pensions rising in proportion to wage increases. This is known as the *dynamische Rente* (dynamic pension scheme) which has gradually become one of the fundamental principles of the German welfare state. When the dynamic principle was discussed in the mid-1950s, the decline of the pensioner ratio during the period 1965–80 could be foreseen as a consequence of war losses (Schreiber 1955: 18, 19). Compared with the development of the pensioner ratio we now expect for the years 2010–40, the small 'pensioner mountain' of the 1960s and the 1970s is a tiny one. According to Grohmann's population projections (1981: 58), the rate of insurance contributions will have to double from today's 18 per cent to 36 per cent – or at least reach 32 per cent or 28 per cent, depending on the assumptions made about fertility.[3] Only a slight decrease in the pensioner ratio will follow. (These projections assume a continuous rise in the pension benefits corresponding to the dynamic principle.)

Ceteris paribus, the drastic rise in expenditures can only be reduced by reducing the nominal growth of pensioners' benefits, or by raising government subsidies and so increasing the tax burden. Both these solutions are likely to give rise to considerable political dissent. Another approach could be to alter the dependency ratio, e.g. by raising the age of retirement or by enlarging the economically active part of the 15–65 age group.[4] According to Grohmann (1983) a combination of several strategies could reduce the maximum contribution rate to 25 per cent. However, it is doubtful whether the welfare state will be able to manage a quick and flexible adaptation to this demographic challenge. Time is passing and the demographic circumstances favourable to political intervention are limited to the present decade (Grohmann 1981: 70, 71).

Survey data reveal the bad state of health of the aged. The incidence of illness increases with increasing age, for example, the incidence of cancer increases 61-fold from the 30 and under age group to the 65–70 age group, and 125-fold to the 80 and over age group.[5] An analysis of the health service budget demonstrates that expenditure rises roughly with advancing age, the expenditure for a person of 75 years or more being 5 times as high as for a child aged between 5 and 15 years. For this reason, the ageing of the population will, all other things being equal, lead to an increase in the health budget by 7–8 per cent from 1980 to 2020 (Bericht über die Bevölkerungsentwicklung in der Bundesrepublik Deutschland 1984: 90, 98). This seems to be fairly minimal, but one has to bear in mind that at the same time the proportion of the economically active part of the population as well as the total population will decline drastically.

Eighty-eight per cent of old people's illnesses are chronic, and thereby constitute a potential extra demand for health services. As costs have been climbing rapidly (due to excessive price increases in social welfare services and housing) more and more people have not been able to afford private old-age or nursing homes. Therefore, public expenditure for persons in need of general care (*Hilfe zur Pflege*) increased by 317 per cent from 1970 to 1979, thus becoming the biggest single item in the German social assistance budget (*Sozialhilfe*) which is financed directly by the government (Presse- und Informationsamt 1982: 301). Apart from spending on the disabled, this represents the highest growth rate of any one item in this budget. The problem of public expenditure for general care is one of the major issues in present social policy. Even the question of a new kind of social insurance is now being raised.

A closer look at the *structure of demographic change* reveals that the aged claim an even bigger proportion of social expenditure than is suggested by their rising proportion in the population:

- The proportion of the *very old* is projected to increase more rapidly than the proportion of the old in general (until 1990). The needs of very old people for health services and care are the highest in the population.

- The proportion of *women* among the aged is higher than in the total population. During the last three decades the female/male ratio in the 65 and over age group has risen to 64:36 (1980), but will gradually diminish in the future. This is mainly due to war losses and to the higher rate of female life expectancy. Since German old age insurance is based on the idea that the relative level of benefits corresponds to previously paid contributions and thereby to previous earnings, women's old age pensions tend to be very low, if they get any at all. In these cases supplementary benefits within the general pension scheme or social assistance may be granted, or the women may receive a survivor's pension. Thus, the high proportion of elderly women is likely to raise government expenditure further in the income maintenance system. As to the demand for health services, there is no clear trend. Although the incidence of some illnesses in elderly women is higher, others, such as cancer, are much lower than for elderly men. Altogether, health expenditure tends to be somewhat lower for elderly women (Bericht über die Bevölkerungsentwicklung in der Bundesrepublik Deutschland 1983: 90).

- The ageing process also applies to the 45–65 age group, i.e. the proportion of 'old' people among the economically active persons in society is growing too. The demands for health services among this age group are higher than among the rest of the economically active. Moreover, the growing proportion of disability pensions within the general pension scheme for workers (*Arbeiterrentenversicherung*) is mainly due to this group. In addition, disability means a loss of social insurance contributions.

Thus, the growing proportion of old people leads to increasing demands on social expenditure, while at the same time the proportion of young people is declining. There is a shift from the child component to the old age component of the dependency ratio, i.e. the economically inactive part of society that has to be supported by the active part will increasingly consist of old people. One might suggest that a low child ratio could compensate for a growing pensioner ratio. But the overall dependency ratio will still be increasing by 20 per cent from 1980 to 2030 according to Grohmann's population projection[6] and there is no straightforward way of transferring societal resources from children to the elderly. Children's needs differ from old people's, children are involved in different social security systems, and they get more of their needs from the family (cf. Leisering 1984).

This ongoing change in the structure of the population constitutes a challenge to society and to the welfare state. Whatever the reaction or non-reaction of the political system may be, society seems bound to undergo major changes in the 'production of welfare'. Demographic change may not create new social problems, but it widens the numbers relying on the welfare state for income maintenance and social services. Furthermore, the decline of the economically active part of the population makes it even more difficult to provide the fiscal resources necessary to meet the rising demands.

These problems of today's and tomorrow's welfare policies indicate a more general issue. In any period of the welfare state and for any welfare programme, demographic change is relevant to social expenditure, although it may not be openly recognised as such. The problem for sociological analysis, therefore, is how to appreciate the influence of demographic change, how to determine its *relative causal weight* as compared with other determinants and how to detect the variation of causal weight over time.

A study of income maintenance programmes published by the OECD in 1976 has tried to attack this problem. The study considers three factors that determine the expenditure for a single programme: the level of benefits, the number of beneficiaries, and the number of potential beneficiaries. Thus, the expenditure as a percentage share in gross domestic product (GDP) is decomposed into three components: (1) the so-called 'transfer ratio', being the average payment per beneficiary as a ratio to per capita GDP; (2) the 'eligibility ratio', being the number of beneficiaries as a ratio to the size of the 'target group' of the programme (e.g. the number of pensioners as a percentage of the total number of old people); and (3) the 'demographic ratio', being the size of the target group as a ratio to the total population. Roughly speaking, the transfer ratio and the eligibility ratio correspond to changes in social expenditure due to legal or institutional amendments, whereas the demographic ratio corresponds to changes due to external

influences that occur without political intervention. A causal interpretation in a strict sense, however, cannot be derived since the
decomposition into the three components does not provide a clearcut
distinction between institutional and external change. For example, a
variation in the transfer and the eligibility ratios may be due to demographic change as well.

Bearing these restrictions in mind we can briefly summarise the
findings of the OECD study. *During the period 1962—72 somewhat
over a third of the increase in social expenditure as a share in GDP was
due to demographic factors* and nearly two-thirds were due to changes
in the coverage of programmes (eligibility ratio); the influence of increases in the level of benefits was negligible. This applies to the major
income-maintenance programmes in the OECD countries. Projections
for the period 1972—85 show a changing picture: the influence of
demographic factors almost vanishes, while the coverage factor could
continue to have a considerable impact. (An up-dated computation for
the overall 1960—80 period assigns some 30.5 per cent of the increase
in expenditure for old age pensions to demographic reasons. (OECD
1983: 14.)) Today, the situation has changed again. As pointed out
above, the demographic factor will regain a considerable importance
after 1990. At the same time, coverage of major income-maintenance
programmes is high, and may reach a ceiling. Moreover, real increases
in benefits could be lost due to fiscal constraints. Thus, we may conclude that the next decades of the welfare state will see demographic
change and other external forces such as above-average price increases
in social services and housing as the main determinants of rises in social
expenditure (cf. also Wilensky 1975: 47). Using a complex method of
social budget projection, Linder (1982: 320) has shown that only for
demographic reasons, all other things being equal and prices held constant, the 'social expenditure ratio', i.e. total social expenditure as a
ratio to the number of people in work, would have to double from
1970 to 2030.

Understanding the importance of demographic trends for the welfare state

There is only a rather weak concensus about the meaning of the welfare
state (cf. Kaufmann 1985). Much writing about social welfare tends
to neglect the fact that welfare institutions do not form a separate
political system (such as a 'welfare state' — *Sozialstaat*) but are aspects
of the activities of the same state or government that struggles for
stability and security, for economic growth, against pollution or for the
integration of ethnic minorities. Welfare is only one of several political
concerns and the so-called welfare policies may also be related to considerations of public order and political integration, as we already know
from Bismarck's motives for promoting social insurance. Moreover,

political concern for welfare is not restricted to social services or social insurance but may also operate in other political domains, like workers' protection, consumers' protection or urban planning. Furthermore, welfare institutions are not necessarily a part of public administration. The production of public welfare is operated typically through a mix of public and private organisations. Social policy eventually leads to a blurring of the distinction between state and society (cf. Kaufmann *et al.* 1985: chs 6–9).

Here we have to focus on the relationship of population trends and issues of the welfare state. In this context we shall discuss the following three arguments:

(1) By the emergence of the welfare state the hitherto mere statistical categories of age groups have also become societal relationships.
(2) The redistribution among generations is a basic issue of the welfare state.
(3) Why are demographic issues seldom acknowledged in discussions about the welfare state?

Population problems as a consequence of the welfare state

The term population is linked normally to the inhabitants of a certain territory. It became prominent only after the constitution of authority over a delimited and coherent territory (*Landherrschaft*), a stage of political development reached in Europe in the sixteenth and seventeenth centuries. The 'political arithmetic' was at that time the first attempt at political science, and we can see a keen interest in problems of welfare as well as of population growth in the absolutist European states of the seventeenth and eighteenth centuries. It was only in the light of the predicaments depicted by Malthus that population growth began to be seen as a threat to the promotion of welfare. And the question of whether and under what conditions an increase or decrease of population may contribute to a growth of welfare is still open.[7]

However, our concern here is not with the correlation of demographic and economic growth, but rather with the distribution of goods among the population. Until about 1800 most people lived in agricultural communities, were incorporated in productive households and were largely self-supporting. Under those conditions there existed no structural differentiation of producer and consumer roles, and everybody — including old people and children — took part in production as well as in consumption according to their capacities and needs. With industrialisation and the pervasive penetration of market relationships into everyday life, a mobilisation of the labour force took place and led to the well-known structural differentiation of production (in factories and offices) and consumption (in families and other households). This created interrelationships between geographically distant people and a kind of anonymous dependency on the forces of the market that accounted for the emergence of the new class structures of capitalist society. These market relationships, however, were not linked essentially to the political unit which defines a population. Market forces accounted for migrations, but the consequential demographic changes had a quasi-natural character, and were not perceived. It was only in so far as a political unit like the nation state of the nineteenth century unified the inhabitants of a territory and created citizenship as a boundary-maintaining concept, that demographic change could become an issue.

The structural differentiation of production and consumption was a necessary, but not a sufficient condition for the differentiation of productive and non-productive members of society. Under the typical conditions of early capitalism everybody was forced to sell his or her labour in order to survive. *It is only by state intervention that a non-productive class to be provided for has been created.* This began with the prohibition of child labour in factories and compulsory education. It continued with the regulation of normal or even compulsory retirement. Social policy here had the impact of protecting those sectors of the population that were threatened by unwholesome and exploitative working conditions. The intervention contributed both to regulating or even excluding the work of persons with limited working capacities, and to providing measures of income-maintenance or social services for those who were not able to earn their living in the labour market.

It has been emphasised recently by social historians and sociologists that childhood as well as old age have emerged only in modern times as socially relevant and differentiated stages of life (cf. Lüscher 1975; Imhof 1981). But it is seldom acknowledged that this development has been an effect of the political regulation of work and the corresponding growth of welfare services to provide a decent way of life for those outside the workforce. This is one of the major 'successes' of the welfare state. By regulating working opportunities, the welfare state has attained both a higher conformity to the existing working conditions for those defined as able to work, and has excluded from the labour market those who are defined as undesirable in the workforce. As the establishment of this boundary brings advantages to both the collectivity of employers (externalising costs for sub-marginal workers) and workers (keeping the labour force scarce), it is not surprising that it has become an unquestioned basic social structure in almost all modernised societies.

State regulation of non-productivity seems to link up with calendar age. Children were forbidden to work before the age of 10 in Prussia 1839); men were assumed to be invalided at 70 in the first social welfare laws of Bismarck (1889). This age limit was subsequently extended from industry to nearly all domains of economic life. Since the age limits on the workforce are linked to services, as for example education, and to income maintenance, early retirement and an extension of compulsory education bring about extensions of these formal age limits.

The clustering of the not yet and the no longer productive population in certain age groups makes their provision dependent on demographic variations. At the same time the statistical categories of age groups become indicators of social classes of productive and non-productive parts of the population. The different schemes of social security have created a new kind of interrelatedness among people that is mediated less by markets than by the welfare state.

Redistribution among generations as a
basic issue of the welfare state

In its beginnings modern social policy was not concerned with the population at large but with the lower social classes — groups like the poor or workers acknowledged to be in need. Hence relief or social insurance were not considered a means of an overall redistribution. In the liberal tradition, social policy was considered as piecemeal engineering. Only later, with the advent of the idea of the welfare state, did the emphasis change and a more comprehensive view of redistribution develop.

The welfare state is not only a set of welfare institutions, but also an idea. The notion of public responsibility for the welfare of *all* citizens emerged only in the 1930s and 1940s. It developed in a special intellectual climate that may be characterised as denial of liberal politics under the shadow of the Great Depression. Instead of liberal ideas about freedom, there arose a quest for planned freedom and large-scale social planning under democratic control. Social science, Keynesianism, opinion polls and social engineering contributed to expectations of rational reform through societal planning (cf. for example, Mannheim 1940; Myrdal 1958). Under the pressures of warfare the hopes for a better future were reflected in government action such as the Atlantic Charter of Churchill and Roosevelt in 1941. The idea of social security became the panacea for the illnesses of the time and found its programmatic institutional layout in the Beveridge Report to the British parliament of 1942 (cf. Kaufmann 1973: 108ff.).

This combination of Keynesianism and the idea of social security and social planning shaped the basic concept of the welfare state. Thus public provision had not only to prevent forms of extreme want and destitution, but also *to develop the human capacities of the whole population by providing educational and health services, to grant full employment in order to ensure maximum economic growth, and to redistribute the economic output from the producers to the non-*

producers.[8] It is in this perspective that the holistic terms of economy, population and society gained political attention in the Anglo-Saxon world, as for example the drastic decline in the birth rate which shocked the European countries before the second world war provoked an evident concern about family and population questions.[9] However, the issue soon withered away in the English discussion, and the Report of the Royal Commission on Population (1949) did not have any substantial effect: pension problems were discussed mainly as a matter of financial issues (cf. Eversley 1982).

The most thorough analysis of the questions involved has been given by Mackenroth (1952), who combines in a unique way the German and Anglo-Saxon lines of thought. He starts with the basic Keynesian assumption that all provision for life must be drawn from the production of the current period. From a macroeconomic point of view, social savings for old age by a whole generation is not feasible. The principle of capital security for future payments that social insurance originally had borrowed from private insurance constitutes no security at all, because a substantial liquidation of capital assets and funds would kindle inflation and thus lead to their depreciation. From this follows — whatever the modes of financing the economic provisions for the non-productive part of the population may be — that there is a direct relationship between the size of the dependent population and the level of provision to be furnished by the economically active population. There exists a *necessary* redistribution from the producers to the non-producers with respect to *all* produced consumer goods and services. As we have seen, the existence of an essentially 'non-productive' part of the population emerged as a consequence of welfare state activities. Consequently, we may formulate a basic law of the economy of a welfare state. *All other things being equal, the average welfare as measured in terms of market income and welfare benefits is a function of the relationship of the productive to the non-productive part of the population.* The larger the non-productive part of the population, the more redistribution is needed.[10] As needs and benefits, however, are not given, one has to decide on the satisfaction of needs either by institutional arrangements or by repeated political decision-making.

As a consequence of these considerations the British and (to some extent) the Scandinavian countries institutionalised economic security for dependants as a part of the overall public budget. The redistribution of income was taken over by the state as one of several public tasks and it is now competing every year with other political issues. This development follows the idea of collective solidarity and transforms the macroeconomic idea of redistribution into the microeconomic device of a unified tax deduction on the part of the producers. Mackenroth did not go so far as to abandon the idea of a separate body for income redistribution, but proposed the organisation of social security along the lines of age groups i.e. by a *Jugendamt* (youth administration), an *Arbeitsamt* (labour administration) and a *Rentenamt* (pension administration) (1957: 70, 71). These agencies would operate in the realm of a common social budget and under the same legislation ensuring equal benefits for everybody with comparable needs. Mackenroth's main concern was to integrate *all* benefits for the dependent part of the population in *one* common frame of reference: *the social budget.* It would allow the satisfaction of different claims to become visible and accessible to an open political decision. This, he hoped, would help clarify basic ethical questions and restore the trust in the equity of social policy which had been corrupted by a jungle of deceit and the plurality of institutions operating under separate rules. To keep the social budget separate from the general budget and to finance it by contributions rather than by general taxes not only reflects the German tradition of social insurance, but also serves to obscure the whole redistributive process.

In 1955 these basic ideas had been worked out in a concrete proposal of reform of the social insurance programme for the aged and in a new compensatory programme for children (cf. Schreiber 1955). Schreiber started with the assertion that in industrial society individual lifetime earnings need to be distributed throughout the three stages of youth, adulthood and old age. As this cannot be achieved by individual savings, there must be a collective redistributive process from adulthood to youth and to old age. Therefore, he proposed two separate bodies of redistribution: one for the aged and one for children. Both should be financed by contributions from the economically active population, and the benefits should equal the contributions of the same period. By this simple institutional arrangement two problems of feedback would be solved:

- First, the problem of *inflation* and of *participation in economic growth*. In so far as benefits are directly dependent on the amount of contributions, they will increase in proportion to wages, the relation of the number of contributors to the number of beneficiaries being equal. If wages were rising due to inflation or gains in productivity there would be a parallel growth of benefits. This idea became quite influential in the reform of old age insurance in 1957 and has since been called the *dynamische Rente*.

- Second, the problem of a *changing dependency ratio*. In its pure form an increase in the number of children or old people in relation to the adult population would lead to a lowering of the benefits for the dependent group, contributions being equal. As changes in these ratios are rather slow and a rise in real wages is expected, this would not normally lead to a real loss of income but only to a lowered increase of benefits compared with net wages. This system then makes manifest the interrelatedness of economic and demographic trends which is hidden in other systems.

One may of course question the equity of the assumption that the risk of being in a very large or in a very small age cohort should be borne exclusively by those belonging to that cohort. But the principle could also be mitigated, e.g. by a modification of the contribution rate or of the age of retirement. What really matters is the idea of a general 'contract between generations' that establishes (1) the level of pension benefits relative to previous earnings, and (2) how modifications of the dependency ratio can be borne by the active and inactive parts of the population. In fact, only the first rule has been made explicit, whereas the second problem has been omitted from German legislation on pensions until today.

One may speculate whether the extreme decline in the birth rate in Germany has partially been induced by poor public support for children. A much larger share of the provision for old age as opposed to that for children is financed by public transfers. An estimate of the overall costs of bringing up children in Germany (1974) showed that about 47 per cent of all costs are paid out of individual family incomes. Cash transfers to families (e.g. family or housing allowances) and health services account for a further 23 per cent; the balance being made up of various welfare benefits in kind, mainly education. If in addition the non-paid time of the parents caring for children is taken into account (as estimated by a very modest hypothetical salary), the proportion borne by the individual family increases to 74 per cent (Wissenschaftlicher Beirat für Familienfragen 1979: 102). The system of old age insurance does not take into consideration whether people raise children or not. Mothers who give up their jobs to bring up their children cannot accumulate contribution for their old age pensions. From the perspective of individual economic rationality raising children is a loss. At the same time it is quite evident that today's children are the producers of tomorrow. Although a purely economic interpretation of the birth rate decline is certainly superficial, one should not underestimate these facts, because they may be perceived also as a public disinterest in the family, and hence as a diminution of the status of parents in our society.

In exploring the interrelationship between demographic evolution and the welfare state we have to answer a final question of a purely demographic nature. Setting apart the modes of financing, a decreasing burden of the young obviously could compensate for an increasing burden of the elderly. What significance does a decline in the proportion of the young have for a rise in the proportion of the aged population? The answer to this question demands sophisticated calculations, which we have to simplify here. One must distinguish between the time of transition and later, the stabilised age structure with a persistent low fertility rate. In the transition period there is first a decrease of the child component of the burden of dependence, with the increase of the old age component coming some 40 years later when the most populous age cohorts leave the economically active population. Although Germany is currently experiencing a period of relief from the overall burden of dependence, there is no related profit due to unemployment. (The expected growth after the year 2010 has already been presented in Figure 7.1.)

In so far as the long-term evolution of the burden of dependence (*after* the 'great wave') is concerned, one can demonstrate by comparing population models with constant rates of fertility and mortality that there is an optimum point, i.e. a net reproduction rate leading to a minimal overall dependency ratio in that type of model (cf. Kaufmann 1984). The optimum point, however, varies according to three parameters: the average age of entrance to and departure from the workforce; the income relationships of the average young, adult and aged person; and the life-expectancy of the population. If one varies these parameters within reasonable limits and takes into account recent estimations of these, the optimum point does not deviate much from the stationary population model, i.e. a net reproduction rate of 1.0. The curve of the dependency ratio dependent on the net reproduction rate has the form of a hyperbola. As it is rather flat around the optimum point, one may argue for practical purposes that with a net reproduction rate between 0.8 and 1.3 there are no important long-term differences in the *overall* dependency ratio. A further decline of fertility below 0.8 would lead to a progressive increase in the overall dependency ratio. This is the actual case in Germany where the net reproduction rate has remained below 0.7 in the last 10 years.

Hindrances to accounting for demographic variation in social policy

As we have seen in the English and German cases, social policy does not take into account demographic variations in a systematic way. These variations are considered as external influences to be dealt with when they occur (cf. Eversley and Köllmann 1982). The situation is much the same in most other industrialised countries. Social policies vary in the provision of resources for the elderly and the young and the *public* burden of dependence is of course a product of legal regulations. From the point of view of rational social planning one should start with the economic needs of the young, the adult and the elderly. But that is not the way politics deals with the issue. In fact, redistribution is carried out by a multiplicity of mostly uncoordinated institutional arrangements where nobody knows who gets what and who foots the bill.

Despite the existing links between the generations in terms of provision of resources, institutional arrangements seldom account for these relationships. Apparently the provision for the elderly is taken for granted as an issue of public policy, whereas the fact that children constitute the next generation of producers and therefore have to be incorporated into all calculations, is not publicly acknowledged. This leads to an arbitrariness in family policies.

This disregard for basic demographic issues is related to political forces. Children have no vote and it is difficult to mobilise parents as a pressure group. And parents of two or more children (who are essential for the demographic balance) constitute a minority.

But the reluctance to acknowledge demographic trends as a political issue seems to have deeper roots than the analysis of mere political power shows. The reluctance is rooted in general convictions and political orientations. In the case of Great Britain, Eversley (1982) notes the persistence of Malthusianism; while in West Germany it is the memory of Nazi population policies and a highly privatised conception of the family. For liberals and conservatives alike the state should not interfere with the decisions of prospective parents as to the number of children they have. The very unpolitical character of demographic trends and their 'natural' influence seem to make them uninteresting for socialists as well.

There is yet another type of ideological impediment to accounting for the role of demographic factors that leads right back to our starting point, namely, the question of how to conceptualise the current challenges of the welfare state. Both left-wing and right-wing fundamentalist points of view tend to focus on internal problems of the welfare state, assuming external problems to be of minor importance. As we have pointed out, external problems — such as demographic change, and changes in the costs of social services — exert not only a powerful and growing influence on social spending, they also touch upon fundamental normative and institutional issues of the welfare state such as the 'contract between generations'. As has been demonstrated earlier, the demographic factor explains a major part of the growth of public welfare expenditure in the present and in the coming decades. Fundamentalist critics of the welfare state, however, are more interested in arguments for cutback management or for endemic crisis, than in arguments that explain the growth tendency of social expenditure in terms of non-ideological causes. There is in fact very little evidence that the growth of public expenditure is due to a never-ending tendency of the welfare state to compensate minor disadvantages in all areas of human life.

This lack of political appeal, however, does not prevent the demographic trends from being influential. *Most of the institutional provisions of the welfare state are based on the assumption of demo-*

graphic equilibrium, i.e. they implicitly assume few or no demographic variations. Consequently, demographic variations must become a political issue. But demographic trends operate on a long-term basis whereas politics tends to deal with short-term variations. Thus politics is likely to react too late and too erratically. The only rational way of dealing with this issue is to make the welfare system itself responsive to demographic variations in order to establish a feedback among demographic trends, economic growth and individual behaviour.[11]

Notes

1. The projections refer to the ratio of the 60+ age group to the 20—60 age group and are based on the assumption that nuptiality and fertility will stay at the 1970, 1972 or 1977 level. Each assumption leads to a different growth rate of the dependency ratio (the 2030 peak being 1.7-fold of today's level in the 1972 fertility case) but the shape of the curve remains the same.
   The population trends in other industrial societies are very similar. All countries in the European Community with the exception of Ireland are experiencing a continuous rise in the proportion of old people, delayed by a stagnation or a slight decrease around the 1970s and the 1980s (United Kingdom in the 1990s) (for data and projections for the period 1960—2000 see Eurostat 1981: 22—3; cf. Eurostat 1980: 34 for the 40—65 age group; for United Kingdom see also Office of Population Censuses and Surveys 1980: 27). Among these countries, Germany and UK have the highest proportion of old people, 15.3 and 15.1 per cent respectively in 1981 (65+ age group). In all EC countries (always with the exception of Ireland) declining birth rates have sharply decreased the net reproduction rate from > 1 in 1960 to < 1 in 1981, and even < 0.8 in Germany, the Netherlands, Luxembourg and Denmark. Germany ranks lowest with 0.68 (1980; Eurostat 1983: 76—7, 88). The overall dependency ratio rises high around the 1960s and the 1970s (except in France and the Netherlands), declining strongly in the 1970s and the 1980s and beginning to rise after 1990 (except Denmark; projections for Italy not given) (Eurostat 1981: 22—3). For the Austrian case see Busch *et al.* (Chapter 12, this volume).
2. In this chapter we do not consider the influence of immigration.
3. In the 1957 reform it was assumed that a contribution rate for old age insurance of 14 per cent would be enough given a long-term demographic equilibrium and a government subsidy amounting to about one-third of total expenditures (cf. Berthold and Roppel 1983: 299).
4. Another strategy could be to reopen the labour market to younger immigrants in order to compensate for the fall in the birth rate. All these strategies presuppose an economic growth in terms of the labour force and not only of GNP. The social problems of immigration and the likelihood of long-term labour-intensive economic growth have, however, to be kept outside of the present discussion. For a discussion of the various strategies to cope with demographic challenges to old age insurance, see Lampert (1980: 19—35) and Grohmann (1981: 59—68).
5. Male population of Hamburg, 1977 (Bundesminister für Jugend, Familie und Gesundheit 1980: 125).
6. 1981:66, under the assumption of nuptiality and fertility as of 1972.
7. From the point of view of pure economics a decrease of population should (*ceteris paribus!*) increase the per capita income and hence individual welfare. cf. Reddaway (1939) and Wander (1971). The empirical evidence available shows, however, a correlation between socioeconomic and demographic decline that may be due to losses of adaptive capacities in declining (and ageing) populations. cf. Kaufmann (1975).
8. Thus, the welfare state combines elements of vertical redistribution (among producers) and horizontal redistribution (from producers to non-producers).

Health services and taxation belong to the first category, whereas cash benefits mainly fall into the second. For example in the German case, 150 out of 186,000 million DM of cash benefits were transferred to households of non-producers (1978; Transfer-Enquete-Kommission 1981: 121–3). Public education and child allowances involve both vertical (referring to households) and horizontal (referring to individuals) redistribution. To a certain extent, vertical redistribution represents the egalitarian element of the welfare state.

9. The most important document for the link of welfare and population policy is Myrdal (1945), completed by 1940. Though only secondarily, the Beveridge Report was also concerned with family and population (cf. Beveridge 1942: 154ff.).

10. This 'law' of course not only applies to the problem of resource allocation to young and old persons, but also to the unemployed who are forced into the non-productive category. As these and other categories like housewives or drop-outs are not linked to demographic developments, we shall not deal with the related issues in the present context.

11. See for example, the proposal of a *bevölkerungsdynamische Rentenformel* by Berthold and Roppel (1983), an old age pension scheme with a built-in mechanism for adaptation to demographic change. Cf. also various propositions in Birg (1983).

References

Alber, J. (1982), *Vom Armenhaus zum Wohlfahrtsstaat. Analysen zur Entwicklung der Sozialversicherung in Westeuropa*, Frankfurt/New York: Campus.
Bericht über die Bevölkerungsentwicklung in der Bundesrepublik Deutschland (1984), *2. Teil: Auswirkungen auf die verschiedenen Bereiche von Staat und Gesellschaft*, Bundestag-Drucksache 10/863, Bonn: Bundesminister des Innern.
Berthold, N. and Roppel, U. (1983), 'Gesetzliche Rentenversicherung und demographische Schwankungen', in *Wirtschaftsdienst* 63/VI, 297–305.
Beveridge, W. (1942), *Social Insurance and Allied Services*, London: HMSO.
Birg, H. (ed.) (1983), *Bevölkerungsentwicklung und gesellschaftliche Planung*, Frankfurt/New York: Campus.
Boettcher, E. (ed.) (1957), *Sozialpolitik und Sozialreform*, Tübingen: Mohr.
Bundesminister für Jugend, Familie und Gesundheit (ed.) (1980), *Daten des Gesundheitswesens. Ausg. 1980*, Stuttgart: Kohlhammer.
Eurostat (Statistical Office of the European Communities) (1980), *Sozialindikatoren für die Europäische Gemeinschaft 1960–1978*, Luxembourg/Brussels.
Eurostat (Statistical Office of the European Communities) (1981), *Pensioners in the Community*, Luxembourg/Brussels.
Eurostat (Statistical Office of the European Communities) (1983), *Demographic Statistics 1981*, Luxembourg/Brussels.
Eversley, D. (1982), 'Prospects for a Population Policy in the United Kingdom', in Eversley and Köllmann, op.cit., 425–37.
Eversley, D. and Köllmann, W. (eds) (1982), *Population Change and Social Planning*, London: Edward Arnold.
Grohmann, H. (1981), 'Auswirkungen der Bevölkerungsentwicklung in der Bundesrepublik Deutschland auf die gesetzliche Rentenversicherung', *Zeitschrift für die gesamte Versicherungswissenschaft* 70, 49–72.
Grohmann, H. (1983), 'Anpassungs- und Entlastungsstrategien zur Lösung des demographisch bedingten Rentenproblems', in Birg, op.cit., 13–46.
Imhof, A.E. (1981), *Die gewonnenen Jahre*, Munich: Beck.
Kaufmann, F.-X. (1973), *Sicherheit als soziologisches und sozialpolitisches Problem*, Stuttgart: Enke, 2nd edition.
Kaufmann, F.-X. (1975), 'Makro-soziologische Überlegungen zu den Folgen eines Bevölkerungsrückganges', in Kaufmann, F.-X. (ed.), *Bevölkerungsbewegung zwischen Quantität und Qualität*, Stuttgart: Enke, 45–71.
Kaufmann, F.-X. (1985), 'Major Problems of the Welfare State. Defining the Issues', in Eisenstadt, S.N. and Ahimeir O. (eds), *The Welfare State and its Aftermath*, London: Croom Helm, 44–56.

Kaufmann, F.-X. (1984), 'Demographische Bedingungen einer Optimierung der wirtschaftlichen Gesamtbelastungsquote der aktiv erwerbstätigen Generation', paper read at the annual meeting of the German Association for Population Research (forthcoming).

Kaufmann, F.-X., Majone, G. and Ostrom, V. (eds) (1985), *Guidance, Control and Evaluation in the Public Sector*, Berlin/New York: De Gruyter.

Lampert, H. (1980), *Entwicklungstendenzen und zentrale Probleme in der Altersrentenversicherung*, Cologne: Deutscher Instituts-Verlag.

Leisering, L. (1984), 'Veränderungen im Verhältnis von Jugend- und Altenlasten', paper read at the annual meeting of the German Association for Population Research.

Linder, P. (1982), 'Aufwendungen für die nachwachsende und ältere Generation und Auswirkungen der demographischen Entwicklung', *Baden-Württemberg in Wort und Zahl* 30, 282–7, 314–21.

Lüscher, K. (1975), 'Perspektiven einer Soziologie der Sozialisation – Die Entwicklung der Rolle des Kindes', *Zeitschrift für Soziologie* 4, 359–79.

Mackenroth, G. (1952), 'Die Reform der Sozialpolitik durch einen deutschen Sozialplan', in Albrecht, G. (ed.), *Verhandlungen auf der Sondertagung in Berlin. Schriften des Vereins für Socialpolitik NF Bd. 4*, Berlin: Duncker and Humbolt, 39–76. (Reprinted in Boettcher, op.cit., 43–74.)

Mannheim, K. (1940), *Man and Society in an Age of Reconstruction*, London: Routledge and Kegan Paul.

Myrdal, A. (1945), *Nation and Family. The Swedish Experiment in Democratic Family and Population Policy*, London: Routledge and Kegan Paul.

Myrdal, G. (1958), *Beyond the Welfare State. Economic Planning in the Welfare State and its International Implications*, London: Duckworth.

OECD (1976), *Public Expenditure on Income Maintenance Programmes*, OECD Studies in Resource Allocation no. 3, Paris.

OECD (1983), *Old-Age Pensions*, Paper SME/SAIR/SE/83.06, mimeo.

Office of Population Censuses and Surveys (1980), *Population Projections*, London: HMSO.

Presse- und Informationsamt (ed.) (1982), *Gesellschaftliche Daten 1982*, Bonn.

Reddaway, W.B. (1939), *The Economics of a Declining Population*, London: Allen and Unwin.

Royal Commission on Population (1949), *Report*, London: HMSO.

Schreiber, W. (1955), *Existenzsicherheit in der industriellen Gesellschaft*, Cologne: Bachem (revised version in Boettcher, op.cit., 75–114).

Transfer-Enquete-Kommission (1981), *Das Transfersystem in der Bundesrepublik Deutschland* Stuttgart: Kohlhammer.

Wander, H. (1971), *Der Geburtenrückgang in Westeuropa wirtschaftlich gesehen*, Kiel (Kieler Diskussionsbeiträge zu aktuellen wirtschaftspolitischen Fragen, Heft 9).

Wilensky, H.L. (1975), *The Welfare State and Equality. Structural and Ideological Roots of Public Expenditures*, Berkeley: University of California Press.

Wissenschaftlicher Beirat für Familienfragen (1979), *Leistungen für die nachwachsende Generation in der Bundesrepublik Deutschland*, Stuttgart: Kohlhammer.

Part II Trends and Problems in National Welfare States

8 Social Welfare in Japan and Britain: A Comparative View. Formal and Informal Aspects of Welfare
Robert Pinker

Until recently the study of social welfare in Britain has focused on the formal social services of central and local government. Formal social policies, however, are only one element in the social arrangements of welfare, which also include indigenous patterns of obligation and entitlement based on informal networks of care and mutual aid. In this wider cultural context the study of social welfare includes the values which influence people's notions of obligation and entitlement, and the conventions through which these notions find practical expression. These values and conventions are expressed partly in formal social services and partly in informal services based on the affiliations of family, friendship and neighbourhood.

The culture of welfare includes the complex meanings and values which influence the choices made in social policy and therefore determine in a given society what needs will be met, and on what terms, whether needs will be met by formal intervention, or left to informal care, and what kind of relationship will hold between the formal and the informal sectors.

The way in which the provision of social welfare is organised and located in particular institutional settings is an integral part of the culture of a society, and such national characteristics should be taken seriously not only by upholders of the *status quo* but by those who hope to change it. The conservative tendency to defend traditional patterns of obligation and entitlement takes insufficient account of the extent to which tradition is the outcome of change. The radical challenge to traditional patterns of obligation and entitlement takes insufficient account of the extent to which they reflect authentic and popular beliefs about social welfare. *A well-formulated theory of welfare gives as much attention to the distinctive features of national culture and tradition as it does to the formal context of social policy.*

Statutory provision

The first thing to note in comparing the British and Japanese social welfare systems is that the marked contrast in their recent economic fortunes has a direct bearing on their respective capacities to meet welfare needs. Most welfare arrangements work reasonably well if there is a credible relationship between declared aims and available resources.

During the twentieth century Britain became a richer nation, but in relative terms it fell from the top to very near the bottom of the league table of advanced industrial societies, taking annual income per head of the population as an indicator.[1] Between 1973 and 1979 Britain experienced a real increase in GNP of 1.1 per cent per annum, compared with 4.1 per cent in Japan. As Naomi Maruo observes, the Japanese economy is still growing at 'about twice the rate of other OECD nations', and the unemployment rate is 'only just over 2 per cent'.[2] In contrast British manufacturing output has fallen by 18 per cent from 1979 to 1984, and the level of unemployment has risen to 14 per cent, or 3.2 million. On the other hand, the annual rate of inflation in Britain has been sharply reduced from over 20 per cent to around 5 per cent in the same period.

Comparing social expenditure as a proportion of GDP in Britain and Japan is more hazardous because of differences in the social division of welfare and in the systems of taxation. Gough gives figures of 18.2 per cent for the UK and 9.9 per cent for Japan, based on OECD data for the early 1970s, and limited to income maintenance, health and education. Current research by Nosse confirms that social expenditure as a proportion of GDP in Japan is lower than that in Britain and other industrial nations. In comparing social security expenditure for the year 1978 in Japan and other industrial societies, Fukutake found that Japanese expenditure, expressed as a ratio to GDP, was 11 per cent, as against figures of 20.6 per cent for the United Kingdom, 25.5 per cent for France, and 30.2 per cent for Sweden.[3]

These comparisons, however, underestimate the extent of Japanese reliance on occupational welfare provision. Although the Japanese constitution of 1945 accepts the principle of universality in its broadest sense, in practice there is a pronounced element of selectivity in the statutory services. This, combined with the widespread reliance on occupational welfare, has helped to create a complicated and sectionalised system of formal social services. The organisation of Japanese social security is a good example.

The Japanese definition of social security is very broad. It includes social insurance (*shakai hoken*), public assistance (*seikatsu hogo*) and a whole range of social welfare services and benefits for special categories such as children, the elderly, one-parent families and the physically and the mentally handicapped. It includes services in cash and kind, and home-help. Public assistance and social work services are combined; social workers are therefore directly involved in the provision of income support.

Social insurance covers medical care, pensions, unemployment benefits and accident compensation. The medical insurance scheme for employees receives a 10 per cent national subsidy, and the scheme for non-employed and self-employed people a 40 per cent national subsidy. There is 100 per cent coverage for employees, and 70 per cent for their dependants and for the non-employed and self-employed.

Chester and Ichien point out that the earliest systems of health insurance in Japan were organised by employers, not as in Britain by Friendly Societies.[4] By 1922 two major schemes had developed — one organised and run by the larger industrial companies, and the other managed by the government for workers in smaller firms. Between the wars there was steady growth in coverage and membership, complemented by new schemes for public sector employees, and in 1938 a basic scheme was started for farmers and the self-employed. However, coverage did not become universal until 1961.[5]

The resulting situation is described by Chester and Ichien as one of 'complexity in universality', in which 'over 1600 . . . societies covering the employees in large organisations'[6] belong to one national federation receiving a small subsidy of about 10 per cent from the state. There are marked disparities in provision among the various occupational health schemes. The national health insurance scheme, which covers 'the self-employed, farmers and the retired and does not, therefore, receive employers' contributions', receives a subsidy of 'not less than 60%'.[7] Despite this high level of subsidy for the government scheme, the levels of benefits and services come nowhere near those provided in the company-run schemes. The very fact that there is a dual system militates against redistribution, and political pressures for unification are naturally resisted by members of the better schemes. Since 1973 medical care has been provided free of charge, subject to a means test, to those aged 70 or over.

According to Chester and Ichien about 58 per cent of all hospital beds belong to the private sector, roughly one-third to the public sector and the remaining 10 per cent to a 'semi-public' sector consisting of the Red Cross and social insurance institutions.[8] This is in sharp contrast to the distribution of health care in Britain, where the bulk of hospital provision is in the public sector and most of the cost of medical care is met out of taxation. Like Britain, Japan is faced with sharply rising costs in medical care and a rapid increase in the number and proportion of the elderly.[9]

Japanese pension, unemployment and accident insurance schemes are similarly complex and diverse. On the other hand, the scope of the public assistance scheme is much narrower than that of the British supplementary benefits scheme. In 1979 just over 1,400,000 citizens were receiving public assistance, and 70 per cent of these recipients were in need because of illness in the family. In Britain (1980–81) the largest group drawing supplementary benefit were the elderly (accounting for 53 per cent), while disability and long-term sickness accounted for only 11 per cent.[10]

Within the statutory sector in Japan the management of social welfare (including public assistance, services for children and families, child guidance and public health) is divided between national, pre-fectural and local administrations. The costs of provision are normally divided on an 80 per cent national/20 per cent prefectural and local basis, compared with a 55/45 per cent ratio between central and local government in Britain. It must be stressed that this type of comparison can be misleading because the distribution of responsibilities between central and local authorities and between the various welfare sectors is not at all the same in Japan and Britain. (No reference is made in this chapter to education and housing, although they are included in the above percentages.)

Voluntary service

In both countries the voluntary sector is attracting more attention than it has done in the past.[11] The British voluntary sector is distinguished by its considerable diversity and the high value which its numerous foundations and agencies attach to their autonomy and constitutional independence from the government, despite their increasing depen-dence in recent years on financial grants from both central and local government. The model of close, formal cooperation between voluntary and statutory agencies which was so strongly recommended by the Majority Report of the Royal Commission on the Poor Laws in 1909 attracted little support, and was never adopted.

Although the provision of welfare in Japan appears to be dominated by sectional groupings based on vertically-structured allegiances, there is also evidence of considerable activity among voluntary associations whose services cut across sectional loyalties. Fukuda attributes the origin of these associations to the influence of western Christianity, but the successive experiences of the 1930s, the war and the American occupation also fostered the development of voluntarism. Immediately after the second world war Community Chest movements were initiated, and the National Council of Social Welfare was set up in 1951. Post-war welfare legislation required national and local governments to develop volunteer services.[12]

By the 1960s new forms of voluntary association were developing nationally and locally, especially in new urban areas. More emphasis was placed on the need for active local participation in community care and cooperation with statutory authorities.

A distinctive feature of the Japanese voluntary movement was the creation of a new category of 'appointed volunteers' recruited by public authorities to undertake specific tasks. The active government sponsorship of the post-war years originates from the establishment of a system of 'goodwill banks' in 1961. Goodwill banks receive offers of help in cash, kind or personal service from local citizens, whose contributions are subsequently called on as the need arises. the National Council of Social Welfare maintained a continuing role in sponsorship and coordination, with the help of government funds.

In Japan, however, the tradition of close, direct government involvement in voluntary service goes back much further than 1961. The best-known category of appointed volunteers is the Minsei-iin which originated at the end of the first world war.

By the mid-1930s programmes of this kind had been organised throughout Japan, with government support. After the second world war the public assistance programme was reconstituted and Minsei-iin became no less than 'the auxiliary agency through which public administration made public assistance available to people'.[13] In effect, Minsei-iin now stood in almost exactly the relationships to statutory assistance that Charles Loch and the Charity Organisation Society had tried for so long to foster in the British voluntary sector before the first world war. Minsei-iin volunteers were appointed on a legal basis between 1948 and 1951.

In the statutory reforms of 1950 and 1951, however, a revised Daily Life Security Law (1950) and a new Social Welfare Service Law (1951) created new publicly administered welfare offices staffed by professional public assistance case-workers. As a result, Minsei-iin volunteers ceased to administer the public assistance funds and assumed their present advisory role in cooperation with the new statutory case-workers. They continue to be appointed by the government for three-year terms, but although they still work closely with the public assistance case-workers, their future role is currently under review.

Despite this evidence of community-based volunteer services cutting across traditional systems of vertical affiliation, it is not possible to infer from the available literature in translation the full extent and significance of these new forms of horizontal affiliation. Fukuda suggests that roughly 5.8 per cent of the total Japanese population have had some volunteer experience[14] compared with about 2.5 per cent in Britain,[15] but neither of these estimates makes any claim to accuracy.

Occupational welfare

In Japan the importance of occupational welfare has significantly affected the whole of the statutory social services. Employer-based welfare provision is a major determinant of individual life-chances. After the Meiji Restoration of 1868 the Japanese economy became increasingly dominated by a small number of vast business empires known as *zaibatsu*, which owed their expansion to preferential treatment from the government and close informal links with political leaders. Although the monopoly powers of the pre-war *zaibatsu* were ostensibly broken after the second world war, they have since recovered some of their influence and they continue to be a very important factor in Japanese economic life.[16]

After 1945 trade unions won formal recognition and were given legal protection and active encouragement to organise. For a short period the new unions came under communist influence, until the left-wing revolutionary leaders were removed from office in 1950. Union membership then declined from 'a peak of 56% in 1949' to 'no more than 32%' in 1978,[17] and the Japanese labour unions became 'enterprise' unions, conducting negotiations at the company level. Morishima states that 'in many enterprises the head of the union subsequently became president or director of the company'.[18]

From these post-war beginnings emerged the now widely recognised phenomenon of the Japanese company, a closely-knit corporate and cooperative enterprise in which 'both management and employers are bound together by a common fate and common interests; in extreme cases they are communities which share a communal philosophy'.[19] Not only work but social benefits and services provide the material basis for such extensive cooperation. In effect the life-chances of employees are so closely associated with their companies that it is difficult to distinguish in Japanese society between the significance of work and that of welfare.

Company loyalty, lifetime employment and seniority as a criterion for advancement are the three cardinal principles on which Japanese occupational welfare is based. The inculcation of loyalty is carried out through intensive induction training programmes. The practice of lifetime employment originated in the years before the first world war when skilled labour was in short supply.

Membership and advancement are contingent on a high degree of conformity but they bring substantial material benefits. In western societies respect for persons and individual autonomy are cardinal values which paradoxically coexist with extensive reliance on collectivist social services financed by the state. In Japan much less attention is paid to individual autonomy and much more to the welfare of the group and the harmonious accommodation of individuals within groups. Japanese employers, as Nakane observes, 'do not employ only a man's labour itself but really employ the total man as is shown in the expression *marugakae*, "completely enveloped"'.[20]

The welfare responsibilities of the company extend to the immediate kin of employees and they include the provision of company housing, shared recreation and holidays, family allowances which supplement the statutory children's allowances, and lifetime employment. Occupational welfare is an increasingly important feature in British social policy but in Japan it is vastly more comprehensive and its membership includes a much larger proportion of the workforce. There are, however, marked disparities in welfare provision between the best companies — which are usually the largest — and the poorest ones, and these welfare disparities are complemented by wage differences. This has led to intense competition for entry into the large companies, with profound effects on the educational system.[21]

The system of lifetime employment also has its drawbacks. The age of retirement is early — often as early as 55. In many of the larger companies retired employees are allowed to go on using certain services such as health care and holiday homes, and some of them find a second job in one of the smaller associated firms. However, as Morishima points out, few of the small companies are able to look after former employees in this way. The size of lump-sum 'retirement allowances' also varies considerably. Many retired workers find that they need additional private health insurance and alternative housing. Consequently there is a high propensity to save against these contingencies during the working lifetime. None the less, because of the close relationship between wages and occupational welfare benefits, those who are at greatest risk find it most difficult to practise self-help.

In Japan the statutory and voluntary social services are particularly important to workers who are employed in companies with poor quality occupational welfare services and to small-scale entrepreneurs, farmers and 'casual workers' in city and countryside. Then there are minorities like the 2 million Burakumin, who do not even 'belong' to conventional Japanese society. Despite longstanding formal incorporation into Japanese society, the Burakumin still suffer from forms of discrimination and exclusion which have much in common with the treatment of racial minorities in Britain.[22]

Finally there is the principle of seniority, which has considerable but possibly declining importance in Japanese industry. Morishima suggests that it was incorporated into industry from the traditional culture in the early stages of modernisation. It provided an incentive for workers to give lifetime loyalty to their companies.[23] The danger that considerations of seniority might conflict with those of merit is recognised in Japanese companies, but it is argued that the creation of good working relationships on the traditional basis of deference to seniority is conducive to greater efficiency.[24]

To sum up, company loyalty, lifetime employment with its associated welfare benefits, and the seniority principle illustrate the importance of group affiliations in Japanese society. Although Japan's prosperity is based on a highly competitive and entrepreneurial ethos, it is not an individualist society in the western sense of the term. *In Japan the ethic of collectivist welfare is expressed through the company rather than through statutory social services.*

Japanese social welfare in a cultural context

The division of welfare in Japan developed out of a unique set of historical and cultural circumstances. In order to understand the present arrangement of Japanese social services it is necessary to study the cumulative effect of social change on the traditional institutions of Japanese society and the manner in which these institutions shaped and regulated the forces of change.

In *The Japanese Social Structure* Tadashi Fukutake describes Japan at the time of the Meiji Restoration as a society held together by 'an emotional kind of patriotism which served as a bridge between the local communities and the national community'. This 'bridge', or rather the trunk and roots of the society, was the Imperial family.[25]

Traditional notions of mutual aid in Japan were based more on the household than on extended kinship. Morishima draws attention to the influence of Confucian thought in Japanese social organisation, but he adds that in Japan Confucianism attaches greater importance to the virtue of loyalty than to that of benevolence, which was a cardinal feature of Confucianism in China.[26] In Japanese culture, loyalty to members of one's household takes priority over loyalty to extended kin. Nakane comments that 'The wife and the daughter-in-law who have come from outside have incomparably greater importance than one's own sisters and daughters who have married and gone into other households'.[27]

The Japanese word *ie* includes the family but extends beyond it, to include notions of a household and a corporate residential group.[28] As Nakane explains:

> The kinship which is normally regarded as the primary and basic human attachment seems to be compensated in Japan by a personalised relation to a corporate group based on work, in which the major aspects of social and economic life are involved.[29]

The continuing pervasiveness of the *ie* family system supported by a law of primogeniture helped to preserve patriarchal authority and the traditional status system. Social solidarity was effectively maintained throughout a period of dramatic economic change but, as Fukutake remarks,

> In social terms the *ie* system was a strongly negative factor, keeping wages low and work conditions harsh, and preventing any demand for social welfare services from becoming powerfully articulated.[30]

Traditional rural life based on family and village was also profoundly affected by modernisation. As early as 1888 a new system of local government combined groups of four or five villages into single units for purposes of administration and taxation. The introduction of compulsory education in 1872 as well as military conscription also helped to broaden public loyalties and mould the people into a nation of patriots.[31] From the 1920s onwards Japan developed into a major industrial and military power within which traditional social institutions and arrangements persisted. It was a hierarchical society in which 'everyone was equally a child of His Imperial Majesty',[32] although effective power was vested in a ruling élite of the military and industrialists. Fukutake tells us that the distinctive qualities of social solidarity in pre-1945 Japan were 'supremacy of custom' and 'submission to authority'. The conventions of neighbourly obligation (*giri*) imposed conformity and suppressed individuality so that 'Behaviour was for the most part guided and regulated not by internalised conscience or rational judgement but rather by custom and authority'.[33] Takeo Doi argues that although these conventions of neighbourly obligation give rise to highly formalised relationships, they derive their authority and pervasive influence from emotional needs and values which are intrinsic to the informal relationships of Japanese family life. He suggests that Japanese culture sustains and is sustained by a general tendency to structure all close relationships on the pattern of a parent–child relationship.[34] The process of socialisation in Japan nurtures the desire to depend on the affection of another person: dependency is a condition to be valued rather than avoided.

Familial emotions and values are so pervasive in Japan that they provide the model for other kinds of relationship between friends, workers, employers, and so on. Such relationships naturally become more formal the more distant they are from kinship; nevertheless, as long as they serve for the discharge of customary obligations and the perpetuation of group loyalties, they retain some of the quality of familial relationships.[35] Formal relationships of this kind are called *giri* relationships and they define the boundary between an inner world in which there need be no 'holding back' (*enryo*) and an outer world of strangers to whom no obligation whatever is felt.

According to Doi these are the characteristics of Japanese relationships which account for the strength of group solidarities, the weakness of individualist sentiments, and the difficulty of extending the range of obligation and entitlement beyond the separate groups and factions which still dominate Japanese culture.

In seeking to apply this analysis to issues of social policy, one notes how closely the relationships at work and the connections between work and occupational welfare appear to replicate and extend the values of the Japanese family. Each occupational welfare scheme is a bounded expression of loyalties and obligations which are far more intense and encompassing than their British counterparts. The pattern of occupational welfare in Japan is an extension of the traditional culture. Limited forms of universal statutory provision exist in Japan, but these services have so far struck only shallow roots in the culture. They are of most importance to the section of the workforce which is excluded from occupational welfare or belongs only to the least adequate schemes.

Taken together, these social and psychological features help to explain some of the marked differences between British and Japanese notions of obligation and entitlement in social welfare. First, there is the British practice of locating most social services *outside* the workplace in contrast to the Japanese tradition which gives the workplace a position of paramount importance not only in the lives of individual workers but in those of their families. Secondly, the two societies display very different forms of social solidarity based on markedly different notions of 'public' and 'private' interest. In Britain the most important social services are statutory ones, of which the majority are universal in scope and relatively impersonal in operation, although selectivity and discretion also play a major role within this framework. Although feelings of loyalty and welfare obligation and entitlement in Britain are universal, they are relatively diffuse and not very intense.

In contrast the strength of the corporate loyalties engendered by the Japanese approach to welfare is profound, though narrow in scope. The near total inclusion of members in these groups is complemented by a greater tendency to exclude non-members and a relative indifference to the welfare of strangers. This sense of group identity based on common interests is far more profound than the sense of association based on a contractual principle.

These qualities of Japanese social life are widely believed to militate not only against universalist notions of statutory welfare but also against voluntary services which cut across the vertical loyalties of Japanese culture.[36]

This leads, however, to a third distinctive feature of Japanese social welfare. In addition to the voluntary networks of mutual aid based on work and closely linked to formal provision of occupational welfare, other kinds of voluntary service have developed to compensate for gaps in statutory provision and to help those who do not belong to adequate occupational welfare schemes.[37] New religions like Soka Gakkai significantly enough appeal to citizens who do not have stable working relationships, especially casual labourers.

Traditional arrangements and notions of group membership and mutual aid have changed under the impact of industrialisation, urban growth, the post-war democratisation of political life, agrarian reform and widespread internal migration. The radical post-war revision of the civil code undermined the older traditional network of affiliations based on the *ie* household. Although primogeniture remains popular, other forms of inheritance are now permitted and the formal authority of the head of the household has been considerably reduced.

Most Japanese authorities believe that their society is still in a state of cultural transition. Traditional notions of community have been weakened without a complementary growth in other forms of social solidarity. Fukutake argues that the conventions of *giri* obligations sustaining *ie* have broken down, and that the Japanese who were 'tradition oriented' in the modern period are now becoming 'other directed' rather than 'inner directed'. The new loyalties based on the workplace and other institutions of mass society are taking the place of the old traditions, but now the new schemes of occupational welfare inhibit the growth of more universal forms of statutory social service just as they were once inhibited by the old *ie* system of mutual aid.

The few universal schemes which exist, such as the national pension scheme, are effectively residual services for citizens who do not have access to adequate occupational schemes, or do not belong at all. Japan has become a major industrial power, but is still seriously deficient in the provision of statutory social services.

Fukutake's apprehensiveness about the quality of any emergent form of community loyalty which might develop in Japan springs from his historical awareness of the frailty of individualist sentiments in comparison with the depth of feeling associated with community and group affiliations. It is difficult to infer the significance of these affiliations simply by studying the formal processes of social policy and administration. We can, however, begin to understand why the Japanese division of welfare acquired its distinctive character when we see it as part of a broader tradition which has adjusted to political change without ever being overwhelmed by it.

Differences in the division of welfare
Comparison is more rewarding when we consider the social division of formal welfare provision in its historical context and also see it as a process of redistribution over the lifetime of individuals whose personal expectations are shaped by the values of specific national cultures. As Titmuss observed, social policy is dynamic and it therefore affects personal welfare throughout the lifetime of the individual. He called his

preferred model of welfare the 'institutional redistributive model of social policy', in which welfare is defined as:

> a major integrated institution in society, providing universalist services outside the market on the principle of need. . . . It is basically a model incorporating systems of redistribution in command-over-resources-through-time.[38]

In comparative social policy we should be concerned, therefore, not only with national differences in the breadth or coverage of social services, but with variations in their coverage over time, and particularly the lifespan of individuals. In Britain the statutory social services are generally universal; they are available throughout the lifetime of individuals but they are only marginally related to the informal aspects of social welfare.

In Japan the statutory social services are less universal and much less important in the overall division of welfare. Occupational welfare, which is the dominant form of welfare provision, is usually available during the *working* lifetime of the individual, but for this limited period it covers both the formal and the informal aspects of social welfare. Most Japanese workers who are members of the large occupational welfare schemes retire between the ages of 55 and 60.[39] Although their pension rights continue, their claims to occupationally-based health care and housing services cease, and their rights to statutory assistance do not begin until the age of 70. Among the numerous Japanese occupational welfare schemes, there is considerable variation in provision, but as a rule most Japanese workers move from one division of welfare to another on retirement, and move again on reaching the age of 70.

It is the existence of these transitionary gaps in the Japanese division of welfare which mainly accounts for the growth of statutory and voluntary social services based on horizontal networks of care and service, although another important factor is the need to provide for minorities in the population who do not belong — and cannot belong — to the large occupational schemes.

There is no reason in principle why Japanese occupational welfare schemes should not be extended to cover the whole lifetime rather than the working lifetime of their members, and it is interesting to speculate about why this is not already happening. It may be that the dominant cultural pattern of vertical relations based on working loyalties is resistant to this kind of extension. Since these relationships include not only work but leisure and other shared informal activities, it would be culturally difficult to separate these formal and informal links after retirement. If the present schemes were extended there would be a sharp increase in the cost of occupational welfare, which, in default of government subsidy, would fall directly on the companies.

Japan is currently feeling the effects of the recession, and in an occupational welfare scheme the connections between economic and social policy are direct and unequivocal. The causal connections between the formal and the informal levels of social welfare provision in Japan are much more difficult to unravel. It is clear, however, that the analysis has to be carried out at both levels.

Finally, comparative analysis needs to be conducted with as much impartiality as possible. Social welfare may be about choices, but the first step in comparative scholarship is descriptive not evaluative in the light of some ideological paradigm. It is obvious, for example, that the provision of social services is more universal and consistent over the individual lifespan in Britain than it is in Japan. The Japanese system, however, provides a much more comprehensive coverage for the majority of citizens (and their families) during their *working* lifetime.

Moreover Japan has been far more successful than Britain in maintaining high levels of employment, and in Japan the connection between work and welfare creates patterns of continuity which bear little resemblance to their British counterparts. In a society like Britain with a high level of unemployment the risks are scattered haphazardly over the working lifetime, as they are for a small minority of workers in Japan. But for the majority of the Japanese workforce it is known in advance that the period of greatest risk will begin with retirement. Britain faces a seemingly intractable problem of high unemployment, and Japan will soon have a higher proportion of elderly people in the total population than most other European societies.[40] If the economic recession deepens in Japan it remains to be seen how occupationally-based welfare will be protected.

Conclusion

Japan is a paradoxical society. It has ostensibly 'borrowed' much from other nations, but whatever it has taken has been carefully reshaped to conform with traditional imperatives. Throughout a period of dramatic change Japan has remained remarkably true to its own culture. The concept of a national culture bears the implication that there is a considerable degree of homogeneity in the lifestyles, life-chances and expectations of a given population. As a rule, however, complex industrial societies are so highly differentiated that it has become necessary to think in terms of various sub-cultures rather than a single culture. Britain is a case in point. Only in the most general sense is it possible to talk of *a* British 'way of life'. On the other hand, most of the basic concepts we use in social policy — universality, selectivity, residual, institutional — are crude summaries of the dominant features of what are in fact complex and often ambiguous phenomena.

Although there are many paradoxical elements in Japanese life, Japan is a remarkably unitary society in a cultural sense. It is a society of infinitely subtle social gradations in which relationships at all levels are carefully ordered in accordance with due form and detail. Sentiments of obligation, entitlement and loyalty are deeply felt, strictly regulated and precisely demarcated. Despite all this preoccupation with the definition of group memberships and the drawing of sectional boundaries, Japan, among all the complex industrial societies, comes nearest to preserving a homogeneous, unique and exclusive national culture.[41]

More important than all the internal demarcations between groups and factions is the difference between being Japanese and not being Japanese. There have been no significant migrations to Japan since the seventh century. There are scarcely any minority groups apart from a very small number of Koreans and Chinese. The Burakumin are an outcast group but they are Japanese and they enjoy full legal rights. For anyone else it remains almost impossible to acquire Japanese nationality.

Britain has always been a more open society, receiving over time numerous immigrants who have become minority groups. In a formal sense Britain has been more receptive than Japan, but in many informal ways, as the history of British race relations demonstrates, there has been a good deal of ambivalence and sometimes open hostility to newcomers on the part of British host communities. Japan has avoided this problem by excluding outsiders and by simply ignoring the few deviant minorities who have always lived inside the country.

In Japan we have a society in which the formal welfare arrangements closely reflect and complement the informal patterns of the traditions and culture. This has long ceased to be true of Britain, where there is more cultural diversity and where formal welfare policy may easily conflict with various sub-cultures based on class, ethnicity or other distinguishing social features.

Comparative analysis is unlikely to reveal striking similarities between societies if the formal and informal dimensions of welfare are taken into account and both are then related to cultural variables. Analysis of the differences may, however, add to our understanding of the unique development of welfare arrangements in each individual society. This might at least make us a little more circumspect in our predictions and prescriptions for their future.

Notes

1. Ralf Dahrendorf (1982), *On Britain*, London: BBC, 20—1.
2. Naomi Maruo (1982), 'The Development of the Welfare State in Japan: An Alternative Model', *The Journal of Economics*, XXIII, no. 3, May, The Society of Economics in the Chuo University, Tokyo, 2.
3. Ian Gough (1979), *The Political Economy of the Welfare State*, London: Macmillan. See also Maruo, op.cit., 7; T. Nosse (1982), *Econometric Analysis of Public Finance*, Tokyo: Sobunsha; and Tadashi Fukutake (1982), *The Japanese Social Structure: Its Evolution in the Modern Century* (translated and with a Foreword by Ronald P. Dore), Tokyo: University of Tokyo Press, 200.

128   *Comparing Welfare States and their Futures*

4. T.E. Chester and Mitsuya Ichien (1983), 'Health Care in Japan: Its Development, Structure and Problems', *The Three Banks Review* 137, March, 17—26.
5. Ibid., 17—19.
6. Ibid., 19. See also Joan Higgins (1981), *States of Welfare: Comparative Analysis in Social Policy*, Oxford: Basil Blackwell/Martin Robertson, 140—4.
7. Chester and Ichien, op.cit., 20.
8. Ibid.
9. Maruo, op.cit., 8; and Chester and Ichien, op.cit., 23.
10. *Guide to Health and Welfare Services in Japan* (1981), Ministry of Health and Welfare (Koseisho), Tokyo, 27 ff.
11. See *Social Workers: Their Role and Tasks* (Barclay Report) (1982), published for the National Institute of Social Work by Bedford Square Press/NCVO, paras 5.5—5.9, 74—5; and N. Johnson (1981), *Voluntary Social Services*, Oxford: Basil Blackwell. For information on informal caring networks, see P. Abrams (1980), 'Social Change, Social Networks and Neighbourhood Care', *Social Work Service* 22, 12—23; and P. Abrams (1978), 'Neighbourhood Care and Social Policy: A Research Perspective', The Volunteer Centre, Berkhamsted.
12. Fukuda (1978), *The Japanese Volunteer*, National Volunteer Activity Promotion Centre, 3-3-4 Kasumigaseki, Chiyoda-ku, Tokyo 100.
13. Ibid., 21.
14. Ibid., 15.
15. Quoted in the Barclay Report, 75.
16. Michio Morishima (1982), *Why has Japan 'Succeeded'?: Western Technology and the Japanese Ethos*, London: Cambridge University Press, 159.
17. Ibid., 167.
18. Ibid., 168—9.
19. Ibid., 170.
20. Chie Nakane (1981), *Japanese Society*, Harmondsworth: Penguin Books, 15.
21. Morishima, op.cit., 171—4.
22. See I. Roger Yoshino and Sueo Murakoshi (1977), *The Invisible Visible Minority: Japan's Burakumin*, Buraku Kaiho Kenkyusho, 1247 Kuboyoshi-cho, Naniwa-ku, Osaka 556; and *Long-Suffering Brothers and Sisters, Unite! The Buraku Problem, Universal Human Rights and Minority Problems in Various Countries* (1981), ed. Buraku Liberation Research Institute, 1-6-12 Kuboyoshi, Naniwa-ku, Osaka 556. Both of these books provide a guide to further reading.
23. Morishima, op.cit., 106.
24. See also Nakane, op.cit., 26 *passim*.
25. Fukutake, op.cit., 15—16.
26. Morishima, op.cit., 4—7.
27. Nakane, op.cit., 5.
28. Ibid., 4.
29. Ibid., 7.
30. Fukutake, op.cit., 28.
31. Richard Storry (1982), *A History of Modern Japan*, Harmondsworth: Penguin Books, 113; and Fukutake, op.cit., 37.
32. Fukutake, op.cit., 65.
33. Ibid., 42—3.
34. Takeo Doi (1981), *The Anatomy of Dependence*, Tokyo: Kodansha International, 1—36.
35. Ibid., 34.
36. Nakane, op.cit., 62.
37. Edwin O. Reischauer (1980), *The Japanese*, Belknap Press of Harvard University Press, 131—3.
38. Richard M. Titmuss (1974), *Social Policy: An Introduction*, London: George Allen and Unwin, 31.
39. I am most grateful to Professor T. Nosse and Professor T. Okada for providing me with information on these schemes.
40. Maruo, op.cit., 8.
41. Reischauer, op.cit., 33.

9 Welfare State Regression in Scandinavia? The Development of Scandinavian Welfare States from 1970 to 1980
Lars Nørby Johansen

Introduction

It seems a commonplace observation that the Scandinavian countries constitute a distinct group within the larger family of modern welfare states. The literature abounds with labels such as 'Scandinavia as a paragon of welfare virtues', 'the Scandinavian model' or 'Scandinavia as a laboratory of welfare policies'. The Scandinavian countries' much vaunted reputation as welfare leaders are bolstered by a variety of indicators. Some commentators point to the high levels of welfare spending prevailing there, or to comparatively high post-war growth rates. Others focus on the composition of public expenditure in general and of social security expenditure in particular and, accordingly, attach importance to the high share of resources channelled into final government consumption or social benefits in kind (e.g. Kohl 1981). Still others play down the significance of quantitative spending indicators, and point instead to a specific institutional profile. Thus, Esping-Andersen and Korpi (1983: 6—7) assert that the Scandinavian welfare states may be distinguished by three features: (1) comprehensiveness of state intervention to provide welfare; (2) institutionalised social entitlements; and (3) a social security system based on universal coverage and solidarity. In short, the Scandinavian welfare states are unique in that they can boast an almost perfect fit with the 'institutional redistributive model' of social policy (Pinker 1971; Titmuss 1974; Mishra 1977).

Yet the widespread belief that the Scandinavian welfare states are something special does not only contain a descriptive portrait whether in terms of spending indicators or institutional profile. It also includes the explanatory notion that the Scandinavian model is inextricably linked with the strength of the Social-Democratic parties and the trade union movement (Castles 1978; Logue 1979; Korpi 1980). Moreover, it appears to be commonly accepted that the Scandinavian model is a product of the post-war era. For one thing, it is well documented that it was the rapid expansion of the public economies in Scandinavia, especially during the 1960s, that pushed the Scandinavian countries ahead of other OECD countries in terms of welfare spending (e.g. Wilensky 1975; Cameron 1978; Kohl 1981). But also the institutional shaping of the model is allegedly a post-war phenomenon (Esping-Andersen and Korpi 1983). Put differently, the Scandinavian model is not only a child of Social-Democratic strength; it is also a product of — or at least coincides with — an unprecedented and sustained period of economic growth. It therefore makes sense to ask *whether the Scandinavian welfare state model has been able to withstand the economic stagnation of the 1970s* and what the experiences of that decade can tell us about the future of the Scandinavian model.

Focusing on the performance of the Scandinavian welfare states under conditions of economic stagnation is also justified by the fact that Social-Democratic governments have been less strong and less stable during the 1970s than hitherto. Liberal governments or weak Social-Democratic minority cabinets have more often than not been in office throughout the decade. Moreover, the economic recession after the 1973/74 oil crisis was accompanied by anti-tax and anti-welfare sentiments, most notably in Denmark where, in 1973, Glistrup's Progressive Party dramatically changed the political landscape (Heidenheimer *et al.* 1975; Wilensky 1975, 1976; Hibbs and Madsen 1981). Thus, if we depart from the assumption that there is in fact such a thing as *a* Scandinavian welfare state model, that this model is a product of post-war economic growth and inextricably related to Social-Democratic strength, one would expect that this model has been under severe strain during the last decade. On the other hand, if the changed economic and political conditions turn out not to have altered the essentials of the Scandinavian welfare states, this line of thought should be questioned.

Structure of the chapter

This chapter will pursue a descriptive and inductive approach. Descriptive because it is necessary to provide a fairly thorough mapping of the development of social security expenditure and of institutional changes from 1970 to 1980. This is the only way to cut through prevailing myths about welfare state roll-back, or myths about continuing welfare state excesses. And inductive because we cannot start out from fixed theories or hypotheses. Partly because the subject-matter is of such a recent nature and so badly documented, and partly because most theories or general propositions in the field focus on the *growth and expansion* of modern welfare states. Processes of welfare state roll-back or adaptive processes have only recently attracted students of welfare states.

The chapter starts with a brief description of the economic *malaise* in the Scandinavian countries. In particular, it will show how the economic recession has hit the Scandinavian countries differently. The next section will trace how strategies of crisis management are reflected in the development and composition of public expenditure in general, and of social security expenditure in particular. As far as social security expenditure is concerned the analysis will follow a strategy of disaggregation. In this way it should be possible not only to avoid the usual tendency to employ highly aggregate — and often rather meaningless — indicators, but also in principle to control for automatic growth components, such as demographic changes and increases in the number of beneficiaries. The third section is concerned with institutional changes. This is crucial to the argument. Even though no significant changes (i.e. cuts) have occurred with respect to various spending measures, institutional changes may very well have undermined the tenets of the so-called Scandinavian welfare state model. The following section will provide an outline discussion of possible explanations of the development of the Scandinavian model under economic stagnation; and possible future developments will be addressed in the concluding section.

Economic stagnation in Scandinavia

As shown in Table 9.1, real economic growth has been markedly slower since the 1974 oil crisis compared with the preceding period.

Table 9.1 Average, annual real economic growth (GDP) in the Scandinavian countries, 1960—82

	1960—67	1967—73	1973—80	1980—82
Denmark	4.7	4.0	1.6	0.7
Norway	4.7	3.8	4.7	1.3
Sweden	4.5	3.6	1.8	0.7

Source: OECD, *Economic Outlook*, historical statistics 1960—1980, plus national sources.

This gloomy picture of reduced economic growth is of course shared by most OECD countries, but in this context of inter-Scandinavian comparison it is striking that Norway was able to maintain its pre-1973 economic growth rate. In fact, Norway's economic growth increased after 1973, whereas Denmark and Sweden both experienced a substantial drop in economic activity.

The major reason for this difference is obviously that sky-rocketing energy prices have been a severe blow to Denmark and Sweden, whereas Norway has profited greatly from the very same factor. Put differently, the traditional vulnerability of open, dependent and small economies and the concomitant ineffectiveness of traditional macroeconomic strategies of crisis-management have been severely felt in Denmark and Sweden, but not in Norway — at least not to the same extent. Thus, the combination of increased burdens of imports caused by escalating energy prices and stagnant export markets has exposed Denmark and Sweden to mounting deficits on their trade balances. Moreover, the demand for foreign capital and the ensuing burden of payments on loans and interest on debts, aggravated by unprecedented high interest rates, have made the problems of large deficits on the balance of payments ever more severe. In contrast, Norway could tolerate huge deficits on its trade balance and balance of payments reflecting the enormous imports of capital, goods and services to build up an infrastructure for oil speculation, in expectation of future oil revenues.

The difference between Denmark and Sweden on the one hand, and Norway on the other, is reflected in another area of economic imbalance — deficits in the public household. If we take the deficit in the total public budget (including both current and capital transactions) this deficit has been exponentially increasing in Denmark and Sweden, especially over the last few years. In contrast, Norway has maintained a surplus throughout the decade — even strongly increasing towards the end of the period thanks to revenues from oil taxes. In order not to reduce domestic demand further in the already deflated economies by raising taxes or cutting social security benefits, Denmark and Sweden have increasingly resorted to deficit financing. However, deficit financing is not costless. As we shall see, the burdens of deficit financing in terms of interest payments on public debt produce repercussions on the profile of public expenditure.

Public expenditure

It was the rapid expansion of the public economies during the 1960s that led some commentators to single out the Scandinavian countries as a distinct group characterised by markedly high growth rates. If we measure the scope of the public economy by total public expenditure as a percentage of GDP it is apparent from Figure 9.1(A) that this growth did not come to a halt during the 1970s. Quite to the contrary. In all three countries the expansion of the public economy continued at a rate similar to that of the previous decade.

Yet there are some noticeable differences among the Scandinavian

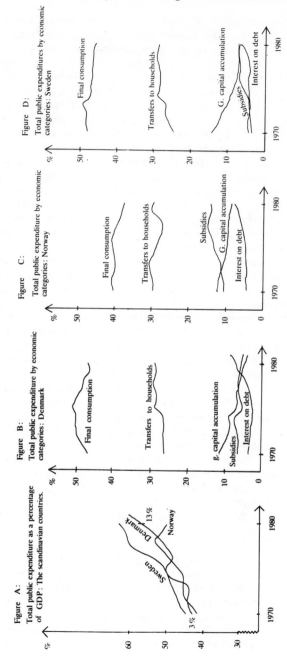

Figure 9.1   Total public expenditure : the Scandinavian countries

countries in terms of level, rate of change and timing. Throughout the period Sweden had the highest level of public expenditure relative to GDP – not only among the Scandinavian countries but also among OECD countries. On average, Denmark had the second highest level, and Norway the lowest level. Sweden also had record growth rates with a spectacular 18 per cent increase from 1970 to 1980. The corresponding figures for Denmark and Norway are 13.8 per cent and 8.2 per cent, respectively. As to timing, it is striking that (1) Norway experienced a marked growth of public expenditure in the early 1970s, in contrast to Denmark and Sweden; (2) the global economic recession of 1973/74 almost immediately manifested itself in Denmark and with a two-year lag in Sweden in terms of marked increases in the public expenditure ratio; and (3) the late 1970s witnessed an accelerating growth of public expenditure in Denmark and Sweden, but deceleration in Norway. These intra-Scandinavian variations to a certain extent reflect national differences in economic growth. The development of public expenditure relative to GDP testifies to a growing *divergence* among the Scandinavian countries in the course of the 1970s. Whereas at the beginning of the decade the 'size' of the public economy was pretty much the same in Scandinavia, the following years brought about a widening gap.

However, one cannot preclude that this divergence hides important similarities in the way in which total public expenditures are allocated to various economic activities. In order to see if that is the case, the relative distribution of public expenditure by economic categories is shown in Figure 9.1(B–D).

If we first look at the distribution of public means absorbed by *final consumption* on the one hand and *transfers* mediated through the public sector on the other, a clear pattern emerges. Denmark and Sweden are distinct in that these countries have relatively more resources to public final consumption than does Norway. This difference is important because government final consumption is a better indicator of the extent to which the public economy really absorbs resources in society compared with transfers, which only signify redistribution mediated through the public sector.

This hints at an important difference in the profile of the Scandinavian welfare states. Denmark and Sweden are to a larger extent 'service welfare states' compared with the Norwegian 'cash welfare state'. Although the difference in this respect is apparently only marginal between Denmark and Sweden, it is none the less interesting that Denmark, on average, allocates relatively more resources to public final consumption than Sweden. Finally it indicates that the Scandinavian countries have not been converging in this respect during the 1970s. In all the three countries there is a slight tendency towards a relative decline of final consumption expenditure, especially towards the end of the period, and more so in Norway than in Denmark and Sweden.

Now, it should not be overlooked that transfers include more than direct transfers to households. Norway has certainly spent relatively more on transfers to households, but only slightly more. The real difference lies in the area of *subsidies*. Throughout the period, Norway devoted twice as much, in relative terms, on subsidies compared with Denmark and Sweden. However, it is striking that from 1975 Sweden significantly increased the proportion of its subsidies. In contrast, the level of subsidies in Denmark has not only been rather low, but also stable.

Though these figures may seem crude, they signal fundamental differences in responses to the economic crisis. Denmark has reacted to the international economic slowdown of the late 1970s by a traditional, liberal strategy relying on the 'cleansing' effects of the market. In contrast, Norway (and from 1975 Sweden to a certain extent) has been pursuing a policy of combatting the impacts of the international economic crisis on the domestic sector by channelling substantial subsidies into private firms and public enterprises. This is probably one of the reasons why the unemployment rate in Denmark soared from 1.1 per cent in 1973 to 9.7 per cent in 1983, whereas unemployment in Sweden did not exceed the 'acceptable' 2 per cent limit of structural unemployment until 1981. Norway followed the same pattern as Sweden.

The 1970s witnessed a steady decline in public *capital accumulation* and investments. This is a general tendency observable in most OECD countries, but in Scandinavia it is interesting to note that the decline of public capital accumulation and investments has been most pronounced in Denmark and least so in Norway. This underscores the intra-Scandinavian variation in macroeconomic and political strategies also found in the differential use of public subsidies.

The accelerating scope of deficit financing in Sweden and Denmark is reflected in the form of rapidly increasing burdens of *interest on public debts* towards the end of the period, a tendency that is more pronounced in 1980—83. In Denmark, public expenditure on interest repayments on foreign debts now exceeds 10 per cent of total public expenditure. Put in a different way, in 1983 interest repayments are estimated to have exceeded expenditure on old age pensions.

The varying distributions of public expenditure by real economic categories among the Scandinavian countries stresses the fact that the borderline between industrial, regional and social policy is blurred. This should be kept in mind when interpreting the development of social security expenditure to which we now turn.

Social security expenditure
In order to overcome some of the shortcomings of highly aggregated

social expenditure measures, the following survey of social spending in the Scandinavian welfare states will depart from some widely-used aggregate measures and subsequently these aggregates will be broken down by programmes and types of benefits (in kind and in cash), before individual social benefits are brought in.

As a starting point it may be useful to show the development of the share of total national economic resources and the share of the public economy that are absorbed by social security expenditure, i.e. social security expenditure as a percentage of GDP and as a percentage of total current public expenditure. In all three countries the proportion of social security expenditure to GDP has risen steeply from 1970 to 1980, most notably in Sweden (14.8 percentage points) and least in Norway (6.4 per cent) with Denmark in between (10.8 per cent). Again, it should be recalled that these differences first and foremost reflect the underlying (and differential) developments of the denominator, GDP.

It is more interesting that, towards the end of the decade, the share of public expenditure allocated to social security decreased. In Denmark and Sweden, this trend may probably be explained by the accumulating impacts of deficit financing (i.e. rapidly increasing debt services). This illustrates the paradox − or rather the vicious circle − of deficit financing: the public economy expands not only as a result of increasing social spending, but also as a result of accelerating costs of *financing* social security (interest and payments on public debt). And due to the fact that these financing costs grow relatively faster than social security expenditure proper, the latter constitutes a decreasing part of the expanding public economy. Deficit financing has paradoxical consequences as well: despite the complexity of the problem, the total distributional effect of social security is progressive (increases income equality); but financing social security in terms of deficit financing is undoubtedly highly regressive.

Broken down by major programmes, the development of the *spending profile* among the Scandinavian countries displays some noticeable differences and similarities. Not surprisingly, the lion's share of social security expenditure goes to pensions, especially *old age pensions*. It is more interesting, however, that national trends differ markedly. In Sweden, the share absorbed by old age pensions has steadily increased, whereas it has decreased in Norway, and even more so in Denmark. One possible institutional explanation would point to the accumulated impacts of the Swedish superannuation scheme (ATP). A similar scheme does not exist in Denmark and was only introduced in Norway some years later.

The second largest item is made up by the *health* sector. Both Sweden and Denmark have experienced a decreasing share of public means allocated to health care in marked contrast to Norway. One would assume that this development may be accounted for by a different timing of the development of public health care systems in the Scandinavian countries. As a laggard — in the Scandinavian context — there has quite simply been more margin for expansion in Norway compared with the more mature health care systems in Denmark and Sweden (Heidenheimer and Elvander 1981).

The most striking difference in the programme spending profiles among the Scandinavian countries is seen in public outlays caused by *unemployment*. In Denmark, the share of social security expenditure paid to unemployment benefits exploded from 3.5 per cent in 1973 to a post-war record of more than 13 per cent in the late 1970s. In contrast, unemployment expenditure in Norway and Sweden is not only at a significantly lower level, but has been kept constant throughout the period. Moreover, in this context it is also noteworthy that public spending on a means-tested *social assistance* assumes greater importance in Denmark, indicating that crisis symptoms are more severely felt there.

In the following we shall focus directly on the *real growth* of social expenditure by types of benefits and by programmes, thus leaving aside the somewhat deceptive expenditure ratios and relative distributions. The overall impression is one of very strong real growth in social security expenditure. From 1970 to 1980 real public expenditure on social benefits and services rose by 124 per cent in Norway, 111 per cent in Sweden, and 88 per cent in Denmark. And there were no signs that the growth rates were falling towards the end of the period. Quite to the contrary. However, the two kinds of expenditure (in cash and in kind) contribute differentially to the overall growth. In the case of Sweden, the growth of total social security expenditure is to a large extent caused by a real growth of cash benefits (194 per cent) as opposed to the real growth of in-kind benefits (40 per cent). In Norway the picture is just the opposite, with Denmark showing equal growth in the two areas. These developments may be interpreted as a sign of growing convergence: Norway is catching up with the high level of social security spending in Denmark and Sweden, and is furthermore approaching the service orientation prevailing in these two countries. But to what extent do these total growth rates hide variations in programme-specific growth rates?

The heavy growth of benefits in kind in Norway is primarily caused by soaring expenditure on health care facilities. The growth in this field is markedly higher than in both Denmark and Sweden (109 per cent vs. 25 per cent and 19 per cent). Also, in Norway, spending growth rates of other services are higher. Although the level of public means allocated to social services in Norway is still rather modest compared with Denmark and Sweden; but again, Norway is rapidly catching up.

In Sweden, increasing public spending on old age pensions appears to

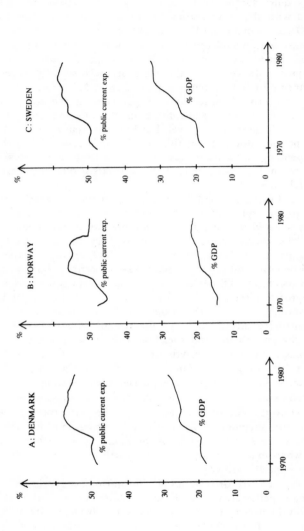

Figure 9.2   Social security expenditure as a percentage of GDP and as a percentage of total, current public expenditure, 1970–80

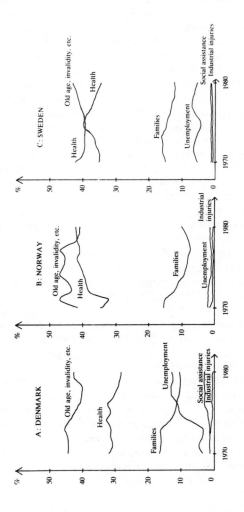

Figure 9.3   Distribution of social security expenditure by programmes, 1970–80, at current prices

be one of the most important factors explaining the growth of social security expenditure in general, and the growth of cash benefits in particular. Considering that outlays on social services display relatively modest growth rates, it appears that Sweden is gradually changing its profile from that of a service-oriented to a cash-oriented welfare state. The Swedish Peoples Home is becoming a Home for the Aged.

The overall growth of social security expenditure in Denmark is heavily influenced by a 710 per cent (sic!) increase in unemployment benefits (i.e. cash benefits). In this area Sweden relies on benefits in kind. Swedish labour-market policies are geared towards the prevention of unemployment and active labour-market policies, such as job training, employment services, etc. In contrast, Danish unemployment benefits aim primarily at alleviating the material costs for the individual by means of relatively generous unemployment benefits. Another distinct Danish feature is that consumption expenditure allocated to the provision of social services for pensioners and families with children grew faster than cash transfers to these groups. Apart from labour-market policies, the Danish welfare state offers more comprehensive social services compared with both Sweden and Norway. In some fields — most notably services for families with children and the aged — per capita spending is more than twice as high in Denmark as in Sweden. These differences in the distribution of benefits in kind and in cash warrant a general warning when interpreting the adequacy of social benefits: adequacy should not only be judged in terms of (cash) compensation ratios or similar cash measures. Due regard should also be given to the public provision of social services.

Amidst the variety of intra-Scandinavian and programme variations one should not lose sight of the basic conclusion: *a spectacular real growth of social security spending from 1970 to 1980.* Still, one cannot be certain how this growth of aggregate expenditures can be 'explained'. The growth of social security expenditure is caused by an interplay of demographic factors, changing criteria of eligibility, changing numbers of beneficiaries, changing benefit levels, as well as changing needs. If we can somehow single out the relative weight of these components we can also provide a clue to the question of whether the individual recipient has been affected by changes in the expenditure profile or has lost ground *vis-à-vis* members of the active labour force.

In the field of pensions, decomposing social expenditure into its constituent parts shows that real growth is not only caused by demographic changes. The other components, i.e. those that are politically determined, do also play an independent role in explaining even pension expenditure (Nørby Johansen 1983). Compensation ratios or earnings replacement ratios are another way of portraying the situation of the individual recipient of social benefit *vis-à-vis* those actively employed.

(Table 9.2 shows compensation ratios in typical cases for a variety of cash benefits.) Generally, compensation ratios have increased over the 1970s, even after the impact of the economic recession.

By now it should be very clear that the Scandinavian welfare states have been able to withstand the strain imposed upon them by the economic stagnation beginning in the mid-1970s. Cuts in social security spending have certainly not been used as a means of reducing the mounting pressure on the public budgets. Quite to the contrary. Whatever indicators or measures are applied, the 1970s have not only witnessed a real growth of social security expenditure, but also continued if not accelerating growth. But, as we have noted, the uniqueness of the Scandinavian welfare state model is not only derived from high spending levels, accelerating growth rates and generous benefits. It is also founded on a distinct institutional profile. And it still remains to be shown to what extent institutional features may have changed.

Institutional changes

If we start with the contention that the Scandinavian welfare states constitute a unique welfare state model, and if this uniqueness is as described above, then the search for essential institutional changes should focus on the following issues:

(1) Breaches of the principle of universalism towards more selectivity. Social legislation based on universal coverage and solidarity is allegedly an important characteristic of the Scandinavian welfare states. Accordingly, we shall look for recent tendencies towards selectivity or changes in social legislation that are targeted towards special problem groups.

(2) Deinstitutionalisation or 'recommodification' of entitlements to social benefits. In the Scandinavian model, social entitlements are not based on market criteria, instead, they are based on citizenship and the principle of equal access to social security for everybody. In principle, social entitlements are not only divorced from market criteria, they are designed to modify or even counteract the distributive logic of the market. As a consequence, attention will be focused on changes that signal a departure from this institutional tenet, such as new legislation that tightens the relationship between labour-market participation and social benefits. Privatisation, payment for services, private pension schemes, or other private insurance-type arrangements will also be conceived of as forms of deinstitutionalised social entitlements.

(3) Legislative changes that reduce the role of the state, i.e. make state provisions for welfare less comprehensive. This set of institutional changes is obviously related to changes towards

selectivity or deinstitutionalisation. But it also points to some specific and identifiable changes, such as a reduction of the scope of publicly-provided social services and cuts of cash benefits.

But before we turn to those institutional changes that may signal a departure from the 'Scandinavian model' it should be stressed that the 1970s also witnessed some comprehensive social reforms that are consolidations or even extensions of that model. In Sweden, a thorough social reform was introduced in 1974: the level of sickness benefits was increased to 90 per cent of previous gross earnings (and made taxable); the traditional maternity leave benefit was replaced by a general parental insurance scheme providing benefits at the same level as sickness benefits and lasting for 210 days; dental care was included in the general health insurance scheme; the level of unemployment benefits was increased to (in principle) 90 per cent of prior earnings (this goal was never fully realised); the duration period for unemployment benefits was extended from 150 to 300 days; and a special labour market compensation was introduced for those who were not entitled to unemployment benefits (e.g. non-members of unemployment insurance funds).

In Denmark, what came to be called 'the social reform of the 1970s' included three components: (1) a 1972/73 reform of daily cash benefits in case of sickness, industrial injury, maternity, adoption, etc. (compensation ratio at 90 per cent of previous earnings, abolition of waiting days, abolition of private insurance features); (2) an administrative reform leaving local authorities with the responsibility for a comprehensive and unified system of social security; and (3) a thorough reform of the social assistance scheme based on the notion that recipients of social assistance (i.e. those who are not covered by the major income maintenance schemes) should receive full compensation in case of a 'social accident'.

In Norway, the most far-reaching reform was the introduction of a sickness pay scheme in 1976, i.e. full compensation or continuous salary in case of sickness.

These impressive reforms were conceptualised, initiated and planned during the economic boom of the 1960s, and were based on the belief that crises would be ephemeral and short-lived. Nevertheless, the reforms were implemented during the protracted economic stagnation of the 1970s and 1980s.

Selectivity
Denmark has experienced changes in its social legislation that portend a selectivist departure. First, child allowances have been made income-related. (In Norway and Sweden, child allowances are still universal and flat-rate.) Secondly, a new concept of 'social income' has been intro-

duced in order to tighten the relationship between income and social benefits. This concept deviates from normal taxable income in that it includes the value of certain assets (plus the value of pensions for civil servants) and excludes the value of certain tax deductions. The social income was justified by a need to establish a 'fair' measure according to which income-related benefits could be granted. However, this new measure has been applied to a number of social benefits that were not previously incomes related. Efforts to target social benefits towards special problem groups (or the 'truly needy') in Norway and Sweden have been less successful, and the phenomenon of incomes related benefits is not as pronounced in these two countries as it is (and has become) in Denmark.

Deinstitutionalisation of social entitlements
The most important example of a direct link between labour market participation and welfare entitlements are the superannuation schemes in Sweden and Norway. In fact, one could make the case that these superannuation schemes (especially the Swedish one) can be compared with the continental model: a contributory social insurance system with benefits (pensions) being based on the individual's labour-market participation record. In contrast, Denmark's pension system is still non-contributory, and solely financed through taxation with universal flat-rate pensions (plus some incomes related supplementary benefits). Denmark has in fact an embryonic superannuation scheme.

However, Denmark has other forms of occupationally-defined pension schemes. For example, civil servants have their own pension scheme, and most other public employees are protected by statutory pension schemes that are heavily subsidised by the employer (i.e. the state) and based on members' contributions. Moreover, a great number of employers in the private sector offer attractive pension schemes as a kind of fringe benefit, especially for white-collar workers. Most importantly, private pension and savings schemes, heavily subsidised by the state through tax deductions, have assumed great importance during the 1970s, to the extent that some speak of a 'dual pension system' in Denmark (Vesterø Jensen 1982): the public and universal pension system on the one hand, and a hybrid consisting of occupational and private or semi-public pension schemes on the other. It goes without saying that the two coexisting pension systems are based on conflicting distributive logics.

Another kind of relationship between labour-market participation and social welfare entitlements can be established by making temporary periods out of the labour market very costly for the individual, for example, by varying such parameters as waiting days before benefits are paid, duration, amount of benefits, and other restrictions. The Scandinavian welfare states have traditionally been comparatively lenient on this score. However, some minor retrenchments did occur during the period. Thus, the present Liberal government in Denmark (elected 1982) reintroduced one waiting day in the case of sickness benefits in 1982, as did the Swedish Liberal government in 1981. However, this was repealed by the subsequent Social-Democratic government. Waiting days in case of sickness have also been brought to the fore in Norway. The Conservative government and business associations there proposed introducing two waiting days and reduced compensations, but without success.

If the Danish experience testifies to a regression in the case of sickness insurance, there are other institutional changes that run counter to this development. Thus, entitlement to unemployment benefits and duration periods have become less restrictive — part-time employees, younger workers and workers with little or no participation record in the labour market have gained easier access to benefits, and existing duration periods have been increased (in fact, the cut-off point has been temporarily suspended). These changes were introduced in the mid-1970s when it was believed the recession would be short-lived. However, towards the end of the period, a number of restrictions were put on entitlement to unemployment benefits.

Fees for services have increasingly been applied in all three countries. In Norway, since 1980, fees have been introduced or increased for medical consultations, lab. tests, drugs, physiotherapy, travel expenses and home-help for the aged. However, fees amount only to about 2 per cent of total social security expenditure. In Denmark fees have not been introduced (but are hotly debated) in the health care sector: both in-patient and out-patient treatment is free. But there have been some minor reductions in the subsidies on drugs, glasses, etc. and day-care charges have been slightly increased. Sweden has some token fees for hospital provision, and in 1981 prescription charges increased.

The scope of publicly-provided social services
The scope of publicly-provided social services did not diminish during the 1970s. Quite to the contrary — health care, nurseries, home-help and other kinds of care for the aged all increased. The Scandinavian 'womb-to-tomb' protection became even more comprehensive. As mentioned above, the major income-maintenance benefits have not been subject to cuts during the period. Yet, there have been some examples of direct or indirect cuts. Manipulating the complicated indexation parameters constitutes one method. In Norway, new indexation procedures apparently have reduced social expenditures, especially regarding the base amount in the pension system (Kolberg 1983). An example of direct cuts may be drawn from the field of social assistance in Denmark, where a benefit ceiling was introduced in

the late 1970s. Other cuts in the Scandinavian countries can be shown, but these cuts (or retrenchments) are *marginal*, both to total social security expenditure and to the basic institutional tenets.

In conclusion, certain institutional changes did occur in response to mounting pressures for reducing the growth of public expenditure and social security expenditure. Yet, it would be inappropriate to interpret these changes as fundamental violations in the Scandinavian welfare states. The essential institutional pillars are still intact. The only systematic departure from the model is found in Denmark in terms of increasing selectivity and the increasing importance of private pension schemes. But even there it appears premature to announce an institutional breakdown.

Discussion

It now seems obvious that the problem is not *whether* the Scandinavian welfare states have survived the economic stagnation and political turmoil of the 1970s, but *how* they have survived. That this is a real puzzle is also stressed by the fact that the 1970s brought about political changes which might have been expected to inaugurate some kind of regression in the welfare states. In parliament the Social-Democratic parties generally enjoyed less strength than hitherto. Rather weak Social-Democratic minority cabinets or liberal cabinets have been the rule in Denmark and Norway during this period, and Sweden has experienced protracted periods of Liberal governments as well. Moreover, the objective of reducing public budget deficits has increasingly gained political momentum, even among the Social Democrats. The political—administrative apparatus in all three countries has in fact produced an abundance of proposals, budget reforms, administrative reforms, plans, etc. with the explicit purpose of curbing the growth of public expenditure and social security expenditure. Also, the widespread existence of anti-tax and anti-welfare sentiments in Denmark during the early 1970s might indicate a lack of popular support for the welfare state: Denmark in particular was seen as an archetypal example of welfare state backlash (Wilensky 1976). If it is a puzzle why a so-called welfare state backlash occurred in Denmark and not in neighbouring Sweden (Heidenheimer *et al.* 1975), it appears no less puzzling why this backlash apparently evaporated in the course of the following years *in spite* of continuing, highly visible taxation (which has even become more visible according to Wilensky's own operationalisation); *in spite* of an incessant channelling of state resources into labour-intensive, publicly-provided services (Hibbs and Madsen 1981); *in spite* of new increases in the aggregate tax rate (especially towards the end of the period) (Wilensky 1976); and *in spite* of an ever-growing divergence between pre-tax income and post-tax earnings (Hibbs and Madsen 1981).

A first tentative answer to the question of how the Scandinavian welfare state model survived both economic stagnation and political attacks may be provided by the following two interrelated hypotheses: (1) economic stagnation itself has engendered an increased political mobilisation of popular support for the welfare state; and (2) the institutional nature of the Scandinavian welfare states produces in and by itself a safeguard against political onslaughts.

That the economic recession and the ensuing vulnerability among the populace have prompted a mobilisation of popular support for the welfare state is indicated by survey data. Thus, it has been shown that popular support for the welfare state in Denmark and Norway increased significantly from the mid-1970s (Kolberg and Pettersen 1981; Andersen 1982). In Norway, the proportion of those among the electorate who favoured an expansion of social policy increased from 20 per cent in 1973 to 42 per cent in 1977. In Denmark, the proportion of those who favoured either the status quo *or* a further expansion of social reforms rose from a record low of 39 per cent in 1974 to 55 per cent in 1978.

Both clients of and employees providing social benefits have become increasingly mobilised and organised. Old age pensioners, the disabled, day care clients etc. all have associations through which they can express grievances against cuts in the budgets. And public employees have not only increased in number, they have also become increasingly organised and mobilised in their support for the welfare state. The number of public employees rose dramatically during the 1970s — in Denmark and Sweden, one-third of the total labour force. In Denmark, public employees number almost twice the number of blue-collar workers. In this context, it is interesting to observe that the single best predictor of popular support of the welfare state is neither traditional class variables nor 'middle mass' notions (Wilensky), but employment in the public sector (cf. the private sector). Finally, it should be recalled that the neo-corporatist setting in the Scandinavian countries gives public employees' unions easy access to the centres of public decision-making.

In order to understand why the political mobilisation of support of the welfare state has grown so markedly, and why it has been so politically effective, we can go a step further back in the causal chain. Korpi (1980) has suggested that an institutional type of social policy — as opposed to a marginal type — produces pro-welfare state coalitions among the electorate. Since most programmes are universal and therefore affect large sections of the population, most households benefit directly from these programmes. If individuals act rationally, there will consequently be a strong impetus towards the maintenance or expansion of such programmes. Korpi suggests further that an institutional type of social policy tends to encourage coalition-formation between the working class and the middle class in support of continued welfare state policies. The question is what groups constitute the middle class. If it is the *petit bourgeoisie*, self-employed craftsmen or smallholders and farmers, Korpi's line should be questioned: in Denmark and Norway, at least, it is precisely these groups who express strong anti-welfare sentiments. A potential for coalition-formation in support of the welfare state is much more likely between the working class and public employees. As we have seen, public employees are not only distinct in their pro-welfare state attitudes, they also constitute the single largest working constituency among the electorate.

If we accept the assertion that an institutional type of social policy produces its own safeguard, it still has to be explained why the growth of social security expenditure varied greatly across programmes, types of benefits and countries, and why certain institutional changes did in fact take place.

In order to account for such variations we can tentatively elaborate on the argument that institutionally-entrenched resistance and a potential for mobilisation against retrenchment are not equally distributed across programmes and types of benefit. One would assume that reduced growth, reversals or direct cuts are more likely to occur where institutional resistance is low. An analysis of the development of social security expenditure in Denmark shows that apart from unemployment benefits, the growth rate was most pronounced for benefits in kind. Therefore a distinction between cash transfers to households and social services could be useful. The point is that the provision of the two kinds of benefit is subject to two different logics of decision-making. The production of social services is characterised by a somewhat atomised decision-making process in which the producers themselves (i.e. public employees) play a dominant role. There are, of course, differences in the potential for coalition-formation between producers and clients based on differences in organisation, professionalisation, etc., but it seems a reasonable hypothesis that politicians in general will experience difficulties in counteracting institutionally-entrenched interests of this kind. Just to take one example: the reported growth of day-care facilities and various social services for the aged can *not* be traced to any overall reform or to specific decisions made by parliament. The growth is largely the accumulated result of myriads of decisions made by the public employees. In contrast, decisions pertaining to cash transfers belong by and large to the realm of politicians. One would hypothesise that it is easier, *ceteris paribus*, to control expenditure devoted to cash transfers. Therefore, it is no accident that the provision of child allowances has become more targeted, and benefits cut. Similarly, assistance and certain benefits for the handicapped have been made more selective and reduced.

If we accept the hypothesis that an institutional type of social policy generates its own safeguards and reduces the likelihood of welfare-state backlash, we must also accept that Social-Democratic strength is not a precondition for the maintenance of this type of social policy. Social-Democratic strength may or may not have been conducive to the formation of the Scandinavian welfare state model. But the fact that this model, *grosso modo*, survived economic stagnation and political attacks during the 1970s cannot simply be reduced to a question of Social-Democratic strength, or partisan politics for that matter.

The future of the Scandinavian model?

A great many lessons can be learned from the history of the performance of the Scandinavian welfare states from 1970 to 1980. First, is the importance of time-lags: it appears that social policy lags behind the problems they are designed to solve. A number of social reforms implemented in the mid-1970s were conceived in the 1960s. These include the impressive Swedish 1974 reform, the social reform movement in Denmark, and the sickness pay scheme in Norway. These reforms were typically based on the belief that economic growth and prosperity would last – if not forever, then at least for the foreseeable future, and as a consequence there would be no problems of financing social security, and additional costs stemming from the expansion of the public economy would be financed either by continued economic growth and wealth, or shifted over to the generations to come.

Yet, the welfare state of the 1960s was not only costless in economic terms; paradoxically, it was also politically costless. The expansion of the Scandinavian welfare states during the 1960s was strikingly uncontroversial. Social policies and reforms were generated within a framework of broad political consensus: the fundamental values and principles of the welfare state were rarely at stake – not even discussed. There was enough for every group competing for a 'fair share' of the means distributed through the public sector. The welfare state was transformed into a distributional machine, fuelled by economic growth.

The point is that the social policies of the 1960s continued into the 1970s, despite the fact that the economic and political conditions were dramatically changed, not only in the sense that some radical social reforms conceived in the 1960s were not implemented until the 1970s, but also in the more general sense that the formation of social policies responded strikingly slowly to the changed environment. And to the extent that the welfare state adapted itself to the challenges of the

1970s, these adaptations took the form of decremental changes. It is in this sense that one may speak of a time-lag in social policy.

Yet there is another time-lag: social science models appear to lag somewhat behind those social policies they are designed to explain. The welfare states and social policies of the 1970s are still analysed and explained on the basis of models of expansion and growth, and few (if any) social policy models include the time-factor — the time-lag — just mentioned. This problem in actual social policy as well as in social science makes it extremely difficult to forecast future developments. However, one thing seems certain given the problem of time-lag: one cannot conclude from the analysis presented here that no changes will take place in the course of the 1980s in the Scandinavian model. Any attempt to forecast the development must also take into account that the economic strain imposed on the Scandinavian welfare states will last for the foreseeable future. There are no easy ways out of the problems generated by the enormous deficits of the public households especially in Sweden and Denmark. The cost-control imperative will be self-perpetuating. Combined with the recent mobilisation of political support for the welfare state, the basic expectation will be this: incremental adaptations of social policies to the imperatives of cost control in combination with a politicised revival of the fundamental values and principles of the welfare state. Put differently, the Scandinavian welfare state model will survive — economically at a more modest level, but politically revitalised.

Notes

1. This is a revised version of a paper presented at the Workshop on the Comparative Study of Distribution and Social Policy in Advanced Industrial Nations, ECPR, Freiburg Joint Sessions of Workshops, March 1983. For a more detailed statistical analysis and for further documentation see that paper.

References

Andersen, J.G. (1982), 'Den folkelige tilslutning til social politikken — en krise for velfærdsstaten?', in D. Anckar, E. Damgaard and H. Valen (eds), *Partier, ideologier, väljare*, Åbo: Åbo Akademi, 175—209.
Cameron, D. (1978), 'The Expansion of the Public Economy: A Comparative Analysis', *American Political Science Review* 72, 1243—61.
Castles, F.G. (1978), *The Social Democratic Image of Society*, London: Routledge and Kegan Paul.
Esping-Andersen, G. and Korpi, W. (1983), 'From Poor Relief to Institutional Welfare States: The Development of Scandinavian Social Policy', paper presented at ECPR Joint Workshops, Freiburg.
Heidenheimer, A.J. and Elvander, N. (1980), *The Shaping of the Swedish Health Care System*, New York: St Martin's Press.
Heidenheimer, A.J., Heclo, H. and Adams, C.T. (1975), *Comparative Public Policy: The Politics of Social Choice in Europe and America*, New York: St Martin's Press.
Hibbs, D. and Madsen, H.J. (1981), 'Public Reactions to the Growth of Taxation and Government Expenditure', *World Politics* 33, no. 3, 413—35.
Kolberg, J.E. (1983), *Farvel til velferdsstaten?*, Oslo: Cappelen.

Kolberg, J.E. and Pettersen, P.A., (1981), 'Om velferdsstatens politiske basis', *Tidsskrift for Samfunnsforskning* 22, nos 2–3, 193–222.

Kohl, J. (1981), 'Trends and Problems in Post-war Public Expenditure Development in Western Europe and North America', in P. Flora and A.J. Heidenheimer (eds), *The Development of Welfare States in Europe and America*, New Brunswick and London: Transaction Books, 307–44.

Korpi, W. (1980), 'Social Policy and Distributional Conflict in the Capitalist Democracies. A Preliminary Comparative Framework', *West European Politics* 3, no. 3, 296–316.

Logue, J. (1979), 'The Welfare State: Victim of its Success', *Daedalus* 108, 69–87.

Mishra, R. (1977), *Society and Social Policy*, London: Macmillan.

Pinker, R. (1971), *Social Theory and Social Policy*, London: Heinemann.

Titmuss, R. (1974), *Social Policy*, London: Allen and Unwin.

Vesterø Jensen, C. (1982), 'The Dual Pension System in Denmark', mimeo, Firenze: Istituto Universitario Europeo.

Wilensky, H. (1975), *The Welfare State and Equality*, Berkeley, Calif.: University of California Press.

Wilensky, H. (1976) *The 'New Corporatism', Centralization and the Welfare State*, Beverly Hills and London: Sage.

Table 9.2 Post-tax social benefits for a male industrial worker as a percentage of post-tax income by type of benefits, 1970–81

	Sickness benefits		Unemployment benefits		Retirement/invalidity pension		Old age pension		Survivors' pension	
	(a)	(c)	(a)	(c)	(a)	(c)	(a)	(b)	(a)	(c)
Denmark										
1970	42	55	63	65	77	90	42	57	38	66
1972	54	68	67	68	80	88	41	59	37	63
1974	64	66	61	61	71	82	48	62	39	63
1978	79	82	79	82	70	82	42	57	—	—
1981	79	80	79	80	76	88	47	65	—	—
Norway										
1970	37	46	37	46	41	48	41	59	38	67
1972	51	62	51	62	43	56	43	61	39	66
1974	51	59	51	58	39	61	56	66	36	61
1978	100	100	64	64	64	81	75	96	—	—
1981	100	100	73	77	75	85	75	—	—	—
Sweden										
1970	83	74	79	69	85	92	85	91	74	98
1972	80	75	80	84	80	90	80	92	74	90
1974	90	90	67	67	73	75	66	77	68	75
1978	94	94	77	77	68	72	68	92	—	—
1981	97	87	78	80	81	87	81	—	—	—

Source: *Social Security in the Nordic Countries*, various volumes.

Notes:
(a) = single man; (b) = married man, childless; (c) = married man with 2 dependent children; includes child allowances.

10 The Changing Hungarian Social Policy
Zsuzsa Ferge

A note on terminology

Hungary, like other socialist countries, does not use the term 'welfare state' when describing its national system of distribution. This is probably due more to theoretical than to political reasons. In a Marxist approach a 'socialist welfare state' would be a theoretically redundant and awkward concept. Even if the 'classical' socialist principle of distribution is 'to each according to his/her work', Marx had specified that a number of central funds serving common needs were to be financed from the social product before the distribution among producers could take place. In Marx's view a fund serving the 'common coverage of needs' — education, public health and so on — would be part of the new society, and from the very outset would be 'significantly greater than in the present society, and will continually increase with its development'. The direction of the expansion of the needs 'covered by the community' is not elaborated. Logically, though, one may assume that the communist principle of distribution 'to each according to his/her need' would slowly gain ground.

On this premise, a socialist society is supposed, theoretically, increasingly to fulfil all the functions which are now identified as the '*welfare* state', hence the redundancy in the terminology. The awkwardness stems from the reference to the *state*. The term 'welfare state' suggests that the state is the active agent in the definition, instead of society as a whole. A socialist society is supposed — though again, theoretically — to become increasingly democratic and participatory, while the role of the state should decrease.

All in all, the Marxist concept of a 'socialist society' seems to be theoretically clearer in terms of the 'welfare' functions to be fulfilled than the pragmatic concept of the 'welfare state'. One may wonder whether the term 'welfare state' was not coined, originally at least, for the sake of avoiding any reference to socialist principles.

Although the rejection of the term 'welfare state' can be explained on theoretical grounds, it is a very different matter how reality conforms to the theoretical blueprint. In this chapter we shall take a closer look at the 'welfare' functions in socialist Hungary — a responsibility assigned either to 'social policy' or to society as a whole. Since the past and its traditions have been important in shaping subsequent events, an historical approach is warranted, starting with a glance at the situation before 1945.

Pre-war Hungary: A weak and manipulative social policy

The dominant classes of this period had a difficult riddle to face: how to contain the social tensions generated by massive poverty without touching the *basis* of poverty, namely, the quasi-feudal system of landownerships where 22 per cent of the land belonged to 0.8 per cent of the landowners, while only 11 per cent of the land belonged to the vast majority of small farmers and other smallholders. The small landowners numbered about 1.5 million out of a population of 9 million; another 1.5 million people were employed in agriculture, but owned no land.

In fact, there was no simple solution to the need for redistribution. The poor could not get more land without dismantling the big estates. If, however, all the oppressed classes had united to attack the large landowners, the existing structure would have been strongly threatened. Perhaps due to this imminent threat the dominant classes skilfully isolated the problems of the period, and handled them separately.

The destitute and militant *working class* were subjected to strong police oppression, but they also obtained some concessions, mainly in social insurance provisions. The coverage and the level of benefits remained low, and the concessions did not weaken capitalist relations. An unemployment insurance was never enacted; the first payments of old age and disability pensions were postponed until 1939; the schemes covered less than one-third of the population; and the whole of the rural proletariat was left out.

The *urban* (and some of the rural) *poor*, including the unemployed, the aged and the disabled, were the target of state-organised, mainly privately-financed charity, permeated by the spirit of the poor laws.

Finally in 1940, a so-called 'productive social policy' was devised for the *rural poor*. According to official rhetoric, its aim was to enhance the income-generation potential of those among the poor who were of pure Hungarian stock (i.e. excluding Jews, gypsies, etc.), and deserving and industrious. The practical instruments were limited to a build-up of some cottage industries, and the distribution among smallholders of land confiscated from the Jews (about 3 per cent of the medium and large estates). These limited measures were then presented as solutions to major social inequalities.

The combination of forceful demagogy, police repression and some concessions succeeded both in assuring quiescence and in fragmenting the political potential of the oppressed classes. The political logic of the dominant classes so marked the progressive movements and thinking of the time that the Left became divided into many factions, and schisms weakened it and made it self-defeating.

The emergence of a complex social policy after the war

From 1945 on, it became possible to solve the main pre-war problems. Following one of the first decrees of the new government, a radical land reform was carried out, which benefited about 640,000 families (or one-fifth of the population). In addition, vast programmes of reconstruction and industrialisation provided jobs for large segments of the urban poor.

Still, the economic difficulties were tremendous in the post-war period, for the country had been half-destroyed in the defeat. The importance of a 'traditional' social policy was therefore enormous. Accordingly, a new Ministry of Popular Welfare was set up, with a dual task: it was:

> to provide, by means of the state networks of the health services and of social policy, help to all those who are unable to assure their maintenance by means of their own work on account of their sickness, age, war injury or the loss of a provider.[1]

The second task was to assure financial assistance to the still very numerous able-bodied poor. New landowners lacked the necessary equipment; jobs in towns were scarce; the land reform still left about 200,000 of the rural poor without smallholdings. Indeed, the most important concern of state social policy was the attainment of full employment and the enhancement of the earning capacity of the overall population.

In this way an *autonomous social policy* emerged, rooted in radical social and political change. It combined social and economic tasks, taking on responsibility for *all* those unable to earn an acceptable standard of living, whether for 'personal' reasons (such as sickness or old age) or for socioeconomic reasons (caused by involuntary unemployment, lack of equipment, etc.). The main problem was poverty, and under the conditions of universal scarcity and radical change the stigmatising effects of traditional social assistance all but disappeared.

The withering away of autonomous social policy from 1949

From the end of 1948 on, the scene in Hungary changed again. After the fusion of the Communist and the Social-Democratic Parties, the dogmatic and dictatorial wing performed a 'hidden political turn', and took over the leadership of the Party and of the country. The new leadership declared in its first programme that 'the majority of the age-old requests of the working class were fulfilled by the people's democracy'. Therefore, 'the so-called "social policy" of the capitalist system' had to be rejected, because the new achievements 'render superfluous individual assistance'. New job opportunities and social insurance would abolish all 'need'.[2] Any remaining problems were assumed to vanish rapidly and automatically, since 'all the actions and measures of our People's Democracy, of its social and economic system *are* social policy'.[3]

Since everything was social policy, and since poverty and other social problems were declared to have been abolished, no autonomous social policy was needed by the central authority. Consequently, in 1950 the Ministry of Popular Welfare was dissolved and transformed into the current Ministry of Health, stripped of almost all its former social policy powers. Many social policy concerns disappeared altogether; others were taken over by other bodies — for example, the social security system was placed under the authority of the National Council of the Trade Unions. What was left of social policy acquired new political and economic functions. The history of this development is rather tragic, because of its long-lasting impact.

Social benefits were turned into instruments of *political legitimation* of the new system. Each measure was praised as a sign of the solicitude, the care, the benevolence of the state, the leadership, and the leader. It was thereby suggested that not only was the new system *superior* to the old one, but also that it was *unnecessary* to organise interest groups from 'below', since everything was being taken care of from 'above'. Moreover, it was made clear that social incomes were not based on individual or citizen's *rights*, but rather, benefits were the 'gift' of the state.

Simultaneously, socially divisive and politically repressive objectives were built into the social security system. For example, from 1950 defrauding the sickness benefit scheme was considered a political crime, punished by up to three years in prison. As in other countries, 'scroungers' constituted ready-made scapegoats to be blamed for the worsening economic circumstances, which were rather due to an erroneous national economic policy. The social security system discriminated against everybody except workers and employees. This 'anti-peasant' side of social policy measures also had other aims. One was to force small farmers into cooperatives, the other was to drive them out of agriculture to fill the new jobs in industry. Once there, social policy measures were applied 'to strengthen their work discipline' in the above despotic way: many of the 'defrauders' actually worked on family-owned land.

While political declarations and the mass media boasted about the outstanding achievements of the country, practically all the indicators of living or working conditions showed stagnation or even a decline. Between 1949 and 1954, the real income of industrial workers and employees dropped about 10—15 per cent, and that of peasants by more than 30 per cent. Expenditure on social security remained constant at around 5 per cent of the national income. The average pensions amounted to only about 20 per cent of the very low average wage, and only a minority of the elderly were eligible. The only field in which progress could be reported in those years was the significant decrease of open and hidden unemployment. However, the massive rural exodus was not a painless process for those forced to move.

In summary, social policy in those years permeated all spheres of policy, including economic policy, and became, more than ever before, a complex societal policy. An ideal state, if true; in reality, political dictatorship dominated both economic and social policy, devoiding them of their real functions. Formal economic rationality, human needs or the building of socialist social relations counted little. Albeit after 1953 the situation improved in some respects, the basis of these problems was not removed. This explains to a large extent the political and social crisis of 1956. Only then did a complete change of leadership and a renewal of the forms and contents of policy become possible.

The silent revival of social policy after 1956 —
the split between theory and practice

Hungarian economic and social history of the two decades after 1956 may be read as a success story. (See Table 10.1 in the Appendix.) Real wages increased and the social wage increased even more. The lag in private and public infrastructure was partly overcome, improving access to social services. There was a considerable decrease in income inequality. (See Table 10.2.) The development was further improved through the reform of the economy in 1968, giving more latitude both to economic activity and to social policy.

The success story has of course had its flaws. The economic reform was often hesitant; the democratisation and decentralisation of the political mechanisms went only part of the way; many aspects of living conditions did not improve sufficiently. But here we are focusing only on social policy events. While the economy was expanding, the dominant feeling was (especially among those who had lived through the pre-war years, the war, or the early 1950s) that 'we've never had it so good'. Social policy appeared to be successful. It was only at the end of the 1970s, when the world economic crisis hit the country, that social policy issues came to the fore.

It became apparent that a curious split had taken place between the declared goals and the practice of policy. (The split was curious because reality was *ahead* of political declarations.) As early as December 1956 a firm political stance was taken to increase the standard of living. But in the following decades the conceptual basis of social policy was rarely considered. A number of laws, measures and regulations were issued, schemes were improved and benefits increased. However, the various steps were not coordinated and followed no clear principles. In this respect there was an important difference between economic and social policy. Economic policy — for all its shortcomings — was based on a long period of reflection and theory-building, producing a critical re-evaluation of the past, and clarifying concepts and principles. These efforts led to an *official* and radical break with the economic policy of the 1950s.

In social policy there was no critical political analysis nor a clean break with the past. This ultimately weakened the position of social policy. Social policy was simply practised, without being able to formulate the rationale of its present actions and future plans.

Current trends and problems of social policy

After the economic reform, social policy became a *legitimate* issue, and during the crisis, an *urgent* one. Indeed, the problems of social policy are treated more explicitly than before. This is reflected in the mass media. (A content analysis of the daily party newspaper shows, for instance, the changing frequency of the appearance of social issues.[4]) Government bodies, including the National Planning Board, have now begun to build up separate social policy departments. In 1981, the government assigned to social researchers the task of evaluating the past, and working out a conceptual basis for the future development of social policy.[5]

Clearly, this is a deliberate search for a new and more adequate framework of social policy. But so far there has been no consensus about the desirable directions of change. Several issues have been extensively debated in various public and academic forums. There is a sustained, mostly theoretically-oriented debate between economists and sociologists, and a more pragmatically-loaded one between researchers and policy-makers. In the first debate the central issue is how to avoid the well-known negative social consequences of a more autonomous, and more effective and more competitive economy. The second debate centres on what is desirable and what is feasible in social policy, under conditions of economic constraint.

These problems will sound familiar enough to everybody acquainted with the recent developments in the western welfare states. In fact, many of the recent steps and recently formulated plans bear a painful resemblance to what is happening in the welfare states: restrictions which imply a shifting of state responsibilities to the private sector; price increases or decreases of state subsidies which, even if carefully designed, may hit disproportionately the weaker of poorer groups; measures which cause a relative fall in income for groups living mainly on welfare benefits, and so forth. The only western 'solution' deliberately avoided in Hungary so far has been unemployment.

The relation between economic and social policy

From a Marxist theoretical perspective, the best, or even the only acceptable relation between economic and social policy is their almost complete fusion, where social policy is built into the economy. This implies, in Karl Polanyi's terms, that the economy is simultaneously performing its *substantive* functions, (the coverage of human needs), and its *formal* functions (the optimalisation of the relation between costs and benefits).[6] It also means that it reconciles the 'intrinsic' economic interests (such as technological development and profit-maximisation) with those interests which are usually seen as external, namely the interest of *human beings* and of the *environment*, even if this may not be 'economically rational' in the strict sense.

An artificial fusion of the two policies could easily be detrimental to both the economy and to social interests. That is why even the most sanguine advocates of social policy presently refrain from suggesting their complete fusion. However, these same people are not wholly satisfied with the operation of the 'welfare states' either. No doubt, in these societies social policy has acquired the respectable position of a negotiating partner. But economic crisis rapidly undermines this position, putting social policy on the defensive. Since the 'ideal' state seems impossible to attain, and actual practice is not very satisfactory, the establishment of a new relation between economic and social policy seems desirable.

The essence of this new relation as formulated by those working on the Hungarian social policy project should be an *increase in the autonomy* of both economic and social policy, coupled with a measure of self-imposed restraints resulting from their cooperation. In fact, the only guarantee against major social ills seems to be an economy which, while effective, avoids creating social problems in the first place. In short, *ex ante* solutions have to replace *ex post* remedies. It is no easy matter to define the major social ills which need to be prevented. Up to now a near political consensus has been reached only in the case of massive unemployment. Other more subtle points, such as the role and the limits of the market and the degree of inequality which can be tolerated, are being debated. Regardless of the origin of the social philosophy of the groups engaged in the debate, there exists an awareness of the extreme delicacy of the balance between too much and too little control of the economy. One may expect a long period of trial and error while a viable solution is worked out. For the time being, it can be considered a step in the right direction that a common ground for discussion has been found.[7]

The principles of distribution

The leading principle of distribution under socialism has been defined as distribution 'according to work'. In addition, central government funds for universal needs have long been established. Distribution 'according to need' could become a principle of distribution only in a communist society. To further complicate the picture, 'socialism' itself is not a discrete historical stage, but a transitory process.

In practice, there has always been an uneasiness in Hungary both with regard to the relative weight of the two principles, and with regard to the use of the central funds. If access to the latter had been granted only 'according to work', then their purpose would have been unclear. If applying only the criterion of need, then a 'communist' principle of distribution would have been adopted prematurely, since the economic foundation for such a principle was not available. The solution was to avoid the conceptual difficulties by not making them explicit.

Central funds were set up and greatly increased over time. But the criteria of eligibility were never defined, and the weighting between 'work' and 'need' as relevant criteria is still an open question. In some cases, the principle of 'distribution according to work' has been taken literally, considering work as a performance that can be measured by the wages earned. This has been the case with pension benefits that remained strictly wage-related, and were adjusted neither in relation to prices, nor to current wage increases. Thus, pensions were raised in the mid-1970s, without relating them to purchasing power. Other entitlements are also tied to 'work' and are conditional on participation in the formal economy. Family allowances, for instance, are paid provided one of the parents is 'working'. However, the definition of 'work' as a basis for entitlement has changed over time. At first only industrial workers and employees were considered to be 'working'. Later, the definition was extended to members of the agricultural cooperatives, and more recently to the self-employed. But the interpretation of 'work' differs from one benefit to the other.

There is a growing uneasiness about the present ambiguities. Some would like to emphasise the role of work and merit in the distribution of benefits, on the basis that more work incentives would be beneficial to the economy, and that Hungary has advanced too far in accepting a 'need approach', thereby creating shortages of services and maldistribution in the economy. The current universal or near-universal system of benefits is considered wasteful by others. (Owing to full employment, benefits conditional only on 'work' participation yields a practically universal scheme.) Some would like to concentrate scarce resources on those in 'real need'. The advocates of more selectivity usually acknowledge the shortcomings and the arbitrary nature of the current welfare system. Their proposal therefore includes the creation of a new network of social workers who would identify genuine clients in need of 'help and care'.

Public opinion polls consistently show that the population in general, and the worse-off groups in particular, are increasingly in favour of more social benefits, better protection of all vulnerable groups, and less emphasis on differentiation according to merit.

The current confusion may be illustrated by complaints voiced by pensioners. They resent the still existing practice of representing pension benefits as signs of state munificence, as they have contributed themselves to the insurance fund. They are simultaneously claiming full price and wage indexation of the pension benefits on the same grounds, thereby applying a false argument to a just cause.

The group working on the social policy project work along the lines of constructing a more flexible and consistent system of allocative principles. In this approach distribution according 'to work' and 'to need' should continue to coexist, but with less ambiguity. The need approach should be strengthened, both at the macro-level of allocation and in social policy. From the perspective of social solidarity, of human reproduction and of social inequalities, social policy cannot be viewed as having gone 'too far'. The opposite would be closer to the truth.

The principles of the individual contributory insurance scheme should be clarified (whether it should be work- or wage-related, and how differentiated the social wage should be), as should the principles of collective security (whether they should be flat-rate, universal, or possibly indexed to incomes). The scope of needs to be covered as of *right* should gradually increase. This right should be expanded to reach in a not too distant future, the right to an acceptable minimum standard of living.

The policy project acknowledges the restrictions in the present economic climate, but it will go ahead to assess the merits or demerits of the forced choices, using as a yardstick the guiding principles of the future. Thus, it opposes institutional changes which could trigger irreversible negative processes, e.g. increasing social distance and inequality, more selectivity measures, or dual systems in the delivery of services. It sees the importance of improving the situation of the weakest social groups; it advocates increasing predictability in the payment of all social incomes, whether universal or selective. Present emergency measures should not be allowed to weaken the basic principles of more acknowledged needs, more rights, more solidarity, less inequality and less uncertainty. Also, public information and explanations for social policy should be more available.

The case for a more autonomous social policy

All the previous arguments support the claim for a stronger and more autonomous social policy. This raises a perplexing question. In the realm of social policy no autonomous mechanisms can be conceived of in an unequal structure which would assure that all valid claims are identified and fulfilled. Almost by definition, the interests of social policy beneficiaries are those of the socially or economically weak. This holds true even for universal benefits, as they are more important for the weak than for the strong. Hence, the assertion of these interests requires legal and state-enforced guarantees. This inevitably means that the role of the state increases in social policy. To ensure that the policy operates smoothly probably requires a high-level central state organ, for example a ministry, as well as a local distribution network. The paradox is that a strong state organ may well lead to over-centralisation and over-bureaucratisation, and so lose sight of the socially distant needs and interests for which it was set up in the first place. The counterpart to a strong state is strong popular control, public accountability and a democratic system to organise and transmit interests. Some steps have already been taken in this direction. The most important is the recent separation of the social security system from the trade unions. The unions may continue in their function as interest groups, while social security has become the first strong central social policy organ, placed directly under the Council of Ministers. A more independent and more decentralised economy increasingly moved by individual and group interests, requires a 'dual' social policy of the type described above. The lack of a strong state policy leads to the neglect of the weak. An over-centralised social policy, however, forced on the economy, would be contrary to the whole logic of the economic reform.

There seems to be a case for a strong and autonomous social policy under the present Hungarian conditions, operating with state guarantees and popular control. It should not work against the revitalised economy, nor should it be dominated by it. In the absence of disproportionately strong private interests, their cooperation on an equal footing seems to be a distinct theoretical possibility. Whether this new model of the relation between economic and social policy will materialise or not, is an open question. But its desirability seems to have been established.

Notes

1. Szociális Szakszolgálat, *Social Service* (1947), Circular of the Department of Social Administration of the Ministry of Popular Welfare, January/February, 2.
2. Dobó, István (1949), 'The Organisation of the Ministry of Popular Welfare and the Perspectives of Work in Social Policy', *Szociálpolitika*, August, 12.
3. Ratkó, Anna (then Minister of Popular Welfare) (1950), 'Editorial', *Szociálpolitika*, January, 1.
4. The analysis of the press from the perspective of social policy is performed by a team headed by János Péteri; the research is part of the project mentioned in note 5.
5. The research project on social policy is under the auspices of the Institute of Sociology of the Hungarian Academy of Sciences. The Secretary-General of the Academy is responsible for the programme. The present author is heading the project.
6. Polányi, Karl, *Carl Menger's Two Meanings of 'Economic'* (in Hungarian).
7. Angelusz, Róbert, Nagy, Lajos Géza and Tardos, Róbert (1983), 'Public Opinion on Social Policy Issues', paper prepared for the social policy research project of the Hungarian Academy of Sciences.

Table 10.1   Some economic and social trends*

	Per capita national income, in real terms	Real wages per employee	Real income per head of the population	% S.S. expenditures of national income, 1st year of the period
1950–55	125	105	115	5
1955–60	133	147	134	7
1960–65	120	109	117	8
1965–70	136	119	135	10
1970–75	133	118	125	11
1975–80	115	104	109	15
1950–80	415	243	334	—

*First year of period = 100.

Table 10.2   Some characteristics of the distribution of personal incomes

Indicator	1962	1967	1972	1977
Average monthly per capita nominal income (forints)	823	1138	1486	2333
Multiplier between the highest and the lowest decile	5.8	4.6	5.0	4.1
% receiving less than average income (in %)				
< 75 per cent	34	29	31	26
< 50 per cent	10	10	9	5

Source: Central Statistical Office.

11 The Future of the New Zealand Welfare State
Avery Jack

Introduction

In the analysis of welfare states account has to be taken of the complex interplay between a variety of factors. Important among these are the value systems of policy-makers and their base in the community. While the values of the powerful are likely to influence policy, in a democracy they cannot deviate too far from the values of the people, at least in theory, without the power base being undermined. Hence the importance of an understanding of the institutional and societal power structures which form the focus of most approaches to the analysis of welfare states. More recently attention has been paid to the influence of the economic environment on the functioning of contemporary welfare states and this has provided the context for discussion of 'the crisis of the welfare state'. By viewing these various approaches as a configuration some understanding can be gained of the reasons for the significant differences between the welfare systems of various countries in spite of their general convergence.

This chapter looks at New Zealand in the light of its history as well as its values, politics and economy in an attempt to elucidate why the New Zealand welfare state has developed in the way it has, and how these elements may influence its future.

Background

New Zealand comprises two main islands and a number of smaller ones and is somewhat larger than the United Kingdom. Its present population is just over 3 million, mostly of European origin, but about 9 per cent are Maori and 3 per cent are from other Pacific islands. New Zealand was colonised by the British from 1840, after having been inhabited for several centuries by the Maoris, a Polynesian people. There were land wars between the British and the Maoris, and it is now accepted that the Maoris emerged at a disadvantage, though equal legal status and widespread intermarriage have blurred their true position.

The welfare state in New Zealand has its own peculiar history, its evolution being strongly influenced by the conditions of its colonisation. The early settlers, the vast majority of whom were 'respectable' working-class people, found themselves in a completely undeveloped, forest-clad country. There were no physical facilities, such as roads and buildings, and no established social institutions to which to turn for support. During the early decades, self-reliance, resourcefulness and mutual help were essential for survival.

With a population scattered in isolated settlements, and with only a small wealthy class, most of New Zealand's early attempts at organised philanthropy were fruitless. Efforts to establish voluntary hospitals on the British model foundered for want of funds. Schools were set up by religious and secular groups but were attended by few children. The churches themselves were not well established, and provided little help to the needy. There was no effective local government and central government was, until late in the century, largely representative only of the substantial landowners. In Sutch's words, 'New Zealand took over from the mother country a system which bred poverty but omitted to make legal provision . . . for its relief' (Sutch 1966: 22).

Neither private benevolence nor enforced self-responsibility, both of which were advocated by some early leaders, could protect the colony from the distress consequent upon unemployment which was present from the earliest days of colonisation. Necessarily, central government became involved in the welfare of the settlers as well as of the Maoris. (The earliest social provisions in New Zealand had been education and health services directed principally towards the Maoris.) By the mid-1880s, when the population numbered about 500,000, New Zealand had national legislation providing for a network of public hospitals which not only cared for the sick but also gave outdoor relief to the poor, financed mainly from taxation. By this time, too, a national public education system had been legislated for, making education free, compulsory and secular.

A combination of factors, economic and political, led to extensive social legislation in the 1890s. Severe economic depression, manhood suffrage and the waning of the influence of the early colonial gentry resulted in the election of the Liberal Party as government. This party believed in the potential beneficence of the state and at least one member identified himself as a 'Fabian socialist'. However the Liberal Party's socialism was tempered with pragmatism — it has been said that they 'adjusted their aspirations to fit the facts' (Sinclair 1969: 187). Their period of government saw the introduction before the turn of the century of female suffrage, land reforms aimed at breaking up the largest land-holdings, labour legislation related both to working conditions and to wage negotiations, a workers' compensation scheme and non-contributory old age pensions. 'Their amalgam of democratic and humanitarian legislation . . . made New Zealand for a time the most radical state in the world' (Sinclair 1969: 188).

Exactly why this legislation came about is not fully understood. While comparisons can be made with European countries which were initiating social provisions at the same time, a population of three quarters of a million people, some of whom were indigenous and a high proportion of whom were first-generation migrants, could make only limited use of their knowledge of other countries (Hanson 1980). They sought solutions which were probably based on various philosophies. It has been suggested that paternalism, in the form of control, discipline and efficiency, may have played as much a part as motivations based on humanity, compassion and simple justice (Oliver 1980).

Increased prosperity from the beginning of the twentieth century seemed to reduce the impetus for social reform, though pensions were soon extended to widows and to disabled mine-workers. Everywhere there were signs of confidence, and in 1912 government passed to a party less concerned with equality and more interested in freedom and capitalism. It was ill prepared to meet the social problems arising from the economic depression of the 1920s and 1930s.

But out of that depression New Zealand again, as in the 1880s, forged a strong political party in which 'bitterness against evil times mingled with the most pure visions of tomorrow' (Sinclair 1969: 266). The influence of the Fabians could still be seen in that Labour Party, but the leaders were also influenced by social credit economic principles, by strong nationalism, and by a humanitarianism which at the time was often referred to as 'applied Christianity'. The Labour Party was elected to government with an overwhelming majority in 1935 and given a mandate to overcome the human and economic problems highlighted by the depression.

The government's policies consisted mainly of a return to full employment and the development of social services. The stimulation of the economy was the principal tool used to overcome unemployment but the advent of war helped, for not only did New Zealand send troops to fight alongside the British, but also there was a ready demand for all the primary produce New Zealand could provide.

At this time New Zealand developed its major social security system. The preamble to the legislation set out its intention:

> to provide for the payment of superannuation benefits and of other benefits designed to safeguard the people of New Zealand from disabilities arising from age, sickness, widowhood, orphanhood, unemployment or other exceptional conditions; to provide a system whereby medical and hospital treatment will be made available to persons requiring such treatment; and, further, to provide such other benefits as may be necessary to maintain and promote the health and general welfare of the community.

Following the precedent of the Old Age Pensions Act 1898, the new benefits were non-contributory and means tested. The free health service that had been proposed was achieved only in part, however, the medical profession proving obstructive on some features of it. A more successful venture of the Labour government of the 1930s was the considerable involvement of the state in housing, both for rental and for home-ownership.

In a period of 100 years from colonisation, New Zealand had established a full range of state (central government) provided social services — income maintenance, health, education, housing, as well as some other services such as childcare. It was these broad-ranging social services that could be seen as giving New Zealand from the 1930s the hallmarks of the status of 'welfare state', though that term has not been much used in New Zealand, and certainly was not used in the 1930s or 1940s.

Values

Although it can be said that New Zealand's welfare achievements have been 'as much a practical and emotional response to urgent needs . . . as an expression of the government's social philosophy' (*Social Security in New Zealand* 1972: 46), this places too much emphasis on pragmatism and pays insufficient attention to underlying values. It overlooks the striving for security which fired the politics of the 1930s and which seems to be the foremost aim of most New Zealanders. The benevolence and the humanitarianism which underlay the social security legislation which is now seen as making New Zealand a welfare state was based on the objective of providing security and protection for the whole community, a value shared by the opposition party and the Labour government. The striving for security can be seen as having an economic as much as a social base, with emphasis placed upon the security which comes to workers through full employment, and the security for producers through guaranteed prices and import controls. (Governments in recent years have managed better protection for producers than for workers.)

The emphasis on pragmatism also overlooks another thread that runs through much of the social legislation which stresses the principle of community responsibility. In New Zealand acceptance of the value of community responsibility is such that for most of its history the ideas of insurance, self-responsibility and private provision have played *little* part in social provisions. When legislation has been debated, conservative politicians have argued for a contributory social insurance approach (often to save tax funds) but they have been overridden. Ironically, the only exception to this was the introduction by a Labour government of a scheme for a contributory earnings-related superannuation supplement which lasted for two years from 1974 to 1975 and was repealed by the National government.

If there is a basic philosophy which underpins New Zealand's welfare services it could then be considered to be the responsibility of the state to ensure security for all its people. Although this has not been clearly enunciated it is too deeply entrenched in the thinking of New Zealanders to be ignored. What is a matter of debate though is the actual level of provision required to ensure security, and in this values are tempered both by political forces and by the economic situation.

Politics

The most significant steps in the first 100 years of New Zealand's social welfare history have occurred when a political party representing the working class has taken power from a conservative or farmers' party. Both in the 1890s and the 1930s the governments of the time were strongly committed to improving the lot of the poorest sections of the community. However, after the war, prosperity seems to have changed the political balance and New Zealand could now serve as an example for Downs' economic theory of party competition (Barry 1970). On the basis that political parties are obliged to take account of the preferences of electors, they put forward packages of policies with which they try to attract voters; but to reduce information costs they also create and maintain ideologies. Thus some people vote not on specific policies but on the images of the parties. Each of New Zealand's two major parties has an image which attracts a certain number of voters — National with a more conservative approach championing the rights of the individual and private enterprise, and Labour with a traditional concern for equality. But when these ideologies are elaborated upon, the differences become blurred.

At the level of actual policies the similarities are marked, and have on occasion even appeared to contradict party ideology. For example, in the 1970s the Labour government introduced a scheme for contributory, earnings-related superannuation and the National government replaced it with a universal, tax-based, flat-rate scheme. Similarity between policies was clearly evident in the 1981 election campaign which was fought not on the merits of economic growth as the means of solving New Zealand's problems — this was accepted by both parties — but on the question of whether this should be geared to large enterprises (National) or small ones (Labour). National put forward the proposition that 'New Zealand's economic growth will provide work, prosperity and security for everyone', and the Labour Party stated that their 'top tier policies are economic and essential to get growth back into the economy'.

Both the major parties have taken steps to maintain their centre-of-the-road image. National has resisted those in its ranks who would too vigorously promote free enterprise; in 1983 this gave rise to a new right-wing party. Labour has the support of the Federation of Labour, but has played down any appearance of alignment with socialist activities. The few candidates who have sought election to parliament under the banner of any party with either communist connections or extreme right-wing ideas have so far received little support — only a few hundred votes throughout the country. The National Party has been the government in New Zealand for 28 of the last 34 years but the Labour Party usually receives about the same number of votes as the National Party.

In such an arena it is not surprising that all political parties are sensitive to major collective interests. The smallness of New Zealand does not require that pressure-group activity and lobbying be sophisticated in order to be effective, particularly immediately prior to the three-yearly parliamentary elections. Promises are made, often in haste, and governments hold themselves to honouring such promises. New services have consequently been established and old ones expanded helping to create what Katznelson (1980: 120) has referred to as a social policy surplus. Having established their claims on government to meet their perceived needs, interest groups tend to move on to make yet greater demands and thus the surplus of one decade tends to become the minimum of the next. To refer to this incremental development of social policy as pragmatism, as has often been done in New Zealand (Easton 1981), is to use a euphemism and to ignore the political pressures and motives which have determined such developments.

Social policies stemming directly from pressure exerted by collective interests or designed to secure the political support of such groups are seldom based on an identifiable welfare philosophy. Politicians aim for a substantial pay-off from new or extended policies and they are best rewarded where there is widespread public sympathy for a particular problem or where a large number of people are likely to benefit. Groups which command neither numerical strength nor widespread public concern seldom make gains from this political manoeuvring.

A graphic example of a major social policy development promised just before an election and still widely recognised as being in the welfare-surplus category, was the introduction of National Superannuation — a generous, universal old age pension for all New Zealanders from the age of 60 years with the married rate being indexed to 80 per cent of the average wage. The large number of beneficiaries of this scheme (approximately 22 per cent of all voters) has led both the major political parties to guarantee to keep the scheme intact despite complaints from younger tax-payers and high-level advice to the contrary. This is an instance not only of a failure to weigh a social programme against clearly defined values and welfare objectives, but also of political considerations taking precedence over concern for the economy.

The economy
After the war living standards rose. Governments, both Labour and

National, were prepared to forgo some growth and dynamism in the economy in order to attain full employment which was the key to the well-being and prosperity experienced by most New Zealanders until the late 1970s. Virtually a whole generation passed through the workforce without experiencing unemployment.

Full employment seemed to hide social problems, and while the economic growth of the 1950s and 1960s was accompanied by a gradual expansion in some social services, the value of social security benefits was actually eroded by failure to adjust them to increasing wage rates. There was little debate about the welfare state and its provisions, and a Royal Commission (*Social Security in New Zealand* 1972) reported that it found no evidence of discontent with the social security scheme. The feeling persisted that everything had been achieved, that the security of all New Zealanders was assured, and that as a result of rising prosperity, need was negligible. Employment opportunities exceeded demand and the 'reserve army' of women and Pacific Islanders were incorporated into the workforce. Wage rates increased as trade union negotiations were successful in gaining a share in the increase in national productivity.

New Zealanders became accustomed to affluence where continued progress, greater productivity and the good life seemed to be assured. The mid-1970s changed the reality, but people were reluctant to accept that the aspirations born of the 1960s were unlikely to be met. Three factors were of particular significance. First, when the United Kingdom joined the EEC, New Zealand lost its traditional market for primary produce; second, the oil crisis had a profound effect on New Zealand's terms of trade; and, third, the impact of these factors was compounded by the coincident increase in the labour force. It has been a slow process endeavouring to diversify economic activities and to establish new markets, and the centrality of a full employment policy has been forsaken. The New Zealand economy is not in good shape. Of the 25 countries surveyed by the OECD (OECD 1983), none had a lower growth rate than New Zealand over the period 1975—80, when New Zealand's average annual growth in GDP was only 0.7 per cent.

Yet during the 1970s major expansion in the social services continued. Clearly these expansions reflected attitudes resulting from the prosperity of the 1960s rather than the reduced productivity of the 1970s, but the truth and implications of this were ignored or denied by economists and politicians, who adopted an optimistic stance and kept seeing 'the light at the end of the tunnel'. Increased public expenditure during the decade had a number of causes, an important one being the Report of a Royal Commission on social security which recommended the reinstatement of the value of monetary benefits, some liberalising of eligibility, and an increase in medical benefits. The National government had no hesitation in implementing these recommendations, particularly since it was election year. The Labour government, which took office the following year, ensured further increases in public expenditure by indexing most benefits to the cost of living. But by introducing its ill-fated contributory superannuation scheme, the Labour government had intended to find a way to secure investment funds and promise better pensions in the future without increasing government expenditure. This scheme was replaced two years later by national superannuation which made then, and will continue to make, extremely heavy demands on public expenditure.

Growth was also occurring in the 1970s in other social services, but to a lesser extent than in income maintenance. Education expenditure did not respond as automatically to the 1970s reduction in school rolls as it had done to the increasing number of children in the 1950s and 1960s. The increase in health expenditure reflected similar trends in other countries as new interventions and technology became available and expectations of treatment were raised.

The growth in public expenditure on the social services at that time could be seen as leading to a social policy surplus. It reinforced the New Zealand tradition of government provision of welfare, and particularly in the personal social services, took the state a step further into the private lives of New Zealanders. Issues that had previously been dealt with in the informal sector became the subject of formal provision and further consolidated the place of the helping professions. Employment in both statutory and voluntary social services increased and many people, especially women, who had previously been volunteers became employees.

Generally consensus rather than conflict has surrounded the expansion of the welfare state in New Zealand. The pursuit of welfare aims could proceed without controversy in times of rising prosperity when it was possible to finance new programmes out of growth. Some people could be made better off without anyone being made worse off. All sections of the community were able to receive a larger portion as both wages and profits rose and the weakest members of society could be assisted from the increase in national income without changing the existing distribution of income and wealth.

However, if productivity is declining and social services can be expanded only at the expense of some other group in the community, then conflict can be expected. The New Zealand government's means of financing social service expansions during the period of no growth have avoided much potential conflict first by the use of fiscal drag, which in times of high inflation and flexible wage adjustments allowed both workers and the government to increase their incomes, and secondly, by allowing an increase in the budget deficit which in the past decade has risen from 9 per cent to 22 per cent as a proportion of net government expenditure. But the cost of these government policies has been high. Since the mid-1970s unemployment, although still lower than in other OECD countries, has been rising at a faster rate to reach at least 6.5 per cent in 1983. And the annual inflation rate peaked at 17 per cent in June 1982.

Opposition to the high level of government expenditure has come not only from supporters of the market (manufacturers and employers) and from the government's economic advisors, but also from ordinary New Zealanders who are concerned about the ever-increasing tax which reduces their discretionary income. The New Zealand Planning Council, a government-appointed advisory body, spearheaded the view that growth in public expenditure should be curtailed and focused attention on social service spending. It questioned whether New Zealand could sustain its past level of social service spending which accounts for more than half net government expenditure.

The future

It has been suggested here that the condition of New Zealand's welfare state has been determined by the interplay between the country's values, its politics and its economy. There is no indication that in the near future there will be changes in those three elements, and in particular there is not expected to be any major upturn in the economy.

There will be demographic changes. It is projected that the number of old people in the population will increase by about 20 per cent by the turn of the century, though the proportion of old people in the population is not expected to increase until after that time. This is of considerable importance in relation to the social services not only because of the high demands on medical care made by old people but also because of the cost of national superannuation. Even now it accounts for approximately 17 per cent of net government expenditure. However, the dependency ratio will decline over the next 15 years as a result of lower birth rates and this may allow some savings in expenditure, particularly on education. Other demographic features to be taken into account are the likelihood of a continuing high level of unemployment and of the trend to more one-parent families. Numerically, these are less significant than the elderly but they are more stigmatised and are therefore more likely to be the subject of conflict.

Thus in a situation of, at best, low economic growth, there will be more people with legitimate demands on the social services. New Zealand has some hard choices to make in shaping the future of its welfare state. Gough (1979: 151), writing of the UK, has said, 'In a period of prolonged recession like the present, the "need" to restore profitability directly conflicts with the quite different "need" to improve living standards and levels of social consumption'. The New Zealand response has been to focus on growth in the economy with government diverting additional expenditure into 'productive' sectors such as energy, industry and agriculture and, where possible, away from the 'non-productive' social services.

This changed focus has been accompanied by a 'technocratic' or 'social engineering' approach which looks at the margins of the social services to see where a little may be trimmed off or anomalies overcome at no cost. Such an approach relies heavily on the judgement and advice of economists who know more about economic costs than about social costs. It is a long time since Titmuss (1970: 241) expressed his scepticism about 'the belief that moral problems of choice can be resolved or avoided by technological means and by "social engineering" answers'. Left in the hands of economists, decisions are likely to be made without confronting the moral problems of what should happen in a decent society — as Neale (1980) puts it — and instead will be made on the basis of what the economy requires. Questions that used to be ethical (*who* should have *how much* of *what*) are now economic — the 'needs' of the market must be met before the 'needs' of the individual can be fulfilled. Policies are a function of the way in which a problem is perceived, and as Walker (1980: 47) points out, 'unless some attempt is made by social policy analysts to decipher national accounts . . . economic rather than social priorities will continue to dominate policy making'. Strong emphasis is currently given in New Zealand to *generation* of resources, and *distribution* of resources is secondary to this.

In an attempt to bring down the level of inflation, the government introduced a wage-price freeze in June 1982. This has been successful in so far as the level of inflation in the following year dropped to 8.3 per cent but, as with such experiments elsewhere, the freeze is more rigidly applied to wages than to prices thus reducing the real value of wages. Nobody was prepared to predict the outcome of lifting the freeze in 1984 (an election year — the customary time for governments to make generous gestures). It seems improbable, though, that low income-earners will improve their position sufficiently to compensate for the disadvantages they have experienced both from the freeze and from tax reforms introduced in 1982. These aimed 'to minimize the disincentive impact of high marginal tax rates on work, savings and investment decisions' (*Budget* 1982: 20) and the prime beneficiaries were persons earning at least double the average wage. Consequently, *the 1980s have seen growing inequality in real incomes.*

New Zealand has a situation where policies are directed (albeit ineffectively — in 1982/83 the growth rate was negative) towards improving the economy. However, this policy is being followed in the certain knowledge that by-products, at least in the short term, are increasing unemployment and decreasing social service expenditure. The reasoning is that a growing economy will ultimately generate employment, which will in turn make resources available to meet other social needs.

So far, reductions in social service spending have been kept at about 3—4 per cent in real terms for two main reasons. First, some substantial savings have been possible from small administrative changes. For example, new personal social service programmes have been financed from sums saved by paying family benefit and national superannuation according to birth dates rather than government pay periods. But there are limited opportunities for this type of saving in the future. Secondly, and more importantly, the government deficit has been allowed to rise and spending has been financed from borrowing. If the deficit is to be reduced it requires either further cuts in government expenditure or increased taxation. Whichever way is chosen, *low income-earners are likely to be the losers.*

If public expenditure is reduced the traditional social services — health, education and social welfare, which account for approximately 52 per cent of net government expenditure — are unlikely to escape pressure to contract.

Two possible ways to restrict expenditure are to shift some of the services to the market and to make less funding available. Neither of these would be without problems in implementation or in impact. A shift to the market would represent a major change of direction for New Zealand social services. It would have different connotations from those it has in some other countries as New Zealand has no history of market supply of social services, apart from housing. The comprehensiveness of statutory provisions dating back to the last century has led to general satisfaction and little incentive for private provision. Nevertheless there are signs that the market may play a significant part in the provision of health care in the future as medical insurance grows and limited funds lower the standards provided in the public sector. Fougere (1974) was predicting this during the 1970s when the health services were under less threat than they are now, and before the New Zealand Planning Council (1979) gave support to government encouragement of private health insurance. Such a step would be a retrograde one for New Zealand where it has been possible to have some confidence that medical care is available on the basis of need rather than ability to pay. But the possibility of two standards of care, one for the insured and one for the rest, is no longer remote.

In housing, where the market has always been important (nearly three-quarters of all New Zealand dwellings are owner-occupied), there is already evidence of government further retreating from commitment to public provision. And there is the likelihood of some increase in the user pays principle in other social services so that market mechanisms will be used within publicly-provided services. Of course, costs will fall most heavily on those least able to pay.

The personal social services are in a fluid position with the 1960s and 1970s having seen a move to statutory provision not from the market but from the voluntary and informal sectors — a move that could well be reversed in the future as government draws on current philosophies to justify limiting its involvement. Dissatisfaction has been expressed about the delivery of these services by centralised bureaucracies and the recommendations of the New Zealand Council of Social Service (1978) for giving local communities the power to determine their own needs and to apply resources accordingly, can provide fuel to a government desirous of minimising its financial responsibilities: 'When governments can no longer hope to claim credit for the extra benefits made possible by economic growth, their strategy may increasingly emphasise decentralisation, if only to divert blame for shortcomings and inadequacies' (Klein 1981: 177).

The second and more pervasive response government can make to meet its own budgetary needs is to reduce the funds that are available to the social services whether or not they do this under the guise of encouraging higher productivity or of setting new priorities. This could be seen as cutting back on the social policy surplus, of a return to the state's role of providing only basic security. In any case in some areas, particularly in the personal social services, there has been declining marginal utility from a political viewpoint as recent developments have brought under the statutory umbrella people with less common social needs, clients who are few in number and without voting strength. (They are of course among the weakest and most vulnerable members of society.) But while it may be politically feasible to withdraw services from this group of people, it will not save much money. On the other hand, attempts to make major savings, such as by restructuring national superannuation, could well produce a situation where political and economic motives will be in conflict with each other.

Piven and Cloward (1982) have put forward the proposition that in the United States coalitions may form between social service workers and their clients in opposing cuts in welfare expenditure. This is also a possibility in New Zealand where those employed in the social services could be driven by self-interest as well as by compassion to help their clients oppose reduction in services. Because social services are labour-intensive, any reduction in expenditure must threaten the employment of workers, including professionals. It can also threaten their working conditions which became very congenial during the expansive 1960s and 1970s. With the support of their unions and professional organisations, an alliance between the employees of the social services and the numerically significant clients could prove a formidable opposition to a government determined to curb public expenditure. However, such a response would probably be brought about only by cuts much more massive than those which seem imminent. *It is more likely that reductions in expenditure will proceed insidiously and incrementally*, in the same way that the expansions occurred, and any opposition could thus be dispersed.

However, if government wishes to reduce its budget deficit without significantly reducing public expenditure it must increase taxation. Here again there is the potential for conflict as citizens are coerced into parting with more money to support social services. Taxation in New Zealand is highly visible, most (67 per cent) being personal income tax, and the marginal rate even for a person on half the average wage is 31.5 per cent. This means that objections to paying tax come from a wide section of the community and the tendency to 'blame the victim' and to be critical of clients of the social services is not a phenomenon confined to the wealthy. However, this critical attitude applies only to selected recipients of social security benefits — mainly the unemployed and single parents — and no stigma attaches to use of public education and health services. (A greater use of the market for health care could alter this balance.) Criticism of social service consumers can be functional both for capitalism and for a government concerned to control expenditure as, at least in theory, it operates as a deterrent. But politically it is only feasible where the number of social service consumers is relatively small.

The national superannuation scheme merits special reference here for its very generosity and universality make it the most controversial area of public expenditure (New Zealand Planning Council 1979). It is of interest that in New Zealand, concern about means-testing centres on the rich rather than on the poor. Means tests are favoured to select out rather than to select in. Thus national superannuation is criticised because it contravenes the principle of support according to need and it is seen as an aberration within the social security system. But many voters and taxpayers receive it and that fact seems to be ensuring its survival. On the one hand it is the most logical target for cuts, on the other, to make those cuts could be politically suicidal. In the final analysis it highlights the pre-eminence of political considerations in the functioning of the New Zealand welfare state.

Conclusion

The unhealthy condition of New Zealand's economy must dominate decision-making in the short and medium-term future. The reduced but still comparatively high inflation rate, the high internal and external deficits, and rapidly increasing unemployment not only give cause for concern but also restrict the potential for traditional welfare developments. Social services have so far been artificially protected from the consequences of a contracting economy and they, together with other activities, are currently in a state of hiatus brought about by the wage—price freeze.

There are some danger signs indicating that the consensus which has been a feature of New Zealand's welfare state may not be as pervasive in the future as it has been in the past. There are indications of racial tensions, not unrelated to increasing inequalities, but these movements so far are not well organised. The weight of economic issues could well obscure value issues so that resources may be shared on the basis of what is good for the economy rather than on the basis of social need. If the past values of community responsibility, security and protection from distress continue to be widely held, major retrenchments affecting the welfare of the people are unlikely to be introduced. However there are many who question whether these values still influence policies, and there are also those who would replace these values and who advocate individual responsibility. The potential for conflict is clearly present in New Zealand's welfare state.

References

Barry, B.M. (1970), *Sociologists, Economists and Democracy*, London: Collier-Macmillan.

Budget 1982, Wellington: Government Printer.

Compensation for Personal Injury in New Zealand (1967), Report of the Royal Commission of Inquiry, Wellington: Government Printer.

Easton, B.H. (1981), *Pragmatism and Progress — Social Security in the Seventies*, Christchurch: University of Canterbury.

Fougere, G. (1974), 'Medical Insurance: The Market's Quiet Counter-revolution', in D. Beaven and B. Easton (eds), *The Future of New Zealand Medicine — A Progressive View*, Christchurch: Peryer.

Gough, I. (1979), *The Political Economy of the Welfare State*, London: Macmillan.

Hanson, E. (1980), *The Politics of Social Security*, Auckland: Oxford University Press.

Katznelson, I. (1980), 'Accounts of the Welfare State and the New Mood', *American Economic Review* 70 (2), 117—22.

Klein, R. (1980), 'The Welfare State: A Self-Inflicted Crisis', *Political Quarterly* 51, 24—34.

Klein, R. (1981), 'Values, Power and Policies', in OECD, *The Welfare State in Crisis*, Paris: OECD.

Neale, W.C. (1980), 'Market Capitalism as Dispute Resolution: The Loss of Legitimacy and the Problems of the Welfare State', *Journal of Economic Issues* XIV (2), 391—8.

New Zealand Council of Social Service (1978), *Sharing Social Responsibility*, Wellington: New Zealand Council of Social Service.

New Zealand Labour Party (1981), *Manifesto 1981*, Wellington: New Zealand Labour Party.

New Zealand National Party (1981), *This is Your Future*, Wellington: New Zealand National Party.

New Zealand Planning Council (1979), *The Welfare State? Social Policy in the 1980s*, Wellington: New Zealand Planning Council.

New Zealand Planning Council (1981), *Directions*, Wellington: New Zealand Planning Council.

OECD Economic Surveys 1982—1983, New Zealand (1983) Paris: OECD.

Oliver, W.H. (1980), 'Social Policy in the Liberal Period', in D.A. Hamer (ed.), *New Zealand Social History*, Auckland: University of Auckland.

Piven, F.F. and Cloward, R. (1982), *The New Class War*, New York: Pantheon.

Report of the Task Force on Tax Reform (1982), Wellington: Government Printer.

Sinclair, K. (1969), *A History of New Zealand*, Auckland: Penguin Books.

Sinfield, A. (1978), 'Analyses in the Social Division of Welfare', *Journal of Social Policy* 7(2), 129–56.

Social Security in New Zealand (1972), Report of the Royal Commission of Inquiry, Wellington: Government Printer.

Sutch, W.B. (1966), *The Quest for Security in New Zealand*, Wellington: Oxford University Press.

Titmuss, R.M. (1958), *Essays on the Welfare State*, London: Allen and Unwin.

Titmuss, R.M. (1970), *The Gift Relationship — From Human Blood to Social Policy*, London: Allen and Unwin.

Walker, A. (1980), 'A Right Turn for the British Welfare State?', *Social Policy* 10, 46–51.

12 Development and Prospects of the Austrian Welfare State[1]

Georg Busch, Rainer Münz, Helga Nowotny, Hans Reithofer, Hannes Schmidl and Helmut Wintersberger

The national background[2]

In its present borders, Austria originated as the remnant that was left after the break-up of the Austro-Hungarian Empire at the end of the first world war. It comprises the seven historical, predominantly German-speaking, Alpine provinces of the Austrian Empire and parts of Western Hungary with a German and Croatian-speaking population.

The history of the First Republic (1918—38) was marked by the absence of an Austrian national identity, pronounced conflicts between the three main political groups in the country (Catholics, Social-Democrats and German Nationalists) and a catastrophic economy. Not until the Second Republic following the liberation of Austria by the Allies in 1945 was it possible to generate an Austrian national identity.

Thus in its present form, Austria is a very young country. Despite that fact, the social welfare sector, including health services, poor relief and the beginnings of social insurance, goes back at least to the eighteenth and nineteenth centuries. Some reforms, however, originated in Germany, thus industrial pensions were extended to Austria during the German occupation (1938—44). Only after the second world war was this German law formally legislated in Austria.

From the Empire the new Austrian republic took over not only statutory regulations and forms of organisation but also an administrative apparatus that performed important services in the government of a multi-nation state. In the First and Second Republics this apparatus continued to operate smoothly on the whole. But this factor, which at first sight seems positive, is influenced by the fact that confidence in bureaucratic forms of organisation is predominant both in general, and in the welfare sector in particular. Consequently, forms of self-help and the spontaneous organisation of services have been discouraged rather than promoted.

Despite its small area (84,000 sq.km.) and small population (7.5 million), Austria is a federal state consisting of nine provinces. This structure is also reflected in the welfare sector: social insurance is a federal matter, while social assistance is largely dealt with by the provinces and the local communities.

The Austrian economy has a relatively large nationalised sector, including heavy industry, electricity generation, large banks, transport and parts of the finished-goods industries.

Since Austria has a relatively old welfare system, which originated in the wake of industrialisation in the last quarter of the nineteenth century, the level of expenditure is relatively high. Another factor that is said to account for the high level of expenditure is the relatively small military budget of neutral Austria.

There is a considerable gap between nominal and actual taxation. This might pacify public discussion about the level of welfare expenditure. There has been no public outcry about alleged 'welfare scroungers', although this will probably occur in Austria if the present level of welfare expenditure begins to decline.

'Social partnership' is an important feature of the Austrian political system. It is frequently regarded as having been the most important prerequisite for Austrian economic and social development from 1950 to the present, which has been more favourable than in other countries. It began as a mechanism for reaching a consensus between government and employers', workers' and farmers' associations on wage and prices policies, and is now a well-developed and efficient system for co-operation between the major institutions representing the employers and the workers.[3] The social partnership has thus become the most important element in the political and ideological framework of the Austrian social system and there have been few social reforms that have not passed through the institution of the social partnership. This applies particularly to reforms regarding labour relations and social insurance, but not to the locally-based social assistance schemes.

Instruments of social policy: quantitative aspects

Austria has a highly developed social security system.[4] In 1982, total expenditure of social security in Austria amounted to about 280,000 million Austrian schillings, about 25 per cent of GDP, most of which was spent under the title of general social insurance. This comprises three main areas: pensions, and accident and health insurance.

Statutory pension insurance is managed by six autonomous public bureaux covering workers, employees, miners, railway workers, farmers and businessmen. Civil servants' pensions are not covered by the General Social Security Act. The federal government subsidises the pension insurance fund if contributions fall short of payments. In addition, the federal government subsidises very low pensions to the level of a statutory minimum. In 1982 the federal government subsidies amounted to a quarter of total pensions paid, thus in the present discussion about reforming the pension insurance system, government has a vested interest in finding ways of keeping its contributions under control.

In health insurance, discussion on income maintenance in the form of sick pay has receded into the background, whereas benefits in kind, such as medical care, drugs and hospital treatment, are clearly in the foreground. Fourteen large insurance institutions and ten industrial health insurance funds cover 99 per cent of the Austrian population in respect of health care. Insured persons and their dependants have a legal entitlement to standard medical treatment that is largely free of charge. Certain occupational groups have their own insurance institutions, some of whom have to pay part of the treatment costs themselves.

The risk of industrial accidents and occupational diseases is covered by four public accident insurance institutions. Expenditure of health services has risen considerably in the last 15 years and now exceeds 10 per cent of GNP.

Another important sector of social policy is family welfare and in particular the Family Allowance Fund. Originally, family welfare was based primarily on demographic criteria (the horizontal redistribution of income from households with fewer than average children to large families). But since the Social-Democratic Party came to power in 1970, the socio-political aspect (redistribution from rich to poor regardless of numbers of children) has been emphasised.

There remain three other instruments of social security. Quantitatively speaking, their volume is relatively small — in total, approximately 10 per cent of the total social security expenditures. However, deprived groups in particular benefit from them. They are unemployment benefits, supplementary benefit, and special federal pensions (e.g. for war victims).

Unemployment insurance is managed directly by the federal government. Rising unemployment has led to an increase of expenditures for unemployment benefits and emergency assistance for the unemployed. Despite major financial problems, discussion concentrates on the question of how to prevent unemployment rather than on how to adapt revenue to expenditure, and vice versa.

Supplementary benefit for the poor and disabled is provided by the provinces and municipalities. It is an important part of the Austrian social security system, since it protects those who escape the first safety-net of social welfare. It is selective and its degree of social effectiveness is much higher than can be expressed by official statistics.

Special pensions (e.g. for war victims, victims of Fascism, etc.) are paid by the federal government. Between the two wars and after the second world war these were an indispensable instrument of social policy in Austria.

From family policy to welfare policy

According to a government policy statement,

> the burden of family maintenance . . . must be balanced between those who
> carry the burden in the interest of society as a whole and those who do not
> have to carry such a burden but consciously or unconsciously derive benefit
> from the fact that others do so for them.[5]

This has been the guiding principle of the quantitative aspect of family welfare policy in Austria since the 1950s.

Three forms of family welfare and social policy can be distinguished:[6]

(1)   Payments and benefits in kind that cover part of the costs actually incurred in bringing up children. Chief of these are family allowances, maternity benefits (and up to 1977 income tax relief for persons with dependent children) as well as allowances and benefits for children in education.

(2)   Payments, benefits and regulations enabling working women to take leave immediately before and for one year after the birth of a child. These include maternity leave, job protection, entitlement to (a maximum one-year) extended maternity leave without payment, an allowance for employed persons during this extended maternity leave, special emergency assistance for single mothers, and help in running a farm (for farmers' wives) or business for self-employed mothers. Payments and benefits in this category are intended to make up for loss of earnings and to maintain continuity of social insurance contributions and hence pension entitlements.

(3)   Benefits and facilities to improve the general conditions at birth, and for the rearing and education of children (i.e. infrastructure).

Demographic and family policy considerations in the stricter sense were of equal importance for the introduction of a family allowance fund in Austria in the 1950s. At that time, family allowances were not expressly intended to bring about a vertical distribution of income for the benefit of low-income families, since the objective of providing for 'the education and maintenance of children in a manner befitting their station'[7] was in the foreground, and thus indirectly maintained existing differences between social classes. There have been fundamental changes in this concept since the beginning of the 1970s. Today, demographic aims of all kinds are rejected by both the government and the population; income redistribution by means of balancing the family burden is thus borne not merely by childless families but also by richer families.

During the 1970s the family allowance fund was transformed incrementally into an instrument for (vertical) fiscal income redistribution for the benefit of lower-income families.[8] Flat-rate transfer payments replaced tax exemptions assessed on income. In 1977, tax rebates for children were abolished and replaced by higher children's allowances, as a result of which approximately 300,000 low-income households that had previously not been able to benefit from the tax rebates benefited for the first time.[9] In addition, a number of universal payments and benefits in kind were introduced. Further reforms introduced measures that provided better facilities for working mothers and single mothers. If fathers refused to pay maintenance for the child, the family allowance fund also advanced maintenance payments for the children.

Despite these developments of egalitarianism, *family welfare policy continues to favour the Austrian income and cultural élite*. Although persons in the higher income brackets are no longer entitled to larger allowances, they are *de facto* entitled to longer periods of payments and benefits whether as family allowances or in education, because, as a rule, their children's education lasts much longer.

From its modest beginnings in the 1940s and 1950s, family welfare policy in Austria has developed into an integral part of government social and income policy. In 1982, the amount redistributed in this manner was about 39,000 million schillings. Family welfare provision represents roughly 42 per cent of all federal government expenditure on health and social welfare, 33 per cent of all transfer payments to private households, and 10 per cent of total federal government expenditure (1984).[10] In quantitative terms, non-specific transfer payments to households with children constitute the predominant part of this family welfare expenditure.

Relating this to the Austrian economy as a whole, this means that in the first half of the 1980s roughly 3.4 per cent of GDP went towards family welfare. That places Austria at the head of the western industrialised states, jointly with France and the Netherlands.[11]

Government family welfare services are financed mainly from contributions made by employers, and by employed and self-employed persons. These payments are specifically designated for this purpose. Following the drop in the birth rate between 1963 and 1978 and the consequent fall in the dependency ratio of children between 0 and 15 years,[12] earmarking such contributions has resulted in an extremely favourable financing structure for family welfare policy. From the mid-1970s the accumulated surpluses were used to expand services, sometimes to a considerable extent, and to finance more areas (albeit that part of the employers' contributions was 'diverted' to financing the pension insurance, which was showing a deficit. As a result of this, there were considerable deficits in the family allowance fund on current account, which were covered out of the fund's reserves). However, since it is assumed that reserves will be exhausted by 1984/85, family welfare policy in the 1990s seems to be faced with the following options:

(1) to increase the employers' and employees' contributions earmarked for family welfare;
(2) to cover the deficits of the family allowance fund out of the general budget; or
(3) to freeze government family welfare benefits at their present level or restrict them either selectively or generally (e.g. by including transfer payments in the taxable income).

In view of the tense budget situation in all public sector institutions, and since resistance to increasing taxes and contributions will doubtlessly grow as the result of stagnation in real income, the present Social—Liberal government (elected 1983) has expressed preference for the third option.

Retirement, disability and widows' pensions and unemployment benefits: two important components of social security

Although these two benefit systems provide for different needs and have different organisational structures, they have nevertheless a number of features in common as far as their recent development and future prospects are concerned. They also share growing financial problems, and so have points in common in their approach to finding solutions to these problems.

Retirement and other pensions

Retirement and other pensions represent about 70 per cent of total expenditure and so are the largest consumers of the social security budget. Contributions to the pension fund are in principle compulsory both for the employed and self-employed and are administered by autonomous offices, each responsible for a particular category of worker — blue-collar workers, white-collar workers, the self-employed in industry and commerce, and farmers. Other workers in the private sector not covered by one of these compulsory schemes have, as a rule, the option of joining a voluntary pension scheme. The unemployed are also covered provided that they were formerly in employment subject to one of the compulsory pensions. Civil servants are not provided for in this system, their retirement pensions being the responsibility of the federal, provincial or municipal government that employs them.

Benefits are paid almost exclusively in monetary form, *viz.* old age pensions for men over 65 and women over 60, disability pensions, and widows' and orphans' pensions. The amount of the pension is calculated from working income during the years immediately before retirement and the number of years' contributions. The maximum pension is just under 80 per cent of income earned during the last years of employment, with a maximum threshold. The widow's (widower's) pension is 60 per cent of the old age pension of the insured person.

Pensions are financed out of the contributions of persons currently in employment, and the contributions paid by their employer, as well as by federal government contributions (currently about 26 per cent for pension insurance as a whole). The federal government currently meets about 12 per cent of the total expenditure on pensions for employed persons, but finances about 70 per cent of pension insurance for the self-employed.

Although the age structure of the Austrian population has shifted since the mid-1970s towards the younger population groups (i.e. the dependency ratio has decreased), the financing problems have become noticeably more acute. The reasons for this are twofold. In the first place the rapid growth in the number of gainfully employed persons in the two previous decades has increased the number of persons now entitled to pensions, while the continuous development and improvement of the social system has given rise to new entitlements. On the other hand, the decline in economic growth since the first oil price shock (1973/74) and the related problems in the labour market means that as the number of pensioners has increased, so the number of contributors in active employment has fallen, relatively. In 1971, 1000 actively employed insured 'took care of' 488 pensioners; the corresponding ratio in 1981 was 1000:531. The direct result of this was that the federal government's subsidy increased, as it must by law meet any shortfall between expenditure and receipts from contributions. However, with persistently weak economic growth, the deficit in the federal government budget also grew, not least because of the effect of the 'automatic stabilisers', and since 1977 the federal government has endeavoured to increase its room for budgetary manoeuvre, for example by increasing employees' contributions. As a result, the federal government's subsidy fell from 34 per cent in 1977 to just under 22 per cent in 1981.

However, this did not solve the cash crisis, as one of the causes — the stagnation in economic growth — persisted. A further increase in contributions cannot be justified politically, and consequently, the strategy in recent years has been to ensure financing by short-term measures such as budgetary adjustments, while entitlement has by and large remained unchanged. In the longer term the pension system is to be financed by a general reform of the system which has been announced for the mid-1980s.

Unemployment benefits
Contributions to the unemployment benefit fund are a form of compulsory insurance and are paid equally by employer and employee.

Unlike the pensions described above though, unemployment benefit is not administered by different offices, but is the responsibility of the federal government. Unemployment benefit is paid for a maximum of 30 weeks, according to the duration of previous employment, and equals approximately 40 per cent of the gross earnings of previous employment. When entitlement lapses, the unemployed can draw supplementary benefit, the level of which is not (or only slightly) lower than that of unemployment benefit. Payment of supplementary benefit is means-tested, i.e. other income in the unemployed person's household is offset against it. The unemployment benefit fund also finances extended maternity leave allowance, i.e. the benefit payable to working women for up to 12 months after the birth of a child.

In the years of full employment there were hardly any problems for financing the unemployment benefit scheme. Benefits were raised, and contributions cut, but reserves still grew. And while full employment continued, reserves were used to finance other budget commitments (e.g. for pensions). With the increase in unemployment from the mid-1970s, financial reserves were soon exhausted and contributions were raised to their present level of 4 per cent. The federal government is not responsible for covering any shortfall between benefit payments and contributions as is the case with pensions, so that contributions have to be increased in line with expenditure.

Future developments and reform prospects
Pensions and unemployment benefits both face an urgent short-term problem of financing. While a number of other countries have made cuts in eligibility, economic policy in Austria has taken a different course: *deficits are to be limited primarily by maintaining a high level of employment; and benefits are to be guaranteed and maintained by increasing contributions or by higher budget deficits.*

This strategy seems desirable not only for reasons of social policy but also for economic policy, since cuts in benefits reduce overall consumer demand and so further aggravate the economic crisis. Every job lost means an increase in public expenditure (mainly in the form of assistance to the unemployed) and at the same time a loss of fiscal income (income tax, national insurance contributions). Comparison with other countries shows that financial problems in the social system cannot be solved by cuts in benefits and that Austria has been relatively successful in combating the consequences of the international recession. Therefore it seems important to continue giving priority to the preservation of full employment, and as a result to ensure that the financial basis for benefits is as broad as possible.

It can also be shown that with *the scope for redistribution on the whole becoming more restricted*, if social policy measures are to be as effective as possible the individual social policy instruments need to be assessed. This may mean the reduction or repeal of some benefits that have become obsolete, on the one hand, and that benefits that are inadequate should be increased, on the other. The central aim is not a desire to control welfare budgets, but rather to improve the efficiency of social policy measures. Accordingly, a balance has to be struck between the needs of the recipient and the burden imposed on contributors.

To strengthen the financial base, it is necessary to bear in mind the longer-term financial equilibrium of the social security budget. However advantageous the principle of adjusting current contributions to the level of current expenditure ('pay-as-you-go' system) may be for flexibility in the financing of social security budgets, its use limits the solution of the problem to the short term. Some of the problems of both the pension and unemployment funds have arisen through neglect of the longer-term aspects, the financial implications of gradual improvements in entitlements not always being taken fully into account.

The labour sector

Austrian experience has not differed from other countries as far as trends in the labour sector are concerned. Productivity has risen by about 200 per cent in the last 25 years; wages and thus material prosperity have grown in a similar proportion. Unlike other countries though, Austria had full employment until 1980, and since 1950 there have been no major strikes.

As already mentioned, most of the sociopolitical reforms of the Second Republic were implemented through consensus between the political parties and the social partners. That also applies to labour policy, and in particular to the Collective Labour Relations Act, which has regulated industrial relations in Austria since 1974 (e.g. elections for and the working procedure of the workers' representatives; workers' participation, etc.).

The Vocational Training Act 1969 codified the dual apprenticeship system in Austria (technical school concurrently with work). Small-scale industry and trade are still able to absorb large numbers of apprentices so that it has been possible to a large extent to avoid youth unemployment — in the narrower sense. The problem is shifted to the young skilled workers who have completed their training, since most of them are not kept on by the small-scale firms for longer than the apprenticeship period, and at the moment they have little chance of finding work elsewhere in industry.

Since the 1960s labour market policy has been directed not to paying unemployment benefits but rather to preventive measures to absorb short-term or seasonal fluctuations in employment, to solve longer-term structural and regional employment problems and to promote training and retraining. However, unemployment figures have grown in Austria as in other countries (1980, 1.5 per cent; 1981, 2.1 per cent; 1982, 3.7 per cent), making it necessary to revise labour market policy. Proposals range from lowering the age of retirement, to the promotion of alternative (self-managed) projects.

The health and safety of workers is ensured through government agencies (e.g. the labour inspectorate), non-governmental institutions at inter-enterprise level (e.g. the general accident insurance institutions, industrial medicine centres) and facilities at enterprise level (e.g. the provision of medical staff in factories). Until 1973, there were very few binding regulations for the provision of medical services at the enterprise level. However, even after the Workers' Protection Act 1973 was passed, the situation remained extremely unsatisfactory. The most recent amendment to the Act includes a wide variety of additional provisions but grounds for criticism remain.

Sociopolitical prospects

The future is likely to be characterised by low or no economic growth and rising unemployment — in Austria as in other countries. Conflicts about the distribution of incomes and social problems will therefore continue to increase.

The future of the welfare state and of social security policy in Austria should be considered first from the standpoint of its *industrial background*. The model of cooperation between government, employers' and employees' associations (the social partnership) will continue in the coming years and will help to contain the situation. However, this system of cooperation will probably be affected by increased tensions and problems, since the social partnership was originally oriented towards economic growth, which was expected to provide the framework for the solution of social problems. Persistent economic stagnation now jeopardises this system, as do the increasingly vociferous demands for stricter environmental protection, including a ban on the use of nuclear power, and limitation of arms production. On these points there are opposing views between the social partners on the one side and certain groups cutting across all party and association lines on the other. Nevertheless, there are good prospects that, in view of Austria's traditional willingness to compromise these new movements can be integrated into the associations and political parties and possibly also into the social partnership system too.

It should be pointed out that Austria is also one of the countries in which there are intensive discussions about new approaches to *self-organisation* and *self-administration*, i.e. self-organisation in the social services, new approaches to self-management in enterprises (production cooperatives) and in general efforts towards some degree of decentralisation of industrial relations. However, in view of the fact that conditions in Austria are traditionally favourable to centralisation, these trends will probably continue to be of only relatively minor importance in the future. In the economic and social sectors Austria still has an 'interventionist market economy system'. This means there is even less expectation than in other countries that market forces will play a primary role in improving the economy — the view being, on the contrary, that appropriate intervention by the government and the employers' and employees' associations is necessary to maintain a balanced society.

But the central effort to maintain the welfare state in Austria will still be the aim of *maintaining a high level of employment*. Employment policy has three strategies. First, *intensifying public sector capital investment and employment programmes*. For instance, in the recent past, federal government employment programmes have been adopted to improve the infrastructure: public transport, energy (district heating), urban renewal and housing construction; as well as extensive additional capital investment and a job-creation programme which in turn are directed towards the improvement of the economy. In labour-market policy on the other hand, the focus is on marginal groups: youth, disabled persons and women. Also, a general *reduction in the number of foreign workers* is taking place by not granting work permits to new applicants, but giving special protection to workers who have already been in Austria for a long time and to their children who have grown up in Austria.

The second line of employment policy is the *reduction of the working week*. In 1975 the last stage of introducing the 40-hour week was completed, and in 1977 annual paid holidays were extended. In addition, early retirement was facilitated so that men threatened with unemployment can retire at 59 and women at 54, while night-shift workers can retire at 57. Furthermore, the qualifications for disability pensions have been relaxed. The Austrian parliament has now adopted a further extension of annual holidays, to be introduced in stages between 1984 and 1986. Other measures under discussion are further reductions in the working week and restrictions on overtime, as well as extending compulsory education.

The third line of employment policy is *incomes policy*. This entails a wages and prices policy by the social partners geared to macro-economic conditions that will help maintain Austria's international competitiveness and keep the inflation rate low and the balance of payments healthy, despite the public sector measures taken with regard to the length of the working week.

As far as *social security* is concerned, it should first be pointed out that Austria has a high level of social expenditures by international standards. The substantial expansion of the social security system is now more or less concluded. But the view of all political forces seems to be to safeguard what has been accomplished. As a result, it is not new overall provisions that are in the foreground of interest but rather improvements in the quality of benefits in certain areas and for the individual. This applies in particular to the prevention of sickness, accidents and disabilities. In the health sector, rationalisations are in the foreground (e.g. improved efficiency in hospitals in order to reduce costs).

In the case of social benefits in general, one principle is that existing rights should not be cut. Additional benefits, however, are to be scrutinised in the future. This reconsideration of benefits will take place mainly in cases where an insured person has more than one source of income (e.g. two or more pensions, or pension plus an earned income). These limited curtailments will not solve the future financial problems of social insurance, so these will probably have to be met from increased contributions.

The development of social services financed by the provincial governments is also likely to be continued, but at a slower pace. In this case as well, closer concentration on qualitative aspects can be expected.

In the labour sector, the situation of working women is to be improved. An Equal Opportunities Act was adopted some time ago and an Equal Opportunities Commission has been set up. It is intended to standardise and improve judicial procedures in all social matters and to codify all laws on labour and social matters.

On the whole, social progress will, in the future, proceed at a slower pace than before and safeguarding what has been accomplished will take priority over the creation of new social programmes. In addition, the efficiency of the various social benefits will have to be scrutinised more closely than before, not only from the economic and financial perspective but also from the social point of view.

Conclusions

In terms of the distinction between pluralist and corporatist welfare states (see Chapter 2), there can be no doubt that Austria is subsumed under the corporatist paradigm. Economy regulations are both demand- and supply-oriented, functional relations between the economic and social sectors are clearly recognised, and class cooperation and consensus are safeguarded by the institution of the social partnership.

In comparison with other countries, Austria managed the first seven years of the international economic crisis quite well on the basis of this system. Since 1981, the economic situation has also been deteriorating in Austria, unemployment figures are rising, and it is becoming increasingly difficult to improve or, in some cases, to maintain the social and welfare standards achieved in the post-war period. The future development will very much depend on economic recovery at the international level.

Nevertheless, Austria is often referred to as a 'success story' or a 'model' which could be adopted in other countries. However, one should be cautious of promoting the transfer of experiences from one country to another. Austria's success, which started after the end of the war, and which was preceded by a most unhappy history between 1918 and 1945, was both a product of conscious action of the political actors and of favourable circumstances as well as of some of the special characteristics of the country (small size, geographical position, economic structure, large nationalised sector, etc.).

In this sense, Austria has a unique configuration, and therefore its response to the challenges of the current structural crisis is not necessarily applicable to other countries. In addition, the authors are aware of the fact that highly corporatist political systems such as Austria's, tend to promote pragmatic, but not ideological approaches; incremental or decremental, but not structural changes; authoritarian, bureaucratic and centralised solutions, but not popular participation; conservation, but not innovation. One could, however, imagine that the future economic and social development in Austria will demand a different type of crisis management, namely, selection among controversial political options, fundamental and comprehensive restructuring of the economy and the welfare sector as well as integration of traditional and newly-emerging social forces through participation. In this case, it would not be legitimate merely to extrapolate the smooth development of the Austrian system for the years to come.

Notes

1. This paper was prepared under the coordinating sponsorship of the European Centre for Social Welfare Training and Research. The authors, however, are giving their own opinions.
2. For more details see: Bundesministerium für soziale Verwaltung (ed.) (1982), *Soziale Struktur Österreichs*, Vienna; Fischer, Heinz (ed.) (1982), *Das politische System Österreichs*, Vienna; Fischer-Kowalski, Marina and Josef, Buček (eds) (1980), *Lebensverhältnisse in Österreich*, Frankfurt, New York; OECD (1981), *Integrated Social Policy, a Review of the Austrian Experience*, Paris; Reithofer, Hans (1979), 'Sozialstaat Österreich', in *Zeitgeschichte*, Österreichische Gesellschaft, Vienna, April; Reithofer, Hans (1982), 'Sozialstaat Österreich', in *Zeitgeschichte*, Österreichischer, Bundesverlag, Vienna; Talos, Emmerich (1981), *Staatliche Sozialpolitik in Österreich: Rekonstruktion und Analyse*, Vienna; Weinzierl, Erika and Kurt, Skalnik (eds) (1972), *Österreich: die Zweite Republik*, Graz, Vienna, Cologne.
3. OECD, *Integrated Social Policy*, op.cit.; Reithofer, Hans (1978), *Die ausgleichende Gesellschaft*, Vienna.
4. For more details see also: Bundesministerium für soziale Verwaltung (ed.), op.cit.; Bundespressedienst und Österreichischer Verband der Sozialversicherungsanstalten: *Soziale Sicherheit in Österreich*, Vienna, 1980; Holzmann, Robert (1979), *Quantitative Sozialpolitik, Finanzsystem und Pensionsversicherung*, Vienna; Mandl, Christoph (ed.) (1982), *Österreich — Prognosen bis zum Jahr 2000*, Munich.
5. Report and submission of the Finance and Budget Committee, no. 419 of the annexes to the verbatim record of the Proceedings of the Austrian *Nationalrat* (Lower Chamber of Parliament) VII G.P. (consultations regarding the adoption of the Family Allowance Fund Act of 1954).

6. Münz, Rainer (1980), 'Familienpolitik. Eine Einschätzung konkreter Massnahmen', in Institut für Demographie (ed.), *Kinderwünsche junger Österreicherinnen*, Vienna, 107—22; Münz, Rainer, 'Familienorientierte Verteilungspolitik', in Fischer-Kowalski and Buček, op.cit., 115—28.
7. See note 5 above.
8. Münz, Rainer (1982), 'Quantitative Aspects of Family Policies in Austria', in *International Social Security Review*, March, 302—18.
9. Bundesministerium für Finanzen (ed.) (1980), *Auf dem Weg in ein neues Jahrzehnt. Der Bundeshaushalt 1980*, Vienna.
10. Bundesministerium für soziale Verwaltung, op.cit.; Rainer, op.cit.
11. Kitzmantel, Edith (1979), *Steuern — wer sie zahlt, wer sie trägt*, Vienna: Bundesministerium für Finanzen; Rainer, op.cit.; OECD (1976), *Public Expenditure on Income Maintenance Programmes. Studies in Resource Allocation*, no. 3, Paris.
12. In 1970, the dependency ratio represented by children reached its highest value after 1945, with 44.3 inhabitants under 15 per 100 inhabitants between 15 and 60; in 1983 the ratio was only 31.5 per 100 15 to 60 year olds (Findl, Peter (1982), 'Bevölkerungsprognose des Österreichischen Statistischen Zentralamtes für Österreich 1982—2010', in *Statistische Nachrichten*, October, 540—6). No comparable reduction is to be expected in the 1980s and 1990s.

13 Debureaucratisation and the Self-Help Movement: Towards a Restructuring of the Welfare State in the Federal Republic of Germany?
Dieter Grunow

Introduction

It is not just fiscal crisis which increasingly puts the welfare state on trial. Often there is sufficient money available to finance the welfare state, but it is syphoned into other channels (e.g. defence budgets). The efficiency, effectiveness and responsiveness of welfare state provisions have been questioned, and the deficiencies in its problem-solving and legitimacy have been criticised. All of which has encouraged influential sectors in West Germany who favour the abolition of the welfare system entirely, rather than reductions in social expenditures. Reductions have been made in recent years, but the abolition aims at a universal eradication of statutory entitlements.

Two trends in the recent public debate and in practical experience seem to reinforce this notion: demands for 'debureaucratisation' and the growth of the self-help movement. These trends will be analysed more closely and it will be shown that they do *not* indicate the end of the welfare state in Germany as some groups assert. But they are important and effective catalysts of a *re*structuring of the future welfare state which builds upon the achievements of the last 100 years of welfare development in Germany.

The situation seems paradoxical: at a time of *economic* crisis in almost all western industrial countries, public debate and scientific argument are focusing on the crisis or even on the end of the *welfare state*. During a time of economic recession, massive structural changes in the industrial system, and consequent high unemployment rates, the welfare system seems to be at risk as if the recent economic problems were a test or a proof of the functioning of the welfare state. As we witness the adoption of such views in decision-making processes in some western countries (especially the UK and the US), a self-fulfilling prophecy unfolds: by emphasising malfunctions in the welfare system, a legitimation is sought to withdraw resources from the system which will bring about the perceived negative results. It is therefore the predominant task of the social sciences to draw a line between facts and fiction contributing to the discussion about the future of the welfare state. Here we shall concentrate on the situation in West Germany where the social security system recently celebrated its centenary. This means that we shall argue about a country in which a high degree of state responsibility and legal accountability for social security have been developed.

Criticism of the welfare state

Although state responsibility for the development of the welfare system in West Germany was reaffirmed in the constitution after the second world war, there have always been criticisms of the development of the welfare state. Two lines of criticism can be distinguished: on the one hand, an ideological criticism of the principle of the welfare state in general; and, on the other, a criticism of the functioning of the welfare system in practice. Whereas the second criticism developed in line with changes in the system itself, ideological opposition to welfare has not changed much during the last 100 years. When the social insurance system was first introduced, it was immediately argued by the conservatives that it would ultimately lead to a socialist government. The Social Democrats were afraid of losing the support of the union-oriented workers and preferred to expand the self-governed health cooperatives they had already established, rather than expanding social insurance into health insurance.

In the discussion and criticisms today we can see the main arguments follow these same traditional perspectives:

(1) For authors in the tradition of the liberal—conservative perspective, the development of the welfare state restricts individual freedom and increases the danger of overwhelming bureaucratic power centres in society (de Tocqueville 1956).

(2) For authors following a Marxian perspective, the welfare state has long been seen as an inadequate device for solving economic inequality, as it does not interfere with the private ownership of the means of production. Such authors have been predicting the crisis in or the end of the welfare state for years because the function of universal welfare and the function of realising preconditions for profitable capital investment are (seen as) incompatible (Offe 1969).

(3) For authors in the Durkheimian tradition the welfare state is an inadequate solution to the problems of social and moral integration of all members of society; the welfare state, to the contrary, seems to increase the erosion of intermediate structures and primary social networks (Durkheim 1893, 1964).

At a more pragmatic level, in the debate on the expansion of the welfare system — which in general is seen as necessary — the following arguments dominate in Germany:

(1)   Social policies for social security have been oriented too much to an income strategy and too little to a personal service strategy (Badura and Gross 1976).

(2)   Social policies for social security have been oriented too much to the equivalence principle and too little to a demand principle (von Ferber and Kaufmann 1977); i.e. they ignore differences of need and demand in different groups of the population.

(3)   Social policies for health insurance have been guided too much by legalistic and monetary considerations of health care and medical treatment, and have been oriented too little to the impact of services and treatments delivered (von Ferber and von Ferber 1978), thus lacking the necessary responsiveness to patients' needs.

(4)   The administration of the different social security systems does not function adequately, thereby giving ever more room to interventions by the powerful interest groups (professions, pharmaceutical industry, etc.) (Sozialpolitik und Sozialverwaltung 1978).

(5)   The lack of cost-consciousness of the participants in the welfare system — especially the powerful interest groups — has led to a situation where the financial basis of the welfare system is in danger of collapsing.

Altogether, social policy has tended to be reactive: it lacks responsiveness to clients' needs and flexibility to accommodate new developments, needs and demands, and to adapt to more economical and efficient forms of problem-solving.

In the last few decades sociologists working from an academic framework have described quite clearly the problems and deficits of a social policy that is based on the ideology of the market economy. They have shown how a lack of impact-orientation and disregard of 'secondary' inequality and disparity of public support and services are *produced by social policy itself* (Achinger 1958; von Ferber 1967; Widmaier 1976). From this point of view sociologists ask for a thorough evaluation of service and support systems in relation to intended goal fulfilment and cost-consciousness.

But in spite of all these critical comments the welfare state has always had overwhelming support from the various political forces which contributed to its development, because of its widespread coverage of social needs and the many vested interests of service providers and managers; and because it served as a major tool for the stabilisation or expansion of the constituencies of the political parties (Alber 1980).

Recent signs of a crisis in the welfare state in West Germany

Although there are many different approaches to understanding the welfare system in Germany, most authors agree upon four important functions of the welfare state (Flora 1979):

(1) balancing economic growth and social welfare by an efficient redistribution system;
(2) stabilising the legitimacy of the political and administrative institutions;
(3) reducing social conflicts; and
(4) integrating minority and marginal groups into society.

Taking these functions as a starting point for our analysis, a crisis of the welfare state can be diagnosed if these functions cease to be fulfilled or if the development of the welfare system becomes counterproductive with regard to these functions. 'Crisis', in this sense, does not mean 'malfunctioning' but *a lack of problem-solving capacity* which can only be overcome by a radical restructuring of at least parts of the welfare system.

Signs of such a development have been observed since the mid-1970s. Initially, this was seen as a response to the 1973/74 oil crisis: the problems were defined in financial terms: cost increases could not be covered by the growth of GNP. In addition, there was severe disappointment about the marginal redistributional results of public transfer payments, especially in terms of the redistribution of property. The main reactions to these financial problems were (and still are) passive or regressive, in the sense that the former expansion of the welfare system was now reversed: benefits were cut; a number of services were abolished; the scope of entitlements was reduced; and the quality of services declined. Politicians showed little initiative. If one sees the welfare *crisis* as an increasing discrepancy between societal problems and the tools at hand to solve them, this demands the potential for *major transformations* in the welfare system. *Ad hoc* financing changes — spending or expanding financial support according to short-term (opportunistic) goals — undermine public support for the welfare system, and reduce the basis of legitimacy of the politico-administrative system as such.

An example from pension insurance can be used as an illustration:

In 1978, 53 per cent of the population aged 18 to 65 were afraid that pension insurance was an institution which could suddenly deteriorate. 35 per cent thought that one could totally rely on this institution, and 12 per cent had no opinion about it. Compared with the year 1967, when a similar survey had taken place, this shows a clear change in the climate of confidence. At that time, only 33 per cent were afraid that their pension could suddenly deteriorate, while 47 per cent thought they could rely on it. 20 per cent had no opinion at this time.

> This scepticism corresponds also to the opinion of a majority of the questioned population that pensions would increase less during the next years. 75 per cent had this opinion whereas only 10 per cent thought that during the next years pensions would increase as much as before. 8 per cent of the interviewed persons even thought that pensions would not be increased at all for the next one or two years. Just a little less than two years before, only 54 per cent had the opinion that pensions would rise less during the next years, whereas 28 per cent thought that during the next years pensions would be adjusted as before. (Umfrage 1978: 253)

Such a change of attitude in the light of the current discussion about pensions is very plausible because there is little public understanding of the financial structure of the pension system and little confidence in the abilities of the responsible institutions to solve problems. A survey showed that:

> According to the opinion of 75.8 per cent of the population aged between 18 and 65 years, the security of pensions depends essentially on the economic situation of the Federal Republic, 58.5 per cent thought it depended on how much work will be done in the future, 49.3 per cent think it to be dependent on the federal government, 45.8 per cent mention the situation of the world economic system, 22.2 per cent the employers and industrialists, 21.4 per cent the trade unions, and 21.4 per cent the political opposition as factors which promote this development. (Umfrage 1978: 253)

In public discussion as well as in the published literature the main focus is on the economic situation; very seldom are the modalities of retirement or the quality of service delivery considered. Rather emphasis is placed on the perceived insolvency of the insurance institutions, the increases in contributions, and the freezing of pension rates, and so forth. Thus in 1967 62 per cent of the citizens interviewed recommended a *dynamic pension* (i.e. an annual increase in pensions in line with increases of the GNP); and 29 per cent the traditional settlement of pensions (*Jahrbuch* 1974: 410). In the same year 48 per cent of the people interviewed supported an increase of pensions linked to economic growth; 31 per cent thought that pensions should be linked to the cost of living. About ten years later (1976), 51 per cent of the population (and 70 per cent of the pensioners interviewed) believed that pensions should be increased as in the past in spite of financial problems; 36 per cent believed that pensions should be supplemented by personal savings. However, only 28 per cent expected pensions to increase at the same rate as before (*Jahrbuch* 1974: 174). Put another way, 49 per cent believed 'that one need not worry about the possibility of getting less than expected on reaching retirement age' (EMNID 1977).

The same shifts in attitude are shown in regard to other functions of the welfare state in:

(1) the increasing number of protest groups (*Bürgerinitiativen*);

(2)   the widespread conflicts about the criteria for the distribution of scarce resources, leading to new allocation processes which hit the lower strata of society the hardest; and

(3)   the increasing hostility against foreign workers (*Gastarbeiter*), people seeking political asylum from the Eastern bloc, and other minority groups who are believed to take a disproportionate share of welfare benefits.

So far these trends have been moderated in West Germany by the general support for the welfare system by the public at large. In a study on 'Citizens and the Welfare State' (1978), between 70 and 90 per cent (depending on the form of question asked) of interviewees said they were in favour of the welfare system, believed in its stability, and were willing to pay for it. In a later study (1980), 44 per cent were said to be in favour of even more state social security, whereas 56 per cent preferred more individual initiative and self-reliance (Lebensziele 1981). Thus, there is evidence that the German population in general supports the existing welfare system. But, at the same time, there is increasing evidence that *many people would support changes in the system if this would help fulfil its overall functions.*

It can be argued that the politico-administrative system has not taken the initiative to bring about such changes in a constructive or creative way. From the financial crisis perspective the alternatives have been to punish 'social security scroungers' and to cut back the content, level and quality of services and eligibility to welfare benefits. Although there have been many counter-proposals to develop a more active, preventive and outcome-oriented social policy, actions taken fall far short of potential. The time for reflective and well-planned action is diminishing and *ad hoc* crisis management seems to be the order of the day: laws are repealed, re-enacted, and amended again.

Debureaucratisation and the self-help movement as new elements in the welfare state

It is difficult to define the relationship between the symptoms of crisis in West Germany on the one hand, and political actions taken, on the other. It could be argued that there is no crisis in the system yet, in spite of the budgetary problems in the pension system, the health insurance system, and, increasingly, in the unemployment insurance system. 'Muddling through' is still seen as a sufficient reaction to the problems. It appears that a still powerful coalition exists which supports this muddling-through politics (a 'technocratic-étatist' option) for future developments. This comprises (1) large parts of the Social-Democratic Party who still follow a Keynesian-type fiscal and economic policy of state intervention which tries to balance investment with the growth and modernisation of the economy and the moderate reduction (but general preservation) of the welfare system; (2) the professional groups which profit most from the existing welfare system are afraid of major structural changes; (3) the union representatives of those public employees who might be affected by, and so are reluctant to see major changes in, the welfare system; and finally (4) the large non-profit-making voluntary welfare organisations which carry out important parts of social service provision and depend on public finance.

From the perspective of their ideological orientation, these interest groups form an 'unholy alliance' — 'unholy' because their motives and aims are very different. The same holds true in regard to two recent developments in West Germany: the demands for the 'debureaucrati-sation' of the welfare state, and the emergence of the self-help movement. Independent of the origin of those notions, they are used as an argument for an incremental contraction of the welfare state by different interest groups with partially opposing aims. The advantage of using these 'catch words' in favour of a radical reduction or even the abolition of the welfare state lies in the high acceptance and general support those issues thus receive. In addition, a two-pronged attack is self-reinforcing and so further underlines the demand for a reduction in public responsibility for the welfare and well-being of the population.

The concept of *'debureaucratisation'* includes:

(1) A criticism of the day-to-day practices of public institutions — their location, opening hours, complex administrative procedures, unfriendliness, and the like. Such criticisms are voiced by protest groups and the general public, as well as by small-scale industries.

(2) Criticism of the administrative system — its organisational and interorganisational structures, general inflexibility, lack of co-ordination between departments, and the like. This is voiced by all political parties though from different points of view (e.g. for inefficiency, lack of data protection, lack of problem-solving capacity), and by public-funded organisations (e.g. voluntary welfare organisations).

(3) Criticism of the increase in rules and regulations, as well as of the increase of budgets in the public sector. The most important aspect here are the arguments against state intervention in (profitable) private economy (i.e. against consumer protection legislation, restrictions relating to the working conditions of young people, costs which firms have to incur as a result of welfare programmes, and the like). This criticism is voiced by the conservative parties and the business community specifically, and by the public generally.

(4) Finally, criticism of the extent of state intervention in all spheres

of life especially of its expanded welfare functions. This is voiced by many powerful groups from their own perspective — e.g. the 'power of the unions', the 'power of big business', or the 'therapeutic role of the social administrators' are amongst the conflicting definitions of the situation.

The advantage of using the 'umbrella' term *debureaucratisation* for a heterogeneous concept lies in the overwhelming public acceptance it receives. The hopes which the word carries for those in favour of the dismantling of the welfare state are based on a multiplicity of arguments attacking welfare provisions. Although many of these arguments seem remote from welfare issues, they are important components of a perspective which we have called the 'neo-liberalist—authoritarian state option', which seeks to reduce state functions to the policing and control, and needs to enhance the 'freedom' of private capital. The main target of debureaucratisation are the welfare functions of the state, especially in those areas where they conflict with private enterprise interests.

The second development, the self-help movement, seems to supplement and reinforce these goals, since a decrease in *public* welfare responsibility seems to lead to the expanding of *self-help* activities. Although the movement tends towards anti-*état*ist ('alternative') options, the individual actions have very diverse perspectives and goals. Again though, the all-encompassing term 'self-help' is conducive to its significance in public debate. Because of its non-specificity it seems to fit with the aims of debureaucratisation.

Much deliberation is spent on the question of whether the shortfall in the budget of public institutions — as a result of cutbacks — can be bridged by individual self-help. The opposition to such cutbacks — which are partly associated with job losses amongst the professional groups — has raised the question in the medical profession of why some strata of the population do not visit a doctor or do not follow medical advice. In this field, professional interest is directed towards *increasing* the use of this professional service. Other interest groups (e.g. pharmacists and the pharmaceutical industry) are not opposed to this kind of self-help (i.e. self-medication) provided the consumption of self-prescribed medicines increases. Similarly — *alternative medicine* — chiropractors, acupuncturists, herbalists, faith-healers, astrologers, and so forth, profit from 'self-help', and try to direct the discussion towards their more esoteric forms of self-help. Finally, there are those groups which see self-medical help as a golden opportunity to abolish excessive technocracy and expertise, and to develop alternative life-styles. (For further details see Grunow (1981: 125ff).)

In spite of these wide-ranging perspectives, the self-help movement is increasingly used as a legitimation for the cutbacks in welfare benefits, especially in the provision of the social and health services (organised and/or financed by the state). The main front of the 'attack' is directed at the heart of the recent developments of the welfare state: the personal (professional) services.

This attempt to dismantle public social services on a large scale (by referring to the self-help movement) can be seen as an attack on the welfare functions of the state in general. As this is put forward by very powerful groups in Germany (which do not necessarily support the 'alternative' goals of the self-help movement, but 'profit' from their criticisms) it is difficult to question successfully the assumptions of these propositions. Data from a recent study throw some light on the question. In a representative survey of German households it was found: (1) that only 3.2 per cent of the population have experienced self-help groups; (2) that most of those in favour of self-help are middle-class; (3) that most of the people who use self-help groups do not see them as an alternative, but as an important *addition* to the public services; and (4) that in spite of all the talk about excesses and misuse of the social and health services, three-quarters of all social and health complaints are met by primary helpers — e.g. 80 per cent of the bedridden are cared for in the family home; only 5 per cent of whom use additional out-patient nursing services.

These as well as many other data can be cited to contradict the claim that the self-help movement could become another step towards the undermining of the welfare system and hence the welfare state.

In sum, we have identified three different options towards the further development of the welfare state. The first follows a line of incremental changes — reducing welfare provisions, and increasing control over welfare delivery. The two others seek a reduction in the welfare state in the sense of limiting state responsibility for social security. Debureaucratisation and the self-help movement are (especially in combination) influential options, because they do not just refer to the growing financial problems, but also imply a fundamental criticism of the concept of the welfare state. Hegner (1979) describes these as the result of the inability of the system to change its basic structures without massive external pressure.

But, in spite of all the ideological claims, the two options do not justify such far-reaching hopes (or fears) about the future, i.e. the end of the welfare state. Even within each option, very different motives and aims are represented, each using the political appeal of debureaucratisation and the self-help movement for their own ends — which might eventually be opposed to each other. In addition, there is still overwhelming public support for the welfare state in Germany, which is seen as an historic national achievement. This makes it all the more plausible to see these new trends *as initiatives toward a transformation of the welfare state*, for instance: by decentralisation; by making it more responsive to the changing needs and demands of its clients; by supporting the 'co-production' of services and the self-assertion of its clientele, thus reducing the power of the professionals; by abolishing ineffective services; and by reducing future demands and costs. There are signs that, while supporting the concept of social welfare, the German people are increasingly interested in a change in its modes of operation. This makes it worthwhile observing more closely some of the recent reform initiatives as well as the concrete propositions (or implications) of debureaucratisation and the self-help movement in search of (possible) catalysts for future developments.

Debureaucratisation and the self-help movement as strategies for modernising the welfare state

The crisis symptoms described above should be seen as a starting point for the restructuring of the welfare system. Although the financial problems in West Germany are not yet severe enough to *force* political action, some steps towards remodelling have been made already:

(1)   Certain laws and regulations relating to the welfare system have been integrated into a 'Social Legislation Book' (*Sozialgesetzbuch*). This has strengthened the position of the 'clients' of the welfare system.

(2)   A commission has been set up to investigate new proposals for the pension scheme. A likely outcome is the ending of discrimination against women, thereby strengthening their position.

(3)   In unemployment offices emphasis used to be given to the counselling and retraining of the unemployed, instead of simply paying out unemployment benefits. This has now been reversed because of the recent increase in unemployment, and the staff are now predominantly occupied with the administration of unemployment benefits.

(4)   In long-term geriatric and psychiatric institutions, attempts have been made to reduce the number of, or abolish, those which had the characteristics of a custodial institution.

So far, minor reforms have had only a slight impact on the overall structure of the German welfare system. However, with debureaucratisation and self-help the promotion of structural changes could be quite drastic.

The self-help movement has potentially three basic functions:

(1)   to develop new forms of dealing with personal or social problems in primary social groups, the main purpose being mutual help between those who share the same problem.

(2)   for the individual to become aware of personal or social competence in dealing with health and social problems; i.e. the competence

of the layman is set against professional expertise. (This does not mean — as Illich (1976) supposed — that everybody becomes an expert.)

(3)   to force the institutions to become more responsive to clients' needs. The self-assertion of the clients of the welfare system is not only applied to their capability of solving their health and social problems, but also used in contact with institutions and professionals organising and delivering welfare services and benefits.

Although only 3 per cent of the German population are members of self-help groups, about one-third of the population said, in our household survey, that they were interested and might become members of such groups. The major motives for participation were: (i) to receive and give help to people with similar problems; (ii) to help people in need; (iii) to do something useful for society; and (iv) to limit bureaucratic and professional inflexibility and arrogance, which is seen as endemic in the welfare system.

These arguments demonstrate that it is not sufficient simply to add alternative modes of dealing with health and social problems in society, if what is needed is a restructuring of the welfare system. Self-help groups and similar micro-social arrangements have to influence the relationship between the layman and the professions (or institutions) directly or indirectly, through intelligent non-compliance against professional advice and through a more active and self-assertive role when in contact with professionals. The self-help movement can thus help increase effectiveness and responsiveness to clients' needs; and should in the long term lead to cost-effectiveness in the welfare system as well.

The difficulties of overcoming the expensive, largely ineffective and arrogant professional service delivery are intensified by the welfare bureaucracy which, in general, endorses the professional system. Thus, the debureaucratisation of centralised welfare institutions (e.g. the pension system for employees is administered by a central agency in West Berlin, with some thousands of employees) is an important prerequisite for the restructuring of the welfare system. Debureaucratisation does not mean transfering the welfare mechanisms to the free market. It is used here in the *sociological* sense of structural and procedural dimensions of bureaucratic organisations and their asymmetric power relationships with their environment. Debureaucratisation means decentralisation, deconcentration, more discretion for the 'street-level bureaucrats'; flexible forms of work (part-time jobs, cooperation between professionals and non-professionals, etc.); responsiveness to the demands of the public; participation and co-production as accepted principles, and so forth. Instead of bureaucratising (co-operating) existing organisations, the advantages of *different organisational types* responsible for service delivery could be acknow-ledged; especially the potential cooperation between professionals and non-professionals, full- and part-time employees, employees and volun-teers, and hierarchical and egalitarian organisations.

Initiatives towards debureaucratisation have made little progress so far. This is probably the consequence of the absurdity of asking the bureaucrats themselves to develop plans for debureaucratisation. Although there are many commissions at all government levels dis-cussing the possibilities of debureaucratisation, another political and/or financial push may be necessary to enforce a restructuring. Also, it is important that the concepts of self-help and debureaucratisation be strengthened and consolidated rationally. At the same time, those pro-positions can be questioned or refused (on the basis of the empirical evidence) which see the crisis symptoms of the welfare state as the beginning of its end, foresee the massive decline of state responsibility for many welfare benefits and services, and predict the reintroduction of the 'survival of the fittest' principle.

If the self-help movement becomes less associated with an image of a life-style of 'dropouts' on the one hand, and if traditional forms of self-help (i.e. within the family) can overcome its specific sex-related bias (as *female* self-help) on the other hand, its impact is likely to increase. These developments could help bring about a reconstruction of the welfare system: from a system 'on behalf of' the population to a system 'with and by' the population. New ways to constitute such a system have to be invented; and old ways may be rediscovered in this process. It is a challenge to look more closely at those countries which are in other phases of welfare development and which so far have been ignored because of their supposed backwardness in these affairs. Instead of trying to abolish the existing welfare state in industrialised countries, a new form could be developed by referring to recent experiences that very different countries have.

References

Achinger, H. (1958), *Sozialpolitik als Gesellschaftspolitik*, Reinbek: Rowohlt.
Alber, J. (1980), 'Der Wohlfahrtsstaat in der Krise? Eine Bilanz nach drei Jahr-zehnten Sozialpolitik in der Bundesrepublik', *Zeitschrift für Soziologie 9*, 313—42.
Badura, B. and Gross, P. (1976), *Sozialpolitische Perspektiven*, Munich: Piper.
Breitkopf, H. and Grunow, D. (1980), *Selbsthilfe im Gesundheitswesen: Einstel-lungen, Verhalten und strukturelle Rahmenbedingungen*, Bielefeld: Kleine-Verlag.
Bürger und Sozialstaat (1978), *Repräsentativerhebung im Auftrag des BMA*, Munich.
Durkheim, E. (1983), (1964), 'The Division of Labour in Society', in K. Thompson (ed.), *Sociological Perspectives*, Harmondsworth: Penguin Books, 94—105.
EMNID (1977) *Erhebungen*, EMNID-Informationen 11/12, 29.
von Ferber, Chr. (1967), *Sozialpolitik in der Wohlstandsgesellschaft*, Hamburg: Wegner.

von Ferber, Chr. and von Ferber, L. (1978), *Der kranke Mensch in der Gesellschaft*, Reinbek: Rowohlt.

von Ferber, Chr. and Kaufmann, F.-X. (eds) (1977), *Soziologie und Sozialpolitik*, Opladen: Westdeutscher Verlag.

Flora, P. (1979), 'Krisenbewältigung oder Krisenerzeugung? Der Wohlfahrtsstaat in historischer Perspektive', in J. Matthes (ed.), *Sozialer Wandel in Westeuropa*, Frankfurt: Campus, 82–136.

Grunow, D. (1981), 'Formen sozialer Alltäglichkeit: Selbsthilfe im Gesundheitswesen', in B. Badura and Chr. von Ferber (eds), *Selbsthilfe und Selbstorganisation im Gesundheitswesen*, Munich: Oldenbourg, 125–46.

Grunow, D. (1982), *Bürokratisierung und Debürokratisierung im Wohlfahrtsstaat: Soziologische Analysen eines gesellschaftlichen Problems, Habilitation*, Bielefeld.

Grunow, D. *et al.* (1983), *Gesundheitsselbsthilfe im Alltag: Ergebnisse einer repräsentativen Haushaltsbefragung über gesundheitsbezogene Selbsthilfeerfahrungen und -potentiale*, Stuttgart: Enke.

Halmos, P. (1975), *The Personal Service Society*, London: Constable.

Hegner, F. (1979), *Praxisbezogene Orientierungspunkte für notwendige Änderungen im System der sozialen Sicherung: Bürgernähe, Sozialbürgerrolle und soziale Aktion*, Bielefeld: Kleine-Verlag.

Illich, I.D. (1976), *Limits to Medicine: Medical Nemesis. The Expropriation of Health*, London: Boyars.

Jahrbuch (1974), *Jahrbuch der öffentlichen Meinung 1968–1973 (Allensbach)*, Bonn.

Lebensziele (1981), *Potentiale und Trends alternativen Verhaltens 1980*, Cologne: Zentralarchiv für empirische Sozialforschung.

Offe, C. (1969), 'Politische Herrschaft und Klassenstrukturen: Zur Analyse spätkapitalistischer Gesellschaftsstrukturen', in G. Kress and D. Senghaas (eds), *Politikwissenschaft: Eine Einführung in ihre Probleme*, Frankfurt: Europäische Verlagsanstalt, 156–89.

Soziale Sicherung (1977), Bonn.

Sozialpolitik und Sozialverwaltung (1978), *Zur Demokratisierung des Sozialstaates*, WSI-Studie 35, Cologne.

Strasser, J. (1979), *Grenzen des Sozialstaats? Soziale Sicherung in der Wachstumskrise*, Frankfurt: Europäische Verlagsanstalt.

de Tocqueville, A. (1956), *Über die Demokratie in Amerika*, Frankfurt: Fischer.

Umfrage (1979), 'Auswirkung der Rentendiskussion', *Arbeit und Sozialpolitik* 7, 253.

Widmaier, H.P. (1976), *Sozialpolitik im Wohlfahrtsstaat*, Reinbek: Rowohlt.

14 Kenya and the Future of the Welfare State
Roberta M. Mutiso

The concept of the welfare state is not normally applied to countries in Africa, Asia and Latin America. The term is used almost exclusively to describe countries in Western Europe, North America, Great Britain and parts of the Commonwealth that are thought to share a particular constellation of economic, political and social characteristics and to have passed through roughly similar historical circumstances which collectively differentiate them from other parts of the world.

This approach to social policy analysis probably accords with the facts. Nevertheless, there are similarities between countries in what are currently being referred to as the North and the South, at least in so far as they are trying to implement social objectives through the use of state policy in a national context that is non-totalitarian, and in a global context that is marked by increasing interdependency and proliferating, seemingly intractable economic problems. Under such conditions one might expect to find some points of comparison related to the determinants of the scope for state action in setting and achieving social aims.

This chapter compares Kenya and industrial welfare states, both in general and in theoretical terms. It examines the present characteristics and historical background of Kenyan society with respect to the concept of welfare and the likely future directions that can be anticipated. Finally, a concluding section brings together the empirical and theoretical discussions, and assesses what there is to be learned from a comparison of industrial welfare and 'developing' former colonial states.

Comparing Kenya and industrial welfare states
In this chapter, the welfare state is taken to be one that is characterised by a basically private market economy — that is, one in which private ownership and control of the economy predominates and has predominated in the recent past although increasing state intervention in varying degrees has produced a mixture of forms of productive organi-

sation. A concomitant of the private market economy is assumed to be a high level of industrialisation. Secondly, a welfare state is thought to include a representative form of government.

Thirdly, it implies that the state has assumed responsibility for citizen welfare and demonstrates this acceptance (1) by providing a network of social services, and (2) by formulating policies at the national level to create the kind of economic, social and political framework that will be supportive of, rather than antagonistic to the effective operation of the social services. Finally, there seems to be enough concern being expressed today over the apparent inability of the welfare state to achieve welfare objectives that one must begin to question whether this failure is actually inherent in the idea of the welfare state itself, or is merely a temporary phenomenon that can be overcome.

To what extent are these characteristics to be found in Kenya?

Kenya, to begin with, has a basically private market economy, as that term is being used here. The private sector share of GDP has consistently been higher than that of the public sector, accounting over the years for approximately 76 per cent as compared with the latter's 24 per cent (Republic of Kenya 1979: 26). Manufacturing has been one of the fastest growing sectors of the economy, but its *relative* importance is still rather small.

Kenya's form of government is that of a parliamentary republic with universal suffrage under a single party.[1] This implies that people do have some means of presenting their needs to the government.[2] If this is so, what has been the content of popular demands, and what has been the government's response?

Ever since the period before independence, the people of Kenya have been pressing first the colonial and later the nationalist government for more extensive and better quality social services (Mutiso 1974: ch. 5). Since independence, pressure has taken the form of pre-emptive self-help activity, in which people put up their own schools, community centres and health facilities in the expectation and on the tacit understanding that government will take over and see to the staffing and running of the service on a recurrent basis. The authorities have generally encouraged this activity, but have often been hard-pressed financially to accept responsibility for as many projects as the people have been able to start. Attempts have also been made to get people to diversify self-help activities more towards economic as opposed to social projects, on the grounds that the latter are both more 'productive' in the short run and no less conducive to welfare in the long. In general, since the current development plan explicitly states government's intention to accept responsibility for providing social services in ample supply to all Kenyans (Republic of Kenya 1979: 1, 18), one can say that a basis has at least been laid for significant government involvement in the provision of social services.

This expectation, however, overlooks the fact that Kenya is not a wealthy country. Hazlewood notes that 'GDP per head even in current prices shows Kenya to be in the poorest group of countries in the World Bank's conventional classification' (1979: 28). Kenya lacks an industrial (or any other) base large enough for the accumulation of capital to finance extensive social services; although tourism is said to be a money-earner, it is doubtful that much of the money so generated comes to or remains in the country. Taxation in theory is progressive, but in practice the system is widely and routinely circumvented by the relatively small number of people (among whom are admittedly some very wealthy individuals) whose incomes are big enough to tax.

What we find, therefore, is that in reality there simply do not exist the kinds of comprehensive, nationwide publicly-financed services in education, housing, health and social security that exist in most welfare states. In every case, what we have is a situation of generally inadequate coverage within an extremely complex picture of partial government provision, combined with varying degrees and types of private individual, group, community and/or voluntary organisational and local authority support. Wide variations also exist between what different sectors of the population have at their disposal. This situation has been well documented both in government publications and in studies conducted by several individuals and groups.[3]

It is, in fact, the question of disparities in access to the social services — and not merely the extent of services available — that has received the greatest attention in government policy formulations since 1963. Concern for 'how the benefits of higher productivity and consumption were distributed amongst different sections of the population' was first voiced in the two post-independence plans (1964—66 and 1966—70), and appeared again in the 1970—74 plan under the theme of social justice as incorporating the reduction of 'serious inequalities in income between a small number of highly remunerated individuals on the one hand . . . and the great mass of the people on the other' (Republic of Kenya 1969: 65—6; Ghai *et al.* 1979: 3). By 1974—78 redistribution in the interests of greater equality was stated as the outright goal of government in planning the development of society.

Performance in terms of securing equality has not, however, been impressive, and government has been frank in admitting this. Commenting on the progress that has been made since independence, the current development plan uses income distribution as an index of relative equality in society. It notes that whereas studies carried out in 1969 and 1976 showed that 'the poorest 25 per cent of the population received approximately 4.1 per cent of the nation's income in 1969, they received 6.2 per cent of income in 1976; similarly, while the richest 10.0 per cent of the population received 56.3 per cent of the nation's income in 1969, their share had been reduced to 37.7 per cent by 1976' (Republic of Kenya 1979: 5). The plan goes on to observe that

> while the comparison of the data in these two studies probably overstates the degree of improvement achieved over the seven-year period, it seems clear that significant improvement has occurred. Despite the improvement, the degree of inequality in Kenya is still very high with respect to long term Government objectives and in comparison with many other countries through-out the world. (ibid: 5)

The statement concludes with a reiteration of the fact that it is a major objective of the plan to reduce further the degree of inequality.

On the significance that can be attached to expressed concerns for greater equality in overtly stratified societies, recent formulations of stratification theory provide useful insights. Court, in comparing the education systems of Tanzania and Kenya, notes that where unequal reward systems prevail, provision of some opportunities for upward mobility that do not 'obviously discriminate against those of lower social status' can serve to legitimise the status quo, proving a useful mechanism for forestalling disaffection in the ranks of the under-privileged majority (in Barkan and Okumu 1979: 212). The same can be said of efforts to ameliorate the worst excesses of inequality and deprivation. If these measures are accompanied by propagation of a meritocratic belief system that stresses equality of opportunity, and by efforts to de-emphasise material considerations altogether in favour of the higher ideals of a participatory society, it is likely that justification rather than progressive undermining and elimination of inequalities is the true operating philosophy of the society.

Court's discussion implies that dominant élite and state interests need not always converge, and that the latter can act in ways which limit the preponderance of the former even where it is economic at base. Pinker's analysis (1979) implicitly supports this view, as he demonstrates that ruling-class perceptions of the legitimate boundaries of state action in formulating and implementing social policies has in Britain varied historically with domestic and international conditions that dictate alternately either a restrained or an interventionist role for the state in economic life. During periods of economic hardship the better-off classes in British society have accepted and encouraged state regulatory and protective action, including the expansion of social security and social service provision, mainly in order to cushion themselves against any erosion of their position and life-style. Under-privileged groups have benefited in the process, and have thus been willing to continue to acquiesce in the prevailing pattern of the distri-bution of rewards.

Clearly, the sincerity of political intentions to bring about greater equality cannot be judged purely on the basis of expressed concerns, nor even on the basis of expanding social services. Rather, consistency in countering disequalising tendencies in the society and tireless promotion of an appropriate supportive ideology seem to offer better indications of what is or is not actually desired. As far as British society is concerned, George and Wilding (1976) contend that the non-attainment of professed equality goals is directly attributable to the failure of the state to enhance the values associated with and required by a true welfare state (mutual assistance, cooperation, collective con-sciousness and concern for social products and goals) over and against those associated with and required by capitalism (self-help, freedom, competition, individualism and achievement).

No one imagines that this is an easy task. In a pluralist society the activities of the state, although apparently far-reaching, respond in fact to the constant shifts in power and position of a number of interest groups (George and Wilding 1976: 18). At best this means that policies cannot be definitive but instead compromise among the range of values represented. At worst it suggests that once a given economic system is established it generates its own congruent value system, so that con-flict and resistance to any alternative value system occur as a matter of course. While some change is possible, it is usually an uphill fight to build sufficient consensus around the need for distinctly different forms of governmental activity and around values that are antithetical to the economic system in question. In other words, the scope for state action is seriously reduced, and only certain kinds of policy outcomes become likely.

Although social policy in Kenya since independence has appeared to focus quite heavily on equality as a long-term objective of the society, there are indications that as unequal as the society was some years ago, it may be even more unequal now (Killick 1976; Ghai *et al.* 1979; House and Killick 1979). Government attributes this problem to Kenya's colonial heritage, which it believes has had the effect of skew-ing the institutions of the society towards foreign rather than domestic and towards élite rather than majority interests and needs. Thus although the takeover of assets by Kenyans is a continuing priority, unless there is a complete transformation of the structures and institu-tions being Kenyanised little lasting improvement can be made. But what is the likelihood that such a transformation can in fact be carried out?

Historical and contemporary contexts of welfare developments in Kenya

To answer that question one has to look at present conditions in Kenya and the events leading up to them. The colonisation process in Kenya began in the 1890s, but Kenya was not officially declared a colony until 1920. By the time of the second world war, it was already well established as a settler enclave with racial segregation and systematic discrimination against Africans, including political disfranchisement, the alienation of their lands to Europeans and the one-sided, protected, development of the 'Scheduled Areas' as compared with the low-potential 'Reserves' to which the indigenous majority had been pushed (Leys 1975: 30; Bigsten 1978: 10; Barkan and Okumu 1979: 20; Hazlewood 1979: 13). During this period, the Colonial Office in London was either unwilling or unable to pressure the settlers toward a more balanced development of the colony's resources (Swainson 1976: 2, 14; Bigsten 1978: 31), and it was deemed not in the interests of the mother country to encourage competition from the colonies.

Britain's changed economic position after the war brought about a reconsideration of the potential of the colonies in supplementing what domestic enterprise could produce. A change in policy toward active promotion of colonial agricultural and industrial development would also open up a whole new investment sphere for British capital. As Swainson argues, in the final analysis the real objective of British colonial development policy was to 'facilitate the ultimate intervention of foreign industrial capital', and that the direct provision of British state aid to industries in Kenya as well as the indirect encouragement and inducements given to private firms (multinationals) must be understood in this light (Swainson 1976: 8).

A policy of active colonial development leading to enhanced productivity required the stimulation of private capital, the building-up of basic infrastructure, and some investment in human resources. Prior to the 1950s funds allocated locally in Kenya for health, education and welfare programmes for the African majority had been the barest minimum, and only such as would enable the population to understand and appreciate the benefits of colonial rule and function reasonably well in the lowest tier of the racially-stratified society (Mburu 1980). The Mau Mau insurrection of 1952–7 and the declaration of the Emergency spelled the death blow to settler domination of Kenya, and placed colonial officials in a more favourable position to exploit African demands for better treatment as a way of preventing further expressions of discontent. Still, administration officials were well aware of the fact that the people's desire for services, and especially social services, could easily outstrip government's capacity to provide them. They therefore relied on three mechanisms besides promoting increased production to try to bring demand into line with potential supply.

In the first place, they began to distinguish among 'productive' services that were likely to make a direct contribution to increased output and 'non-productive' services; the former were encouraged and not the latter. Secondly, they sought to build into the service provisions as many self-limiting features as possible that would nevertheless appear reasonable and legitimate, for example by making the paying of fees and the passing of highly competitive examinations critical determinants of the ultimate accessibility to education to the population (Nkinyangi 1980: 81ff; Gakuru 1982). Finally, colonial officials in Kenya worked tirelessly to instil among the African population the idea that it was their duty to do as much for themselves as they could, looking to government only as a last resort and after they had exhausted all possible avenues of self-help. In this way they tried to replace traditional communal values that they felt provided little incentive for personal initiative and enterprise, with values more like those they themselves were familiar with and felt they could live with in a future independent Kenya.

Although the settlers as a group lost much of their influence following the Emergency, some had the foresight to understand that their best hope for salvaging as much of the situation as possible lay in cultivating and grooming for power a class of Africans whose values and economic interests would be similar to their own (Mutiso 1974: 310ff; Leys 1975). This calculation received official support in 1954 with the publication of the Swynnerton Plan, which reversed the former policy of denying Africans the right to grow any but subsistence foods in the reserves and initiated instead a total restructuring of indigenous agriculture involving consolidation of land fragments, individualisation and registration of holdings by means of title deeds, and the introduction of cash crops.

The Swynnerton Plan explicitly foresaw the acquisition of more land by 'able, energetic or rich Africans' at the expense of 'bad or poor farmers', thus creating 'a landed and a landless class' which Swynnerton, the Assistant Director of Agriculture, took to be 'a normal step in the evolution of a country' (Leys 1975: 52; House 1979: 61). As Hazlewood observes, the Plan in effect substituted a class approach for the former racial approach and class inequality for racial inequality, as a governing principle in the further development of the colony (Hazlewood 1979: 9).

At this time, the newer commercial and industrial interests were also ready to dissociate themselves from the settlers' disastrous position and to seek an alliance with the up-coming African leadership, provided such leaders could be persuaded to accept the private enterprise system and allow them to stay in business (Leys 1975: 42). This was not difficult. The internal logic of the colonial system as it operated in Kenya had succeeded in producing the nucleus of an educated and propertied African élite. This élite had no thought of effecting any fundamental changes in the highly-regulated private enterprise system established under colonialism, other than to take it over themselves (Leys 1975: 60; Mutiso 1975: 77); partly because they had in fact benefited from it and partly because they sincerely believed that it was the best route to rapid development for a newly-independent state.

There were, nevertheless, a number of individuals — considered the radical wing of the Kenya African National Union (KANU) — who were opposed to this formula for development, and who identified closely with such groups as the unemployed, urban unskilled workers, former guerrillas, and squatters and small landholders in the rural areas. They differed from the moderate majority mainly on the issues of land for the landless and free education, which they saw as critical in determining whether the independence settlement would provide security and equality of opportunity for the masses or not (Leys 1975: 214).

Yet their attention in the early 1960s was taken up with securing independence and the general political and economic stability they thought would help to consolidate it. By the time the radicals tried to mount a serious protest and mobilise opinion first in the cabinet, then in parliament and later — after they had been forced to form an opposition party, the Kenya People's Union (KPU) — it was too late (Okumu, in Barkan and Okumu 1979: 51n, 60). The political and economic stability they had helped to build proved to be their undoing, and they were isolated, undermined and harassed continually until their leader, Oginga Odinga, and other party officials were finally detained in 1969.

The latent conflict in Kenya between those who accept as legitimate the prevailing criteria by which rewards are distributed and those who reject these criteria in favour of a more egalitarian society is still present, and lies no doubt at the root of the present concern over government's social policy objectives. While the banning of KPU and the detention of its leaders ended the immediate threat to the regime, government is apparently not convinced that the sentiments represented have entirely died out.[4]

Understandably, there is sensitivity on the part of the authorities to a persistent undercurrent of discontent not very far beneath the surface, and which a second party might presumably tap. This accounts in part for the progressive shifts in policy from an overt concentration on economic growth with its accompanying tendency to exacerbate inequalities, to a voiced concern for a fairer distribution of the fruits of that growth.

Yet many writers, some of whom have been cited in this chapter, conclude that there has in fact been little real change in Kenya over the past two decades since independence, and they doubt the likelihood that the kind of structural transformation the current development plan speaks of can be realised. The colonial antecedents of the present political and economic set-up and the measures adopted since independence that have buttressed it seem to weigh heavily against any peaceful, non-revolutionary effort to replace the concept and model of development that we now witness with one that would be substantially different.

Moreover, in the light of an expressed commitment to structural transformation, Kenya's actual development strategies seem rather modest. According to Killick (1976), Kimyua (1978), and Ghai *et al.* (1979), the government's poverty alleviation and redistribution measures are almost entirely 'dynamic', meaning that they concentrate on alternative ways of channelling the increases in national income and wealth that it is believed will result from growth-stimulating policies; while shying away from any attempt to alter existing patterns of inequitable assets and wealth (Killick 1976: 35–6; Kimyua 1978: 130, 172–3; Ghai 1979: 74, 80). This problem is made worse by the fact that official policy does not concede that a multiplicity of goals encompassing both greater equality and growth may conflict, so it becomes necessary to think in terms of possible trade-offs and the need to prioritise (Killick 1976: 3). Since development objectives are held to be integrated and complementary, ambivalence, ambiguities and inconsistencies in development plans cannot be acknowledged and sorted out.

Anticipating future trends

It has been stated that policy in Kenya often appears to work against itself in the sense that it is trying to achieve objectives that pull the society in opposite directions. On the one hand, government has evidently chosen to work with what Kenya has in the way of social, political and economic institutions in an effort to prime them for growth and more rapid attainment of national development goals. On the other hand, there is repeated reference to the need to make basic structural transformations in order to create a more equal society. Recent policy statements underscore this point, and indicate that the controversy may now be resolved increasingly in the direction of a consolidation of the status quo.

In 1982, President Moi gave a speech on Kenyatta Day, that expanded on two earlier sessional papers, nos 4 of 1980 and 1982. The president here suggested new policy directions that have an important bearing on the subject-matter of this chapter. These initiatives can be summarised under the headings 'debureaucratisation', 'decentralisation', 'privatisation' and 'self-help'. Taken together, they imply that government is now seeking to strengthen in the population the kinds of values the colonial authorities thought were lacking several decades ago and that they studiously tried to introduce. Any interim attempts to develop African socialism or mutual social responsibility as possible cornerstones for an alternative value system in which equality would be stressed now seem to have been quietly set aside.

Privatisation is probably the most critical of the new ideas being voiced. In reality, emphasis on the importance of the private sector in Kenya's economy has always been there. Each development plan has talked of the need to facilitate private sector development. Recently it has been said that the private sector's role in supplying social and economic services to the people must expand, and government will provide the necessary encouragement and incentives to make this possible (Republic of Kenya 1980: 14). Coupled with efforts to 're-juvenate' and expand the private sector, it is strongly hinted that government in the future will be able to do less and less. For example, it is suggested that proposals for new parastatals, public enterprises and joint public—private ventures will from now on be 'carefully scrutinised to ensure that government funds are utilised only when absolutely required' (Ibid.). Meanwhile, the *harambee* (self-help) movement, voluntary agencies, trade unions and associations, cooperatives and private firms will all be 'induced to take up some of the burden which government cannot now finance' (Ibid.). Efforts will also be made to recover the costs of basic needs services increasingly from those who benefit from them (Republic of Kenya 1982: 33).

Phased withdrawal by government from 'over-involvement' in the supply of basic social and economic goods and services is being justified on financial grounds. But beyond this, the authorities are also apparently apprehensive of what they see as the extent to which 'pro-liferation of government activities . . . has diverted scarce management talent away from the *essential functions* of government' (Republic of Kenya 1982: 2; emphasis added). Commenting on this further during his Kenyatta Day speech, the president reminded Kenyans that there was a time when 'growing and far-reaching public investment and government initiative' was justified, and that was when government was concerned with getting the new economy off the ground, developing and controlling necessary infrastructures and industries and promoting Kenyanisation.[5] But times have changed, and it is now evident that government's public sector activities — while having made possible steady progress toward the nation's fundamental objectives — have been tending to get out of hand. Since moreover, the president said, some of these public enterprises have been rather casual about efficiency, it is now likely that they could be more productively and profitably run in the hands of private Kenyans so that government can devote itself once again to its primary function of creating 'a suitable and favourable setting in which the people of this country can develop themselves'.

It is within this context that references in the same speech to de-bureaucratisation, decentralisation and self-help take on meaning. The president said that Kenya is in real danger of creating 'a large and impersonal bureaucracy which, by its nature and complexity, has not fully encouraged or stimulated personal and business initiative'. Besides re-examining the size, structure and deployment of the civil service, one of the ways of countering this trend, the president noted, would be to focus on the district as the basic operational unit. This would 'harness the full impetus of local knowledge and involvement', and 'create for the people . . . a whole new world of opportunity'. Having been presented with such opportunities, it would then be the responsibility of all Kenyans to 'encourage self-reliance as one of the greatest of our African strengths and traditions'.

If we go back to our earlier discussion of some of the issues surrounding equality as a state objective, the significance of these new policy directions in Kenya comes out more fully. It was argued from stratification theory as reviewed by Court that one way of securing consensus to the unequal distribution of rewards in a society is to provide limited possibilities for equality through opportunities for upward mobility that at least appear accessible to all, while at the same time marginally improving the conditions of life for the many who cannot in fact move up. Clearly, the success of this strategy depends on the ability of the rulers to earmark sufficient resources for creating equal opportunities and enhancing life conditions for the society's less privileged groups. In effect, the rulers must act to counter the tendency towards polarisation and conflict that inevitably accompanies the exclusive use of meritocratic criteria in a situation where people are not all equal.

Social policy in Kenya over the last few years had given evidence that it was government's intention to do just this. But recent developments give cause for concern. Financially, government is now indicating that the public coffers have run dry, which suggests that programmes and services directed to lower-income groups that relied heavily on government financing may have to be scrapped altogether or severely cut back (Republic of Kenya 1982: 32, 33, 38). Efforts to increase charges on basic needs services to those who benefit from them and can afford to pay may indeed, as government anticipates, make it possible for similar services to 'be extended to others within the same total cost to government' (Republic of Kenya 1982: 33). The temptation, however, may equally be to offer the services increasingly only to those who can pay.

A much lower than expected growth rate has translated into fewer jobs in the country, whereas government had based its hopes for a more equitable distribution on constantly expanding employment opportunities. There are also fewer opportunities for the large and growing numbers of landless families to acquire even a small plot of land (Republic of Kenya 1979: 282). Yet Kenya's land tenure system, which following Swynnerton is based on the private, individual ownership of small farms, has been considered 'the principal means by which the benefits of agricultural production can be equitably[6] shared among large numbers of people' (Republic of Kenya 1982: 18).

As more and more of the responsibility for the provision of services and goods in Kenya is turned over to the private sector, which is admittedly substantially beyond public control, government loses whatever scope it may have had for applying equity criteria in the determination of who gets what. This can be seen clearly for example in the case of income and wages policies (Republic of Kenya 1980: 17—18). Decentralisation, similarly, can permit more efficient use of resources through local participation in programme selection and implementation (ibid: 15). But where localities differ significantly in terms of existing infrastructure, natural resources, per capita wealth and levels of awareness and education among the people, decentralisation and indeed self-help have been shown to have marked disequalising effects (Bigsten 1978: 385—9). Kenyans have been exhorted to make sacrifices, and the well-to-do, in particular, have been told that they 'must accept their responsibility to make greater proportional sacrifices than the poorer members of our society' (Republic of Kenya 1980: 31). Individual commitment and effort are being held up as the means by which economic inequality is to be reduced, but exactly how this will happen has not been fully explained.

The discussion so far implies that Kenya government has chosen to pull back from an equality-oriented social policy that it earlier chose to pursue, and that it has abandoned its former commitment to use the apparatus of the state in an effort to secure social and economic goals. The authors cited in this chapter tend to believe that the apparent reversal is less a matter of choice than of defeat, though they are not agreed as to who or what the enemy really is. Ghai *et al.* (1979) on the one hand, argue that domestically the influence of the private market effectively frustrates even the best intentioned policies of the state. They describe in detail the effects of market forces on land ownership, access to education and regional and rural/urban imbalances (ibid.: 55—9), and show systematically the extent to which state intervention in the social services sector 'responds to the existing pattern of purchasing power (and of political power . . .) rather than effectively counter-bidding on behalf of the needy' (ibid.: 57). The emphasis on the disequalising logic of market forces 'also underlines the *weight* of intervention that may be necessary' and guards against a tendency to overemphasise the role of the state, which they say 'runs the risk of raising too high expectations about the likely result of certain policy measures' (ibid.: 63).

Within the world economy, moreover, Kenya seems to be tied ever 'more tightly into its role as a primary product exporter and tourist resort in an exceedingly competitive (if erratic) world market', as attested to in part by the existence of a huge capital outflow from the country caused by the transfer overseas of most of the profits of foreign-controlled multinational corporations (ibid.: 52). For these authors, as well as House and Killick (1979), these facts suggest that it will take time as well as considerable effort and commitment before the institutionalised forces that tend to perpetuate poverty and inequality in the society can be neutralised and possibly reversed.

Leys, on the other hand, scoffs at this way of thinking, which he characterises as naive, and suggests that the kinds of problem Kenya faces cannot be written off as an historical accident. He argues that inequality is not 'something which perpetuate[s] itself by mere inertial force'; rather it is something which constantly develops and evolves 'as the result not merely of continued old policies but of new policies adopted since independence which [have] extended inequality in fresh ways' (Leys 1975: 265).

Leys' approach leads him to see the role of the state in bringing about fundamental changes in Kenyan society as basically illusory. The government, in fact, in his analysis exists purely to arbitrate between the different sectors of the alliance between 'foreign capital, the local auxiliary bourgeoisie and the various politically powerful petty-bourgeois strata', whose interests, though largely in harmony, at times do conflict. Government must also try to 'master the tensions and conflicts generated among the mass of the people by the process of underdevelopment' (ibid.: 207). Ultimately, however, the state is seen as having been captured, as it were, by foreign class interests. This has led to increasing polarisation of society so that government no longer truly represents the people. There is, consequently, a need to engage in the deception of populist rhetoric combined with a genuine fear of mass political parties, since mass parties imply mass participation and mass participation implies a mass ideology and a *programme* for the masses (ibid.: 245). Other institutions of the liberal democratic state, although they exist in Kenya, are similarly irrelevant in Leys' view in that they are merely empty imitations of the true substance and form of such institutions found in the typical bourgeois state (ibid.: 244; Anyang'-Nyong'o 1980). Since the factors which originally produced underdevelopment in Kenya arose out of a complex interaction among international, regional and national forces, short of changes occurring in these same global forces Leys does not see any possibility for meaningful change in Kenya (Leys 1975: 275).

Conclusion

We began this discussion of Kenya and the future of the welfare state by comparing Kenya and industrial welfare states on a number of criteria and certain sociological concepts thought to be relevant. As has been observed, significant differences do appear. What is surprising, however, is the degree of similarity. Policy statements aside, both Kenya and industrial welfare states seem to have adopted in practice what Migot-Adholla, after modernisation theorists, calls the 'trickle-down model of development'. This model assumes that the 'critical question is not whether inequality exists, or even whether the extent of inequality is becoming more pronounced, but whether everyone's share of the national pie, large or small, continues to expand'. (Migot-Adholla, in Barkan and Okumu 1979: 164). Placed in the context of Court's discussion of inequality, it can be seen that the trickle-down theory of progress provides the necessary basis and rationale for a stratified society in its suggestion that people will accept inequalities and relative personal deprivation as long as they 'believe that they have an equal chance to benefit and do not choose to question the criteria by which merit and hence mobility are determined' (Court, in Barkan and Okumu 1979: 215).

As Migot-Adholla notes, there is some historical evidence to support the trickle-down model of progress in a society, provided the minimum material security of less privileged groups can be guaranteed. But when this is no longer possible, the *quid pro quo* element in the compromise is undermined and continued acceptance of previously rationalised inequalities becomes precarious. This in fact would seem to be the situation in which both Kenya and a number of industrial welfare states now find themselves. Despite pronounced differences between them in terms of per capita income and wealth, for a brief period in Kenya's recent history the two kinds of societies enjoyed a roughly analogous position: growth rates were high and the possibility of expanding incomes for everyone could be taken for granted.

Kenya's day of reckoning came sooner and after a much shorter period of captivation with exclusively growth-oriented strategies, perhaps because even a growing economy was still insufficient to produce enough of a trickle to reach the bottom. Again, such strategies have not been as successful in obviating questions of inequality here as they have been in industrial welfare states, partly because of the added ethnic/regional dimension that is so potentially explosive. Industrial welfare states are only now beginning to experience a weakening of the social fabric as hostility between more and less privileged groups escalates, conflicts over the rationing and distribution of increasingly scarce resources per head become more pronounced, and attempts are made to apply criteria of merit to areas of life where traditionally other norms have prevailed.

It is in this light that moves toward debureaucratisation, decentralisation, privatisation and self-help both in Kenya and in the industrial welfare states must be viewed with some trepidation. Though such moves are being justified as efficiency measures that will enhance citizen participation and responsibility while rebuilding a sense of identity and community, other, possibly unintended, consequences can also be expected. As was remarked in the case of Kenya, all such policies are likely to have marked disequalising effects. Given that disadvantaged groups in some welfare states are becoming less reticent about registering discontent, this is not an eventuality one would want to take lightly.

Governments caught in such a situation seem not to have too many options at their disposal, and the scope for action by the state may indeed be small. If privileged groups even in times of relative prosperity have not been well disposed toward sharing, and economic hardship reaches the point where a protective floor cannot be maintained let alone extended, political stability may come to be endangered, along with the way of life it ensured. For countries like Kenya, the problem is confounded by lack of autonomy and by the likelihood of intensified exploitation as developed countries struggle to maintain that to which they have become accustomed.[7]

George and Wilding (1976) in their discussion, it will be recalled, place their hopes for the emergence of a just society in Britain on the search for values that can somehow overcome the influence of the private market system, enlarge the scope for governmental action and form the basis of a new consensus as to the meaning of the welfare state (George and Wilding 1976: 135—6). The fact that such a debate can be carried on is in itself instructive. In Kenya, anything that looks like an ideological debate is explicitly discouraged as counterproductive and therefore close to subversion. Perhaps this is, as Leys suggests, a necessary outcome of the fact of neo-colonialism. Certainly colonial policy articulated a consistent and highly-integrated though thoroughly objectionable view of the nature of society and the relationship between the governors and the governed. Policy since independence has lacked this holistic quality. It has focused on problems and objectives but only as if the reasons for them and what should be done about them are all self-evident. Any value system that would upend the colonial value system, yet be equally coherent, would clearly not support the continuation of dominance and dependence.

In many respects, as Yahya (1976) observes, Kenya is still an open society that defies being controlled entirely either from within or from without (Yahya 1976: 121). Kenyans are presently being called upon to take seriously President Moi's *'nyayo'*[8] philosophy of love, peace and unity, to examine these principles carefully, consider their implications and incorporate them fully into every aspect of national life. Whether the deliberations called for will be allowed to go as far as the kinds of issue raised in this chapter is yet to be seen. That cannot happen, however, until the implicit threat of sanctions that has characteristically clouded such discussions is dispelled.

Notes

1. The Constitution was amended on 9 June 1982 to make Kenya officially a one-party state. Previously it had held that status *de facto* rather than *de jure*.
2. Barkan notes that 'participation in Kenya exists for the purpose of selecting one's representatives to central political institutions so that one's community might be more effectively linked to the centre and gain access to the resources the centre commands. It does not occur for the purpose of changing the leadership or character of the system, and the goals — including the conception of development — which the system is already committed to pursuing (Barkan and Okumu 1979: 27; see also Oyugi 1974; and Yahya 1976).
3. Some of these are listed in the References to this chapter.
4. *Daily Nation*, 20 November and 16 December 1982.
5. *Nairobi Times*, Thursday, 21 October 1982. The direct quotations in this and the next paragraph are all from that source.
6. Equity is apparently viewed as a means toward greater equality. See Jones, Brown and Bradshaw (1978: ch. 1).
7. Sugata Dasgupta, in a 1974 paper presented to the General Assembly of the International Council of Social Welfare, Nairobi, Kenya, pointed out that 'twenty-five per cent of the people of the world use, according to Mr [Robert] MacNamara, seventy-five per cent of resources and have secured development. It is common sense, therefore, that the remainder of seventy-five per cent of the people who have access to only twenty-five per cent of resources cannot aspire to the same standard of living that obtains in the North World and is called 'development' (Dasgupta 1974: 1—5).
8. '*Nyayo*' is a Swahili word which means 'footsteps'. When President Moi took office following the death of President Kenyatta, he said on several occasions that he intended to follow in his predecessor's footsteps. 'Nyayo' has now become the slogan, but in a highly honorific sense, of President Moi's regime just as '*harambee*' ('let's all pull together') was the slogan of President Kenyatta.

References

Anyang'-Nyong'o, Peter (1980), 'Electoral Politics and the Democratic Tradition in Kenya', Nairobi: Seminar paper, Department of Government, University of Nairobi.

Barkan, Joel and Okumu, John (eds) (1979), *Politics and Public Policy in Kenya and Tanzania*, New York: Praeger.

Bigsten, Arne (1978), *Regional Inequality and Development: A Case Study of Kenya*, Gothenburg, Sweden: Nationalekonomiska Institutionen, Göteborgs Universitet.

Dasgupta, Sugata (1974), 'Participation in Development', Address to the General Assembly of the International Council of Social Welfare, Nairobi, Kenya.

Gakuru, O.N. (1982), 'Education and Social Class Formation: The Case of Pre-School Education in Kenya', Nairobi: Seminar paper no. 51, Department of Sociology, University of Nairobi.

George, Vic and Wilding, Paul (1976), *Ideology and Social Welfare*, London: Routledge and Kegan Paul.

Ghai, Dharam, Godfrey, Martin and Lisk, Franklyn (1979), *Planning for Basic Needs in Kenya: Performance, Policies and Prospects*, Geneva: OECD.

Hazlewood, Arthur (1979), *The Economy of Kenya: The Kenyatta Era*, Oxford: Oxford University Press.

House, William J. and Killick, Tony (1979), 'Social Justice and Development Policy in Kenya's Rural Economy: A Survey', Geneva: A report commissioned by the International Labour Office.

International Labour Office (1972), *Employment, Incomes and Equality: A Strategy for Increasing Productive Employment in Kenya*, Geneva: ILO.

Jones, Kathleen, Brown, John and Bradshaw, Jonathan (1978), *Issues in Social Policy*, London: Routledge and Kegan Paul.

Killick, Tony (1976), 'Strengthening Kenya's Development Strategy: Opportunities and Constraints', Nairobi: Discussion paper no. 239, Institute for Development Studies, University of Nairobi.

Kinyua, Joseph K.M. (1978), 'Plan Implementation in Kenya, 1974—78', Nairobi: MA thesis, University of Nairobi.

Leys, Colin (1975), *Underdevelopment in Kenya: The Political Economy of Neo-Colonialism 1964—1971*, London: Heinemann.

Mburu, F.M. (1980), 'Sociopolitical Imperatives in the History of Health Development in Kenya', Nairobi: Working paper no. 374, Institute for Development Studies, University of Nairobi.

Musiga, L.O. (1973), 'Organizational Aspects of Social Security in Kenya', Nairobi: MA thesis, Department of Sociology, University of Nairobi.

Mutiso, Gideon-Cyrus M. (1975), *Kenya — Politics, Policy and Society*, Nairobi: East African Literature Bureau.

Mutiso, R.M. (1974), 'The Evolution of Social Welfare and Community Development Policy in Kenya, 1940—1973', Nairobi: PhD thesis, Department of Sociology, University of Nairobi.

Nkinyangi, John A. (1980), 'Socio-Economic Determinants of Repetition and Early School Withdrawal at the Primary School Level and their Implications for Educational Planning in Kenya', Stanford, California: PhD thesis, Graduate School of Education, Stanford University.

Oyugi, W. (1974), 'Public Policy-making in East Africa and the Role of the Social Scientist', Kampala, Uganda: Paper presented at the Xth Annual Universities Social Science Council Conference, Makerere University.

Pinker, Robert (1979), *The Idea of Welfare*, London: Heinemann.

Republic of Kenya (1969), *The Development Plan 1970—74*, Nairobi: Government Printer.

Republic of Kenya (1979), *Development Plan 1979—83*, Nairobi: Government Printer.

Republic of Kenya (1980), Sessional paper no. 4, *Economic Prospects and Policies*, Nairobi: Government Printer.

Republic of Kenya (1982), Sessional paper no. 4, *Development Prospects and Policies*, Nairobi: Government Printer.

Swainson, Nicola (1976), 'The Role of the State in Kenya's Post-War Industrialisation', Nairobi: Working paper no. 275, Institute for Development Studies, University of Nairobi.

Yahya, Saad (1976), 'Urban Land Policy in Kenya', PhD thesis, Department of Land Development, University of Nairobi, Nairobi, Kenya.

15 The Welfare State in Sri Lanka
Kumar Rupesinghe

This chapter will review the implications of export-oriented industrialisation as a development strategy and its implications on welfare policies
in Sri Lanka. Although Sri Lanka is ranked the eighteenth poorest
country in the world, in some ways it can also be called an early welfare
state. But in 1977, Sri Lanka adopted an International Monetary Fund
(IMF) growth strategy based on export-oriented industrialisation.
The adoption of these policies turned out to have fundamental consequences on welfare policies.

The first section of the chapter reviews the evolution of the welfare
programme. It is argued that the existence of parliamentary democracy
ensured the maintenance of an extensive welfare programme. However,
welfare policies were adopted at the expense of development and
growth.

The second section reviews the adoption of Export-Oriented Industrialisation (EOI) or 'free market' policies in Sri Lanka. The adoption
of these policies were ostensibly to emulate the miracle growth rates of
the so-called Newly Industrialising Countries (NICs) of South East Asia
(South Korea, Taiwan, Singapore, and Hong Kong). Unlike the NICs,
Sri Lanka inherited a rigid colonial export economy, and a population
composed of diverse ethnic groups. Also, Sri Lanka was a latecomer in
adopting the strategy of export growth, and the policies were pursued
under different conditions of the world economy, namely a period of
crisis and stagnation.

The third section reviews the implications of this strategy on welfare
policies, and raises some issues as to whether the growth strategy of the
NICs can be successfully adopted in other developing countries.

The case of Sri Lanka

There has been a general consensus that despite low economic growth
Sri Lanka has achieved considerable success in the field of welfare
policies. Sri Lanka's achievements in meeting social needs can be
observed in a series of social indicators (see Table 15.1). Paul Isenman of

Table 15.1   Selected social indicators

	1946	1953	1963	1973
Adult literacy (%)	58	65	72	n.a.
School enrolment (% age 5–14)	41	58	65	78
Life expectancy (yrs)	43	56	63	66
Infant mortality (per 1000)	141	71	56	46
Death rate (per 1000)	19.8	10.7	8.6	7.7
Birth rate (per 1000)	37.4	38.7	34.3	27.9
Indigenous population growth rate	1.8	2.8	2.6	2.0
Total population growth rate (including migration)	2.3	3.3	2.5	1.6

Source: *World Development*, vol. 8, 1980.

the World Bank, compared Sri Lanka's indicators with those of other countries at different income levels, where a regression analysis was carried out on a 59-country sample of countries for which complete data sets were available. He observed that 'in each case Sri Lanka's social indicators relative to its income were the best among 59 countries' (Isenman 1980: 237–58). His findings were corroborated by the Overseas Development Council in the so-called physical quality of life index. The ODC index ranked Sri Lanka amongst the most developed of developing countries in spite of its low ranking in terms of GNP. In spite of the World Bank's consistent criticisms of Sri Lanka's welfare policies, the World Development Report records that 'throughout the post-war period, Sri Lanka was exceptionally successful in protecting the poor from the worst effects of falling consumption and in improving, albeit slowly, the high quality of life as measured by various social indicators' (The World Development Report 1982: 28).

Components of the welfare programme
The achievements which these positive social indicators show can be seen in relation to conditions which Sri Lanka enjoyed during and after colonial rule. The main components of the welfare programmes can be described as follows.

The welfare package
The bulk of the social welfare measures were introduced before Sri Lanka achieved independence in 1948. The maintenance of these measures was continued by all governments until July 1977. By then

the total expenditure for social services and net food subsidies was about 41 per cent of current public expenditure. The extensive welfare programme came in the form of *free education*, *free health care* and a wide-ranging network of *subsidies* which reduced food costs for the poor income groups.

A Bill for free education was introduced in 1943, and provided free education from the primary to the tertiary level. As a result of the high state expenditures on education, school enrolment increased (to 86 per cent in 1983), as did literacy (see Table 15.1).

Expenditures on health services also increased. Sri Lanka's extensive health care system had a dramatic effect on the reduction of mortality as shown in Table 15.1. The malaria eradication programme through spraying of DDT led to a sharp drop in the crude mortality rate. Similarly, maternal mortality declined from 16 per 1000 in 1946 to 12 per 1000 in 1970, partly because of better maternity care. At present more than two-thirds of births take place in hospitals or maternity centres.

The food subsidy programme was a direct consequence of the food shortages experienced during the war, and was continued after the war. The rice and wheat rations have varied between 2 and 4 lb per person a week, half of which was free, whilst the remainder was sold at subsidised prices. The subsidy programme constituted about 20 per cent of public expenditure. Sri Lanka's ration and subsidy programmes had an effective coverage of the poor and rural areas. The positive effect of the food ration and subsidy programmes was the substantially reduced malnutrition, particularly for those living close to subsistence levels.

Policies of income distribution

During the same period, political initiatives and policy measures were taken which attacked and broke up the concentration of private wealth and economic power. For three decades, Sri Lankan governments had emphasised income distribution and sought to lessen inequality. Income distribution measures were sustained in 1970 by the Business Acquisition Act, the Act on the Ceiling of Housing Property, and the land reform in the early 1970s, which nationalised over 1 million acres of tea, rubber and coconut estates.

The development of the peasant economy

Efforts were also made to redistribute incomes to the peasant sector. These measures included land alienation, through the distribution of Crown land and irrigated lands to the peasantry, extensive agricultural support, guaranteed producer prices, subsidies for agricultural inputs, massive investments on irrigation and rural credit. All these measures

helped to achieve near self-sufficiency in rice production and encouraged growth of subsidiary food crops.

The growth of the public sector

Most of the capital-intensive developments took place in the public
sector, particularly in manufacturing. A series of nationalisation
measures and the initiations of state corporations meant that capital-
intensive fields of development were not in the hands of the private
sector. To that extent the accumulation of capital in private, individual
forms was restricted. Policies of import-substitution industrialisation
were attempted to encourage domestic production, with its corollary
of import restrictions, price control and exchange control regulations.

Price stability

A factor which was vitally important up to 1974 was the maintenance
of relative price stability. During this period the increase in the cost of
living, the fluctuation of prices and the rate of inflation were contained.
This was partly made possible through the regulated economy, the
welfare programmes, and the system of subsidised prices for essential
consumer and intermediate goods. The regulated economy also imposed
certain constraints on conspicuous consumption and on the demand for
luxury imports by high-income groups. In this sense import restriction
imposed a higher burden on the higher income groups.

The welfare programme and political democracy

The welfare programme was largely inherited from the colonial administration, but was continued and expanded until July 1977. An
explanation for the continuation of these policies must be seen in a
conjuncture of factors which can be identified as follows:

(1)   The relationship of the welfare programme to parliamentary
      democracy.
(2)   The relationship of parliamentary democracy and its inability to
      maintain equal distribution of welfare to different ethnic groups,
      where language and racial strife played a major role in the politi-
      cal process.
(3)   The readiness of the Sri Lankan élite to administer welfare
      policies at the expense of fundamental reforms and increases in
      productivity.

The welfare programme and parliamentary democracy

The development of welfare policies and political democracy has a
clear historical relationship which is unique for a developing country.
Sri Lanka was the first British colony to enjoy universal franchise in
1931. The conditions for the maintenance of welfare programmes were

largely related to the parliamentary system which Sri Lanka inherited from the colonial period. Due to the fact that all political parties had to secure the vote of the population, populism became the hallmark of all political parties. According to one commentator:

> The semi-autonomous, representative and competitive political structure established under British rule encouraged the development of patronage politics in which political representatives pressed for boons for their constituencies — roads, hospitals, schools, welfare policies, without the power or responsibility to alter either political institutions or the basic economic structure. The political élite emerged as welfare brokers, and distributive policies came to dominate the political process. (Herring 1980: 20)

The conditions of parliamentary democracy, with the periodic and regular changes of government, coupled with universal franchise and the right to vote secured to all those over 18 years, meant that the reduction of the food subsidy and the curtailment of certain other welfare programmes became a serious political issue and could be used against any government in power.[1]

The welfare programme and ethnic cleavages

The political system in Sri Lanka did not allow for equal representation of all the ethnic and religious minorities in the country. The ethnic composition of the population according to the 1981 census is as follows:

Sinhalese	74.2%
Ceylon Tamils	12.6%
Moors	7.7%
Indian Tamils	5.5%

The history of Indian Tamils is closely connected with the establishment of the plantation economy, whilst the history of Sri Lankan Tamils goes back many centuries. Indian Tamils are concentrated in the plantations as labourers while the Sri Lankan Tamils have been able to spread into various occupations in different sectors of the economy.

After independence, the coexistence of the different ethnic groups could not be maintained, and language and race were to play a major role in the political process. In the efforts of the major political parties to satisfy the aspirations and the economic interests of the majority population, serious discriminatory measures were used against the minority Tamils. For example, the plantation workers of Indian origin were excluded from the franchise immediately after the country gained independence in 1948. Being unable to exert pressure through the vote, the estate areas have been sparsely provided with welfare goods and services. The striking impact of welfare policies on the plantation workers was brought out by Isenman:

> For example, the death rate was 55% above that of the country as a whole for 1973 and 130% during the food short year of 1974. In 1969, 52% of estate women had no schooling at all, compared to 23% in the rural sector. Only 1.5% of the estate population had 'O' level qualifications, compared to 7.5% of the population as a whole. Also low income estate dwellers get much lower benefits from the government subsidy and service programmes than does the rest of the population. (Isenman 1980)

The pursuit of hegemony by the majority parties has also led to vociferous complaints by the Sri Lankan Tamils, who before and immediately after independence had enjoyed relatively high status in occupations and education. Discriminatory measures have ranged from the denial of the rights of the Tamils' language, discrimination in public sector employment, and discrimination in education by the imposition of 'ethnic quotas' for university enrolment. The open economy which was subsequently inaugurated in July 1977, with the cuts in welfare, further heightened ethnic conflicts amongst the population.

Welfare and growth

The role of the Sri Lankan state in pursuing economic policies was primarily determined by the colonial economy and administration which it inherited after independence. Basically the country inherited a rigid export economy based on the export of tea, rubber and coconuts, which provided the majority of the revenue for the government. In the 1940s and 1950s foreign exchange earnings from war activities and the post-war commodity boom were more than sufficient to pay for extensive imports. The terms of trade fluctuated but remained more or less stable between 1948 and 1960. But this strategy broke down around 1960, owing to the inability of the export sector to generate enough foreign exchange to pay for necessary imports. The terms of trade have declined continuously since then. The impact of the deteriorating terms of trade was aggravated by stagnation in the production of export crops. The balance of payments crisis meant that the government had to manage the economy based on the restrictions of imports, the adoption of import-substitution industrialisation and the development of a public sector. The growth rate, however, continued to stagnate.

The industrial performance during the period exhibited most of the *malaise* associated with import-substitution industrialisation. The growth rate of manufacturing output deteriorated and the manufacturing sector increased only marginally. There was hardly any perceptible diversification away from the plantation-dominated agrarian economy. The relative stagnation in the manufacturing sector, however, must be seen in relation to the spectacular increases in food production, both in terms of increased yields and in the production of subsidiary food crops.

In sum, Sri Lanka's economic structure has been characterised by an unusual degree of rigidity; over the last few decades both the composition and production changed only to a limited extent. The particular nature of the political process and, after 1960, the shortage of foreign exchange, were two factors that contributed to this rigidity.

Although there has been universal agreement on the impact of social welfare policies, controversy has always surrounded the relative merits of investments on social welfare at the cost of economic development. For instance, according to an ILO study,

> the successful social programmes of Sri Lanka can better be seen as part of an overall compromise 'imposed' on a nation of conflicting interest groups which has left the overall social structure untouched . . . social programmes have substituted for the more radical redistribution of assets and incomes. . . . We therefore feel that one effect of the food subsidies in Sri Lanka has been precisely to perpetuate the structure of traditional relations, particularly in the rural areas. Welfare and subsidy programmes have been heaven-sent weapons in this respect. But we must doubt whether fast growth and modernisation will themselves be sufficient to improve the position of the rural poor without more forthright rural measures. (ILO 1980)

The argument against welfare policies is emphasised continuously in the World Bank's periodic reports on Sri Lanka. However, the World Bank's arguments are often contradictory. For although it was critical of Sri Lanka's heavy expenditure on education, health and nutrition, it commends the results in terms of 'human development'. In the *World Development Report 1982*, it argues that the trade-off between human development and growth 'has not been so sharp as it is sometimes suggested', and that *the growth rate deteriorated 'for reasons generally independent of human development spending'* (emphasis added). The welfare package constituted a declining share of the budget deficit, and *no simple correlation can be drawn between welfare investment and the lack of growth in the economy.*

The adoption of export-oriented policies in Sri Lanka

During the election campaign the United National Party (UNP) levelled a sustained criticism of the economic performance of the United Front government (UF) of 1970–77. Criticisms ranged from corruption to food shortages and the sluggish growth of the economy. Further, the failure of the economy was seen as due to the adoption of import substitution and self-reliant strategies of development where price controls, import controls and exchange controls compounded administrative inefficiency and the misallocation of resources. The manifesto of the UNP therefore sought to free the economy of all controls and regulations, and growth was to be achieved by the adoption of policies associated with Export-Oriented Industrialisation.

The elections resulted in a massive landslide victory for the UNP, which won 83 per cent of the seats in the National Assembly. Soon after assuming office in July 1977, the new government initiated many basic and far-reaching political and economic policy changes. A fundamental shift in policy was the definite commitment towards a substantial degree of foreign capital participation in the country's development efforts, especially for export-oriented industries. In order to attract foreign capital the government initiated a package of policies, including almost all the so-called 'conditionalities' of the IMF.

Changes in the political system
The massive majority in parliament enabled the government to make fundamental changes in the Constitution by establishing an executive presidential system and introducing proportional representation in elections to parliament. The constitutional changes aimed at achieving political stability by reducing the influence of small political parties on the legislature, thus ensuring the rule of a two-party system committed to the economic objectives of export-led industrialisation. Guarantees for foreign capital were provided in the Constitution. The government also armed itself with measures designed to destabilise political opposition.

The explanations for the introduction of the new constitution were several: (1) It was intended to attract foreign investment and to convince international aid donors that Sri Lanka provided the necessary conditions for political stability. (2) It was intended to create continuity in economic policies and promote national consensus on the objectives of the government. (3) It was to enable the executive president to change the welfare system without having recourse to the legislature.

The new president indicated the need for change in the following way:

> You would have noted that we have taken steps to ensure political and economic stability in our country. Our main object is to improve the investment climate as encouraging foreign investment has been a major plank of our economic strategy. We are confident that the new electoral system gives our country further political stability as it will prevent swings in political power due to the previous distorted electoral system. (Jayawardene in *The Sun* 1978)

The IMF conditionalities
The IMF and the World Bank were enthusiastic, and provided considerable financial support for the experiment, at least in the early phase. Sri Lanka was one of the few remaining democracies in the Third

World, and this was all the more reason why this experiment should be supported so as to demonstrate that export-led industrialisation was compatible with democracy.

What the IMF calls its 'stabilisation programmes' often require devaluation of a country's currency, reduction of government spending, curtailment of welfare expenditure, encouragement of foreign private capital investment by providing incentives, removal of foreign exchange controls and import liberalisation. These are the preconditions for the grant of new stand-by loans, credit for the import of consumer goods and for rescheduling maturing debts. The extent to which the government willingly followed the so-called conditionalities of the IMF can be seen in the economic measures which it adopted after its first budget in 1977. These measures included:

(1) Liberalisation of Sri Lanka's import trade, implying the dismantling of the controls and restrictions on external trade and payments that had existed for nearly two decades.
(2) Exchange control liberalisation.
(3) Introduction of high interest rates, unification of the exchange rate and devaluation of the rupee by nearly 100 per cent.
(4) Elimination of the food subsidy and its replacement by food stamp rationing for those below the poverty line.
(5) Gradual dismantling of the public sector corporations.
(6) Increased participation of foreign capital in the economy.

In support of the policies the IMF made available to Sri Lanka a stand-by credit of R5000 million (US $300 million). The IMF for the first time posted a resident officer in the country.

Alongside these general economic policies, the government introduced four lead programmes which were to be the major development goals for the country. These programmes were (1) the accelerated Mahavelli project, intended to irrigate 1 million new acres of land; (2) the establishment of an export processing zone with extensive tax concessions, guarantees and infrastructure facilities; (3) an urban renewal and housing scheme which included the improvement of civic amenities, land reclamation and construction of 100,000 new housing units; and (4) the Greater Colombo development plan, with a new administrative capital.

Some of the consequences of the new policies

The argument for the adoption of export-oriented policies is that these policies would lead to higher growth rates, higher productivity and increases in manufactured exports. The open economy, in contrast to self-reliant strategies, would enable the country to save foreign exchange, increase employment and help raise the standard of living.

Implicit in these arguments is the idea that welfare programmes and subsidies should be abandoned since they are presumed to lead to inefficiencies in the allocation of resources for production.

Import liberalisation was vigorously pursued by the government, and the import controls which had previously existed were abolished and opened the door for unrestricted private sector imports. A consequence of the import liberalisation measures was the abolition of all public sector monopolies for the import of yarn, textiles, oil, fertiliser, milk, medicine, tractors, cement, etc. Although imports increased fivefold the export incomes did not increase correspondingly. From 1978 to 1981 the volume of exports increased by 2 per cent, whilst imports increased by 45 per cent. The terms of trade deteriorated sharply. Between 1978 and 1981 export prices increased by 29 per cent whilst import prices rose by 182 per cent. The terms of trade deteriorated from 100 at 1978 to 46 in 1981 (Central Bank 1981: 64). Import liberalisation had a serious effect on local, middle-sized and small industries nurtured under the import substitution period. Small cottage industries, such as handloom textiles, and wood and paper products, suffered heavily from import competition.

The policy of import liberalisation had a serious and permanent effect on the balance of payments (Central Bank 1981). The World Bank itself sounded the alarm at the massive debt burden of the Sri Lankan economy (World Bank 1982a). At the same time, Sri Lanka's growth rate rose to an impressive 6 per cent in 1978. The growth rate was undoubtedly an achievement when compared with the growth rates for the period 1970—77. But the success of the economic strategy can be brought into question by pointing to the relatively high levels of inflation and deteriorating payments position over the period 1978—82. The increased investment and growth rates, however, cannot be attributed to the much emphasised expansion of exports and increases in domestic savings but rather to a massive expansion of public sector capital expenditure, financed primarily by unprecedented levels of foreign borrowing.

Dismantling the welfare system

Table 15.2 provides a picture of the extent to which welfare expenditures have been dramatically pruned by the government. The expenditure of total social services and net food subsidies decreased from 41.8 per cent of current expenditure in 1977 to 16.7 per cent in 1982, almost entirely due to the dramatic reduction of subsidies after 1979. In relation to GDP, subsidies were reduced from 7.6 per cent in 1977 to 3.04 per cent in 1982. The free and subsidised food ration was substantially reduced, given selectively only to those earning R300 or less per month. Flour, sugar, infants' milk, food, petroleum and kerosene, fertilisers and bus and train fares continued to be

Table 15.2   Major social expenditures in relation to total current budgetary expenditures and to GDP, 1969/70–82

Year	Total current expenditure adjusted[a] (R million)	% of total current expenditures adjusted					% of GDP (current market price)				
		Health[b]	Education[b]	Total social services[b]	Net food subsidies[c]	Total social services and net food subsidies[b]	Health total[b]	Education total[b]	Total social services[b]	Net food subsidies[c]	Total social services and net food subsidies
1969/70	2,577	9.15	18.33	28.44	12.66	41.10	2.00	4.01	6.22	2.77	8.99
1970/71	3,019	7.89	16.01	24.74	17.76	42.49	1.99	4.03	6.23	4.48	10.71
1971/72	4,023	6.31	16.13	19.88	16.36	41.20	2.47	5.06	7.80	5.13	12.93
1973	3,777	6.94	14.90	22.69	17.98	39.82	1.42	3.06	4.48	3.69	8.17
1974	4,565	6.40	12.77	19.98	20.86	40.02	1.23	2.45	3.68	4.00	7.69
1975	5,265	6.15	12.43	19.39	23.37	41.95	1.23	2.48	3.71	4.66	8.37
1976	5,602	6.89	14.07	21.83	16.73	37.70	1.29	2.63	3.92	3.13	7.05
1977	6,553	6.94	13.13	20.86	21.73	41.79	1.26	2.39	3.65	3.95	7.60
1978	10,491	4.95	9.37	14.89	20.33	35.21	1.22	2.31	3.66	5.00	8.66
1979	10,887	5.81	10.40	16.87	21.36	38.24	1.21	2.16	3.51	4.44	7.95
1980	12,730	5.81	10.90	17.42	2.40	19.82	1.11	2.09	3.33	0.46	3.79
1981[d]	15,025	5.71	10.64	17.04	0.55	17.59	1.00	1.87	3.00	0.10	3.09
1982[e]	19,566	4.92	10.56	16.21	0.51	16.72	0.89	1.92	2.95	0.09	3.04

[a]   Total current expenditure adjusted – total current expenditure – gross food subsidy + net food subsidy.

[b]   Expenditures on current account only.

[c]   In 1968–69, Sri Lanka introduced a dual exchange rate. However, food imports, which determine much of the cost of the food subsidy, were valued at the official exchange rate and got at *free* rate thus understating the true cost to the budget. The gross food subsidy, valued at the new R 16 exchange rate, would amount to 6.4% of GDP in 1977.

[d]   Provisional.

[e]   Budgetary estimates.

Source: Calculated from Statistical Appendix Tables 2.01, 5.03 and 5.04, *World Bank Report* (1982b).

subsidised. In 1979 the government decided to abandon the subsidy scheme altogether and replace it with a food stamp scheme. The saving to the government by these measures was approximately R650 million. The changes in the food subsidy and rationing policy had dramatic results on the population. Prior to 1979 free rice rations and food subsidies could cushion economic strains on a family's budget. The food stamps were fixed in monetary terms leading to a reduction in food stamp purchasing power due to inflation and increases in food prices. In reviewing the effects of the changes in food subsidy and rationing policy, Kamp observes,

> It also makes increasingly vulnerable welfare gains such as the food subsidy and ration system which, despite often criticised economic inefficiency, has probably been the most important single factor in Sri Lanka's very favourable longevity and nutrition record. (Lamb 1981: 104)

The current situation is that due to the increasing deficit in the government's balance of payments and deficits in its current account, *the IMF has requested the government to abandon the food stamps scheme altogether* and it is likely that the government will be forced to follow this recommendation.

The argument that the budget deficit had a clear relationship to the welfare expenditure is, however, erroneous. Food subsidy/food stamp expenditure constitutes only 10 per cent of the total deficit. The argument that the food subsidy/food stamp scheme is a major burden on the economy and the reason for the ever-increasing budget deficit is not valid in present Sri Lanka (Oshoug 1983).

In addition to the cuts in the food subsidy, expenditure on education, health and other social services reflects considerable reductions. In education, the government intends to introduce and encourage fee-paying levies and develop a system of private education (White Paper on Education Reforms 1981). In health care, the relaxation of rules regarding private practice is likely to favour the well-to-do and impair the quality of the services for the poor.

Social consequences of export-oriented policies

In a strategy which diverts resources from present welfare to future growth, the inevitable lags between investment and output, i.e. between capital outlay and productive employment, are always certain to work against the poor, unless development strategies are consciously directed towards the under-privileged. The regulated economy functions as an instrument for equitable distribution in a period of scarcities. The present policies, however, will stimulate the demands of high-income groups, with the phenomenon of conspicuous consumption which will exert pressures and divert resources through market forces, to the satisfaction of the demands of higher income groups. In such a process is an inherent tendency to widen the income disparities in society.

Export-oriented policies for the world market require that domestic purchasing power (wages) is continuously reduced or held steady if that country is to retain its comparatively low-wage advantage in the international labour market. This strategy is different from import-substitution industrialisation where domestic purchasing must be enhanced for the sale of goods within the domestic economy. However, the large reserve army of labour available in the periphery and the existence of subsistence agriculture perpetuates low wages in the urban sector.

The combination of policies associated with import liberalisation, continuous devaluations of the currency, and galloping inflation, has contributed to reduce the purchasing power and real wages of the population. Price stability, which was an essential component of the regulated economy, has been abandoned, and Sri Lanka has been vulnerable to externally-induced inflation as a result of rising oil prices, the global capitalist crisis, foreign remittances, and so on. Domestic inflation has been compounded by borrowing from the banks, printing money and the capital investments through foreign aid of huge infrastructure capital investments.

The rate of inflation had reached astronomical heights by 1980, representing a tenfold increase since 1960. The rate of inflation will be in the range of 35—40 per cent during 1983—84. The increase in the cost of living has been felt by all sectors of the population, and most severely by those who earn fixed incomes in the state and private sector. In the agricultural sector, due to the increase in the costs of tractor hire, reductions in the fertiliser subsidy, and increasing costs of inputs in general, there has been a fall in the disposable incomes of the peasantry.

The extent to which inflation affects different income groups depends on their consumption preferences and needs as well as their income level and access to non-market food. According to one study:

> Increases in the prices of basic food items like rice, flour, bread, dried fish, coconut, coconut oil and sugar were exceptionally high both in 1980 and 1981. Kerosene oil increased by 142 per cent in 1980 over 1979 and another 24 per cent in 1981. All these basic items are used in urban and rural areas. The 34% increase in rice, 84% in wheat flour, 78% in bread, 31% in dried fish, 55% in coconut, compared with only 26% average increase recorded in the Colombo Consumer Price Index in 1980, invariably causes increasing difficulties to low income groups, who mainly depend on these basic items for their food needs. (Oshoug 1983)

The consequences of export-oriented policies on income distribution can be seen in some recent studies. The top 10 per cent of Sri Lanka's income-earners now get 39 per cent of the total incomes in the country.

In 1973 the figure was 30 per cent. In the same year, the bottom 40 per cent of the income-earners together received 15 per cent of all incomes; now the share has dropped to 12 per cent. It is expected that this gap will continue to increase in the future (Fernando and Fernando 1982). According to one study:

> Thus the open economy not only made us indebted, but also helped to run down our own production due to the dumping of imports. Yet due to the inflation and low incomes, the poorer half of the population cannot buy these goods. Hence there is malnutrition of about 1/3 of our school-going children and infant mortality has risen by 25%, from 37 to 47 per 1000 during the past four years. (Centre for Society and Religion 1982)

Infant mortality in 1979 (per thousand live births) was 38. In a limited circulation report by the World Bank, infant mortality (per thousand live births) is reported to be 49 in 1981 (World Bank 1982b), *which gives for the two years an increase in infant mortality of 29 per cent.*

A recent survey showed that compared with figures in the first island-wide nutrition survey conducted in 1975, there will be a progressive increase in the proportions of chronically undernourished children with increasing age. In several districts one-third of all pre-school children suffer from chronic under-nutrition. In a country where these adverse conditions persist, there will be a progressive increase in the proportions of chronically undernourished children with increasing age (Ministry of Plan Implementation 1981).[2]

Female employment

The fall in the value of Sri Lanka's currency and the reduction of purchasing power meant that wage expenditures became comparatively cheaper to foreign investors both in the free trade zone and outside. Sri Lanka now boasts in its publicity brochures of having the 'cheapest wage in Asia'. With the changes in government policy the pattern of occupational participation of females seems to have undergone a dramatic change. The loss of the value of the currency has meant that whatever was saved by parents, either for their daughter's wedding or for her dowry, has lost most of its value. This also means that no single wage earner is now able to support a full family. Therefore, families adopt a strategy of multiple employment to retain income levels. In this sense it would be natural for daughters to seek employment in whatever avenues are available to them. It is also within this framework that we must analyse the employment opportunities newly created by tourism and the free trade zones.

It would appear, given the conditions of poverty and the 'revolution of expectations' created by the ideology of modernisation and new consumer goods, that young women are both the beneficiaries and the victims of export-led industrialisation. Apart from female employment in the free trade zones and in the tourist industry, the largest increase in female employment has been recorded in the export of female labour to the Middle East. Up to 1983, more than 100,000 females secured employment as housemaids in the Middle East, the majority being unskilled. Foreign exchange remittances from the export of labour to the Middle East is now the second largest foreign exchange-earner for the government.

According to a study of the social factors which lead to the search for employment in the Middle East, 'these forms of employment now possess a high social value. A trend which did not exist earlier' (Tilakasiri and de Silva 1981). The study goes on to suggest that the age group 20—24 displayed the highest interest to secure foreign employment:

> Reductions in the disparity in material conditions which has existed among the villagers earlier, appeared to be an important feature evident in the post-Middle East situation. The interest in foreign employment had increased depending on the size of their families and problems of seeking an existence based on these incomes. 84% of those surveyed had sought a job abroad due to economic problems and indebtedness.

The Sri Lankan experiment

The Sri Lankan experiment was an attempt to demonstrate the viability of export-led policies with the maintenance of democratic traditions. This was an important experiment according to its international supporters, particularly since the so-called NICs had a known record for the violation of labour rights, as well as human and democratic rights. Exponents of export-led growth had argued that the adoption of this strategy would not only lead to high growth rates but that it would have a 'trickle-down effect' which would have the long-term effect of raising wage levels and purchasing power. Rising purchasing power, it was argued, would inevitably result in pluralism and political democracy.

From this point of view the Sri Lankan experiment can be considered a failure. The open economy and the political and economic preconditions for export-led growth has had far-reaching effects on the democratic tradition known to Sri Lanka. The worsening economic conditions for the large majority of the people, the continuing repression of workers, peasants and the ethnic minorities and the erosion of democratic freedom seem to be the concomitants of the social costs associated with export-led industrialisation.

Measures to destabilise the political opposition have also included the extensive use of violence against political opponents, and parastatal forces have been used against workers, pickets, opposition meetings, students and even against the judges of the Supreme Court. The introduction of the Prevention of Terrorism Act has aroused widespread condemnation, particularly from the International Commission of Jurists, and Amnesty International. This Act enables the security forces to hold persons under arrest for eighteen months without trial. The Act has been directed mostly against minority Tamil youths in northern Sri Lanka. Amnesty International, in its latest report, records widespread and inhuman torture against political prisoners (Amnesty International 1982).

Ethnic violence in July 1983 helped shatter the dreams of export-led growth in Sri Lanka. Tamil grievances, particularly about work opportunity, education and land in the context of a diminishing welfare budget, led to increased extra-parliamentary agitation for a separate state starting in the late 1970s. The agitation of the Tamils was confronted with increased state terrorism which culminated in the holocaust against the Tamils in July 1983. The current phase of violence is unparalleled in the country's history. During the holocaust more than 100,000 Tamils fled to refugee centres in Colombo. According to the Secretary to the Ministry of Industries and Scientific Affairs, more than 100 industrial units were destroyed, the intention being to destroy the material existence of a whole community.

There is little doubt that the open economy accentuated and polarised existing ethnic cleavages. The dramatic decline in welfare provisions, rapid inflation, increased food prices and the expectations created by pervasive consumerism tended to heighten the perceptions of inequality and income disparities. The open economy has also led to the destabilisation of the national capitalist class, whose industries were threatened by foreign competition and import liberalisation. But the Tamils bore the brunt of the changes.

Sri Lanka adopted a strategy of development under the auspices of the IMF in the mistaken belief that a mere change in policies, and cuts in the welfare programme, would automatically lead to growth. The question to be raised is whether the IMF prescription (i.e. repeating the experiences of the NICs in South East Asia) could be generalised for developing countries as a whole. Sri Lanka was a late-starter in export-led industrialisation. The political, cultural and economic conditions which enabled the NICs to record high growth rates do not exist in the 1980s, particularly in a period of recession and stagflation. Although the government's intention was to strengthen export-led industrialisation by promoting an active industrial bourgeoisie, the open economy only served to consolidate and reproduce a dependent merchant class, who seized the opportunities of import liberalisation to amass vast profits by diverting investible resources to trade and import—export activities. This may seem irrational, but it enters the debate as to the nature of the capitalist class in Sri Lanka. Although the peripheral state seeks rapidly to industrialise the economy and promote policies to achieve this end, the character and historical specificity of the capitalist class and the nature of the state set limits to achieving these objectives.

By adopting measures to open the economy, Sri Lanka became vulnerable to all the vagaries of the world economy, as was demonstrated in the balance of payments crisis, galloping inflation and the decline in growth rates in the 1980s. The IMF debt management and its so-called 'stabilisation programmes' seem irreversible when more and more countries are caught in a vicious circle of dependence and political destabilisation. As far as Sri Lanka is concerned, the casualty in the process was, with all its weaknesses, the welfare system and political democracy. These two institutions were the two pillars upon which Sri Lanka built a high standard covering basic needs, including the relatively high nutritional status of the population. By destabilising both, and given the conditions of the world economy, the prospects for retrieving these high standards in the future are indeed depressing.

Notes

1. For example, in 1951 the Minister of Finance decided to go back on the welfare measures which he had introduced in the 1948 budget, which caused the Left parties of Sri Lanka to call a *hartal* (general protest strike). This led the government to declare a curfew and a state of emergency, and eleven persons were shot in the subsequent disturbances. The government of 1956 partially restored the subsidy, but when the UNP government was elected in 1960, it increased the food subsidy. In 1962 the SLFP government sought once again to reduce the ration in the face of a serious balance of payments crisis but had to withdraw it owing to strong opposition from its members. In 1967 the UNP attempted to reduce the food ration by half, but the opposition in a bid to win power promised the restoration of the ration in the original quantity. The UNP government in the election campaign promised 8 lb of cereals free if it were restored to power.
2. There is some controversy with regard to this survey, and criticisms have been levelled at the methodology of the study. The ministry is presently withholding its circulation.

References

Amnesty International (1982), *Report of an Amnesty International Mission to Sri Lanka, 31 January 1982*, London.

Central Bank, Sri Lanka (1981), *Report*, Colombo: The Government Press.

Centre for Society and Religion (1983), Dossier no. 88.

Fernando, Sarath and Helen (1983), 'Development Strategies in Sri Lanka', in E. Utrecht (ed.), *Transnational Corporations in South East Asia and the Pacific*, vol. V, Sydney: University of Sydney, Transnational Corporations Research Project.

Herring, Ronald J. (1980), 'Structural Determinants of Development Choices: Sri Lanka's Struggle with Dependency', Paper submitted to the Ceylon Studies Seminar Conference on Post-War Economic Developments of Sri Lanka, 16–20 December.

International Labour Organisation (1980), *Basic Needs, Poverty and Government Policies in Sri Lanka*, Geneva: ILO.

Isenman, Paul (1980), 'Basic Needs: The Case of Sri Lanka', *World Development*, vol. 8, 237–58.

Lamb, Geoff (1981), 'Rapid Capitalist Development Models: A New Politics of Dependence?', in D. Seers (ed.), *Dependency Theory: A Critical Reassessment*, London: Frances Pinter, 97–168.

Ministry of Plan Implementation (1981), 'Food and Nutritional Status, its Determinants and Intervention Programmes', Food and Nutrition Policy Planning Division, Government of Sri Lanka, October.

Morris, D. (1980), 'The Physical Quality of Life Index', *Political Development Digest*, vol. XVIII, November/January, 95–109.

Oshoug, Arne (1983), 'Impact of Political and Macro-Economic Processes on Price Level, Income Transfers, Real Wages and Credit Institutions in Sri Lanka', Research Programme on Development of Methodology for Nutritional Evaluation of Development Programmes, Progress Report to NORAD, July.

The Sun, 18 March 1978.

Tilakasiri, S.L. and de Silva, Asoka K. (1981), 'Socio-economic Impact of Employment in the Middle East', *Economic Review*, vol. 17, no. 1, 12–13.

World Bank (1982a), *Economic Adjustments of Sri Lanka, A World Bank Report*.

World Bank (1982b), *World Development Report 1982*, New York: Oxford University Press.

Index